Silk Route
The Undying Romance

Silk Route
The Undying Romance

Krishan Gopal Tyagi

SHIPRA

The Indian Council of Historical Research has extended the financial support for this publication. Views expressed in the volume are of the author and do not represent the view point of the Council.

ISBN: 978-81-7541-694-9

First Published in India in 2014

Silk Route — The Undying Romance

Published by:
SHIPRA PUBLICATIONS
H.O.: LG 18-19, Pankaj Central Market, Patparganj,
Delhi-110092, Tel: 91-11-2223 5152, 2223 6152
Br.Off.: 4617/18, Ansari Road, Darya Ganj,
New Delhi-110002, Tel: 9650028065, 9810522367
E-mail: info@shiprapublications.com
www.shiprapublications.com

Dedicated with Respect
in Honour of
Professor Devendra Kaushik

My sincere and special thanks
to
Prof. K. Warikoo

Foreword

Silk Road and its dozens of branches knit together regions of China, Central Asia, India, Persia and right up to the Mediterranean opening into Europe. Before the discovery of Sea routes by the European powers the Silk Road rather the Silk Route – was the intercontinental life-line. It is not important as who travelled on the Silk Route; a more pertinent question is what travelled through the Silk Route? A simple answer to this complexed question is that goods, technologies, commodities, capital, ideas, philosophies, religions and political and military adventurers all travelled on this route. In a word, It was the first large scale human experimentation about Globalization. Before proceeding further, let me pose a simple question. What is Globalization? Globalization is a free movement of goods, capital, technology, people and ideas. Goods and technology have their own attraction. What is even more obvious and fascinating is the free movement of ideas. Great ideas can not remain confined to its village or town of origin. The very fact that they are great ideas means that they are universally valid.

Buddhism, Islam, Christianity and Confucian thoughts were some of the Great ideas which freely travelled on the Silk Route. These ideas belonged to the civilizational category. These ideas were and continue to be the best achievements of the mankind. For students bearing interest in those great ideas, the entire Silk Route is full of this universal legacy. At times these great ideas travelled on this route either as a cause or as an effect of conflict. This was not the norm but an exception. Most of the time, these ideas and ideals travelled and triumphed as a consequence of debate and dialogue. Make no mistake, excepting few occasions when these great ideas triumphed on the force of the sword, the majuscule ideas on majuscule occasions were the product of dialogue and discussions. Such was the case within Buddhism and Chinese schools of philosophy, the ideas of Jesus and even the ideas of Prophet Mohammad. Some of the best endeavors of human creativity and imagination in particular the ideas of Gautam Buddha are literally littered on the entire Silk Route. In a word, dialogue, covenants and mutuality of interests were the Ideals and ethos of this Globalization. The expression Democracy was not born when the Silk Route was at its zenith and one is skeptical about the prevalence of democracy in the countries, located along the Silk Route but one thing is absolutely clear that the inter relations between the Silk Route countries were mainly based on the precepts and practices of democracy. Specialization and equity guided the whole movements of goods and Ideas

With the discovery of Sea routes and later on the discovery of Air routes made Silk Route irrelevant and out of use. Two ideas still remain hugely relevant and if these two ideas are translated into action, the human dream of true globalization and international cooperation will become true. What are these two ideas? First let all those countries that were once the stake holders in Silk Route construct an express high way providing linkages and connectivity. This will facilitate the free flow of ideas, goods, capital, people and technology again. Second, let the ideals of dialogue and democracy triumph among all these countries. If this dialogue/democracy in its nascent and imperfect form could prevail thousand years back, it stands to reason that countries of Asia need it much more. That will be a true tribute to the spirit of Silk Route.

As far as I know, the present work is the first well-researched monograph on the Silk Route and its Revival. I am happy to find that this study throws light on various dimensions of political culture of the region. The theme is timely and relevant to the contemporary society. I hope that the findings are useful to the students of History, research scholars and policy planners from this and other side of Indian borders.

New Delhi
June 2013

Prof. K. R. Sharma

Preface

At the outset of the third millennium, the Silk Route can still be considered a viable network of trade and commerce between East and West. When the Swedish explorer Sven Hedin passed through Xinjiang, the cradle of the Chinese section of the Silk Route, in 1933-1935, on his last expedition, he dreamt of reviving the old Silk Route as a great motorized highway linking China, India and Europe. The Silk Route is not only an expression that refers to sites, monuments or ruins of the past, but is lived vivid experience that indicates a direction for the future. Narratives abound of the Silk Route: of myths both ancient and medieval, historical annals, religious narratives and tales of conquerors, monks, merchants and diplomats. Silk Route stories have been told in several notable exhibitions over the past few years, most using trade or Buddhism-excavated exhibits that reinforce China's role on this famous trading route. The Silk Route has become now almost a brand name that inspires thoughts of prosperity, beauty and strength. The Great Silk Route, the first trans-continental trade and diplomatic route in the history of mankind ran from China to the Mediterranean Roman Empire covering, 6,400 kms. This study analyzes the economic, political and socio-cultural importance of the Great Silk Route in the historical context. The main concern of this work is to trace the origin, development and decline of the Silk Route.

Following the disintegration of the Soviet Union, new independent states of Central Asia came into existence. The course of the ancient Silk Route was through the territories of the Central Asian Republics of Kazakhstan, Kyrgyzstan, Uzbekistan, Tajikistan, Turkmenistan and also through the southern Caucasian Republics of Azerbaijan, Georgia and Armenia. Being landlocked, the Central

Asian Republics do not have direct access to the world transport network and to the world markets. Possessing rich natural resources these republics need economically viable, cheap and safe access to the world markets. The Central Asian states are in the transitional period of their social and economic development. The restoration of the Silk Route opens opportunities not only for expanding trade and regional economic cooperation but also for the interchange of ideas and contacts between Europe and Asia. Hence the revival of the historical Silk Route has become one of the key policy issues of the newly independent Central Asian Republics. This study examines the policies of the Central Asian Republics and adjoining countries of Russia, China, Iran Azerbaijan, Turkey, Georgia etc. towards the revival of the Silk Route.

Numerous meetings have been held on the revival of the Silk Route in Central Asian and other Eurasian Countries. WTO at its General Assembly in Indonesia in 1993, decided to create a long term tourism project to promote a special Silk Road tourism concept. The Samarkand Declaration on Silk Road Tourism adopted in 1999 by 19 participating countries under the inspiration of the President of Uzbekistan and the then Secretary General of WTO was a landmark. A special logo of the WTO Silk Road Tourism Project was subsequently adopted to unite all the countries' organizations and the private sector under a common visual banner.

The transport network connecting Asia with Europe passes through the territory of Eurasia. Russia has been having a monopoly over the transportation network with Central Asia, which has been built assiduously over the past hundred years or so. But after independence, the Central Asian Republics are keen to develop other transport networks and routes, so that they are dependent to the minimum degree on Russia. Hence the proposal to revive the Silk Route connecting Asia with Europe by constructing the transport corridor through Central Asian Republics and the southern Caucasian states to meet Europe has been mooted. The principle objectives of this study are to identify: (a) all feasible rail and land-cum-sea routes forming part of a network of routes connecting Northern Europe with the Persian Gulf through the Caucuses Central Asia and/or the Caspian sea (b) the characteristics of these routes in terms of their lengths and the transit times they can reasonably offer, and (c) the possible presence of operational restrictions which might impede the smooth flow of goods along the routes.

Some external powers like the United States, Germany, France, U.K. etc. are interested in the revival of the Silk Route and widening the scope of their economic activity in the new markets of Central Asia. The huge oil and gas reserves of Central Asia are attracting other countries as these natural resources can fulfill the requirement of energy. The USA has particular economic, strategic and political interests in the countries along the Silk Route. WTO, UNESCO and ESCAP are big organizations which are providing funds for the development of Silk Route. This study evaluates the role of these external powers in the revival of the Silk Route and in the economic development of the Central Asian Republics.

The concept of a Eurasian Land Bridge has attracted serious attention. The Presidents of Azerbaijan and Georgia with the support of the European Union hosted an international conference on the "Restoration of the Historic Silk Route" on 8th September, 1998 in Baku, Azerbaijan. The Presidents of Azerbaijan, Bulgaria, Georgia, Kyrgyzstan, Moldovia, Romania, Turkey, Uzbekistan and Ukraine, transport ministers and experts from 32 countries, and representatives of international organizations attended this conference. The participants emphasized the importance of the revival of the Great Silk Route and highly appreciated the contribution to that end of the TRACECA project, implemented within the European Union's TRACIS (Transportation in Commonwealth Independent States), programmed as a Eurasian Land Bridge. The "Final Communiqué of the Conference", was signed as the "Baku Declaration", foreseeing further international cooperation for the development of TRACECA. Five main corridors were discussed in the Euro-Asian Transport Conference in St. Petersburg, Russia on Sept. 12-13, 2000. These are identified as: the *TRACECA (Transport Corridor Europe–Caucasus–Asia) Corridor*, from Eastern Europe via the Black Sea and the Caspian Sea to Central Asia, the *Central Corridor*, from Southern Europe, via Turkey, Iran and Central Asia to China, the *Southern Corridor*, which runs from Southern Europe to Iran, as the Central Corridor, but reaches China via Pakistan, India and Southeast Asia, the *Northern Corridor*, from Europe via the trans-Siberian railroad to China, North and South Korea, and Japan and the *North-South Sail-*

Ship Corridor, which goes from Northern Europe to Russia, crosses the Caspian Sea to Iran, and via Iran's southern ports across the Arabian Sea to India.

These corridors, along with their numerous branches, form a unified network, providing the foundation for the development of a gigantic economic zone of about 4 billion human beings. The construction of the Gwadar sea port, the extension of the Karakorum Highway, the opening of the Sakhalin Rail Tunnel and the reopening of the Nathu La Pass on the India-China border are some results of the efforts in the direction of the revival of the Silk Route. This study has also examined the problems and prospects in the implications of the Silk Route in Central Asia.

Chapter One gives the geo-political background and historical account of the Silk Route and its role in the socio-economic and political development of Central Asia through history. It also throws light on the political contacts among the countries and territories along the Silk Route. *Chapter Two* analyses the major factors behind the decline of the Silk Route, and its social, economic and political consequences.

Chapter Three deals with the political interests of the newly emerged Central Asian Republics in the revival of the Silk Route. It examines the problems and prospects of the restoration of the historical Silk Route with particular reference to the policies of the Central Asian Republics and their impact on regional cooperation.

The Fourth Chapter focuses on the role and interests of the external powers like Iran, China, Russia, Turkey, Japan, the European Union and the USA in the revival of the route. It also details the support of the World Bank, UNESCO and ESCAP in this revival.

The Fifth Chapter examines the nature of the New Silk Route being built as the Eurasian Land Bridge. It also explores the implications of this route. The focus has been on the role of the revived Silk Route as an idea of prosperity, peace, modernization, cooperation and development.

Acknowledgements

To begin with, it is difficult to put in words, the amount of gratitude I owe to Prof. K. Warikoo who has painstakingly revised and corrected the draft of the book till it was made into a coherent, concise and academically contributive one. Without his perspicacious comments and scholarly guidance I would never have been able to complete this work.

I wish to express my sincere gratitude to my torch bearer, Prof. Devendra Kaushik, whose help encouraged me during the early stage of this work. I must express my deep thanks to Prof. Uma Singh, Prof. Gang Nath Jha, Prof. M.P. Lama, Prof, Nirmala Joshi, Prof. Dilbag Singh, Dr. Nazaf Haider and Dr. G.D. Gulati all the faculty members who rendered invaluable help.

I am indebted to Prof. D.N. Jha, Prof. R. S. Sharma, Prof. T.K.V. Subramaniam and Prof. K.R. Sharma of Delhi University to suggest a historical advance to this work. I also owe thanks to the faculties of the department of History of Ram Lal Anand College, University of Delhi who helped me to complete this book.

I would like to give special thanks to Prof. Yogesh Tyagi, Dr. Ambrish Dhaka, Dr. M.N. Singh, Sanjay, Nalin, Avdhesh, Vidhan Pathak, Mukesh Mishra, S.L. Kaushik and Pramod Sharma for their help in various forms during my pursuit of the present work.

I would like to give a special thank to the Indian Council of Historical Research to give financial grant for publication of this book.

Last but not least, I express my heartfelt gratitude to my beloved mother Smt. Vimlesh Tyagi, father Shri Bhushan Tyagi.

Without the love and support of my wife Ambika, I could not have produced this work. Their robust optimism has been a constant source of inspiration.

Krishan Gopal Tyagi

Contents

Content

List of Tables

List of Figures

1
The Silk Route: History

The term "Silk Route" was first used by the German geographer Ferdinand Von Richthofen in the 19th century when he referred to an ancient trunk road across Central Asia.[1] This Great Silk Route, the first trans-continental trade and diplomatic road in the history of mankind connecting China and the Far East with Europe and India passed through Central Asia covering 6,400 kms. The Silk Route was a network of roads, which followed the wide and varied contacts between the peoples of the Mediterranean countries, Near and Middle East, Central Asia, the Indian subcontinent and East Asia. Silk Route included the so called "Oasis Route", connecting caravan cities in the desert and semi-desert areas of Central Asia; the "Steppe Route", the commercial route controlled by nomadic tribes who lived in the Eurasian steppe region extending to the north of the Oasis Route; and the "Southern Sea Route", which linked the China Sea, the Indian Ocean, the Arabian Sea, the Red Sea and the Mediterranean.

The Old Silk Route

There was not just the Silk Route, but many routes, roads, and paths that headed in an east-west direction. Some routes were well developed and relatively free from bandits, while others were less protected and had fewer oasis towns which offered protection from the bandits. One route along the southern edge of the Takla Makan was quite risky, but it took less time to cross. Kashgar (Kashi) the meeting point of the various roads of the Silk Route, became one of the most important trade centres of Central Asia. The main route was the "Oasis Route" which was the most popular not only because of its historical significance in terms of East-West trade and cultural exchange, but it attracted people also because it evolved through consistent human efforts, with countless people traveling along it for thousands of years. The terminals of the Oasis Route were Changan[2] (Xian) in the East and Rome in the West; and later on Luayang in the East and Byzantium (Constantinople) in the West.[3] The route crossed many hazardous regions such as the Takla Makan desert, the Tien Shan and Kunlun Shan, the Pamirs, the Karakurm and Kyzylkum deserts, and the Hindu Kush. The Takla Makan dessert was called the Land of Death or "the Land of Irrevocable Death"[4] by the local people. At the foot of steep mountains, there were oases of various sizes with streams and springs. Cities were constructed in the oases and protected by gates and walls, surrounded by green trees, farmlands and orchards, ponds and flower beds. Travellers from various lands gathered in the oases to setup markets and depots where they traded in the goods which they had brought from their respective lands. They formed and got engaged in the intermediate activities of the East-West trade.

The Oases Silk Route along which people travelled from one oasis to another, is a stupendous example of human endeavour in which natural dangers and perils for a thousands of kilometers were overcome. The route developed as the shortest trunk road of Central Asia spanning East and West. The 4,000 kms long section of the Oasis Silk Route that ran through East and West Turkistan was located in the heart of Asia.[5] Earlier, people had had to fight many natural hazards including vast deserts, snow covered hills swept by freezing winds, deep valleys with torrential mountain streams and steep cliffs. They were also terrified of evil spirits in addition to bandits and highway robbers. There were four major areas that defied human access in innermost Asia. These were the Bailongdui desert around Lop-Nor, the Takla Makan desert, the Pamirs and the steep cliffs in the upper reaches of the Indus.[6] The Oases Route was far more dangerous than the Steppe Route. Yet, so many people-kings, noblemen, army generals, local governors, merchants, artisans, Buddhist monks, missionaries, scholars, exiles, musicians and dancers, artists, soldiers and refugees – chose the Oasis Route because the Steppe Route was mostly occupied by nomadic tribes, prohibiting easy access, and lacked towns, markets and accommodation facilities. No water, food or other necessities for travel, no entertainment or medical services were made available to caravans and travelers along the Steppe Route.

The second important constituent of the Silk Route was the Steppe Route. It had been used by nomads when they moved from east to west or vice-versa. The Steppe Route originated from the migration of nomadic, horse rearing tribes in pre-historic times. These nomadic equestrian tribes developed the metal culture that is commonly called the Scytho-Siberian style, disseminated to the East and West by way of the Steppe Route.[7] This metal culture was diffused by the sixth to fourth centuries BC in the Kazakh plains, the Altai mountains, the semi-plains in upstream Yenisey in the Central Eurasian continent, as far as the steppe regions in Southern Russia and the Donau river basin in the West and the semi-plain, semi-desert region in Mongolia, and near the Great Wall of China in the east. The ancient nomadic equestrian tribes bore this metal culture along the Steppe Route through which it was spread.

The Steppe Route was not a road but a continuation of plains from east to west which served as an artery of traffic in Northern Eurasia. It was a convenient artery for nomadic equestrian tribes to migrate in any direction and breed cattle or trade at various locations. The Steppe Route was a stage of military activities. It was virtually a huge economic and cultural pipeline through which not only products from both East and West were exchanged, but also technology and information from various parts of the world in which were brought to the nomadic equestrian tribes in Central Asia. The migration of equestrian nomads living in Eurasia was made possible by the Steppe Route and this route served as a natural highway through which the life style of the nomads, their animal rearing and gold culture were diffused in East-West and West-East directions. These nomadic groups (called Hu by the Chinese)[8] conducted trade with neighbouring regions from a very early period. They purchased silks, bronze mirrors and weapons from China; furs and gold from Siberia; nephrite jade and wool from East Turkistan, and horses from West Turkistan.

The opening of the Southern Sea Route made for the third great landmark of the Silk Route in connecting the Orient and Occident both in terms of politics and culture. It was not only by way of Central Asia and the lands of the Parthian that silk came to Europe; it could also be purchased in certain distant ports in India.

The Southern Sea Route was discovered in the course of the use of winds to help mariners along a route, and it was made possible by a Roman ship pilot who discovered the direct route across the Indian Ocean. The Southern Sea Route started from the Southern coast of China in Kuangchou (Canton), round the peninsula of Indo-China, through the Malacca Straits and up to the mouth of the Ganga. Archaeological excavations differentiate between the products which came from southern China by way of north-east India and those which came from northern China via the Central Asian route. Towards the end of the first century AD, the bulk of silk imported by Mediterranean countries was carried by sea and not over the land route through Persia.[9]

Alignment of the Silk Route

The Great Silk Route spanned half the then known world. The earlier alignments of the silk route essentially spanned in the east-westerly direction, carrying oriental merchandise to Europe, and the preferred routes were overland because of a traditional lineage of trading centers that had existed since ancient times. Over thousands of years many alignments of the silk route have been traversed, economic viability, lay of the land, mountain passes and geopolitical constraints favoring one over the other. It started from Changan (literally, eternal peace)[10] which is today's Xian and was the capital of China during the Chi, Han, Sui and Tang dynasties. Passing through Kansu, the principal route bifurcated at Anxi near Dun Huang. The northern route passed through well known oases like Hami, Turfan, Urumqi, and either went farther west to Ili and to the area of the Caspian Sea or branched off south to Korla, Kucha, Aksu and Kashgar. It skirted the Taklamakan desert (Tarim Basin) from the north. The southern route passed through Dun Huang, Niya, Keria, Khotan, Karghalik, Yarkand (Shache) and joined the northern route at Kashgar.[11] There was another middle route which went west from Dun Huang through Yumen Pass (The Jade Gate), to Lop Nor going along the extended Great Wall to the ruined city Loulan from where it either went North-west to join the northern route at Korla, or south west to meet the southern route at Jechiang (Shanshan).

The road again bifurcated from Kashgar which was the junction of the two principle routes. The western route continued over the roof of the world (the Pamirs), towards Samarkand, Balkh, Bukhara, Merv, Nissa and through Parthia to the shores of the mediterranean at Antioch and then on to Rome and Alexandria by ship. The southern route turned to Tashkurghan to cross the Karakoram pass and then on to the great Buddhist University of Taxila or Gandhara.[12] There was no importance of the sea links and therefore the silk route was not developing southwards, it only became visible when the Russian allow began its expansion towards the warm waters of the Indian Ocean and was effectively checked by the British Empire during the ensuing period of the world wars and the cold war era, there was a stalemate on this front till the Soviet occupation of Afghanistan, whereas the Soviets withdrew and eventually the Soviet union collapsed there was for the first time a realization of the emphasis of the Silk Route to shift its flow is in the north-south direction.

There were other routes also, one from Khotan or Yarkand to Leh and on to Srinagar in Kashmir and another over the Taghdumbash Pamirs, through Wakhan to Afghanistan and Iran. Due to its geographical closeness to Central Asia and linkage with the Silk Routes system, Kashmir acted as an important transit emporium in the mutual Indo-Central Asian trade. Traders from Kashmir and Punjab hills would prefer to traverse the Srinagar-Leh-Yarkand-Kashghar-Kokand route via valley of Nubra across the Khardungla pass for their trade and other dealings in Central Asia, mainly because it was safe from robberies and political turmoil.[13] Those traders who conducted small business in Chitral, Gilgit, Hunza, Nagar, Skardu etc. thus bypassing Leh and the valley of Kashmir, used other mountainous tracks – Ferghana-Kashghar-Tashkurghan-Hunza-Gilgit, Bukhara-Kabul-Chitral-Peshawar, Ferghana-Pamirs-Chitral.All these routes were used for the expansion of trade and culture in the Asian continent.

History of Silk

Sericulture or silk production has a long and colorful history unknown to most people. For centuries the West knew very little about silk and the people who made it. Pliny, the Roman historian, wrote in his Natural History in 70 BC, "Silk was obtained by removing the down from the leaves with the help of water…". For more than two thousand years the Chinese kept the secret of silk altogether to themselves. In the 8th century BC, Lei-tsu, the queen of the legendary Chinese Emperor Huang-ti, invented the basic methods of weaving and embroidering with silk thread.[14] Silk is among the fundamental elements of Chinese civilization. Words like silkworm, mulberry and silk itself have been used many times in historical books and in Chinese inscriptions. One more important fact is that Chinese archaeologists found a silkworm cocoon among objects dating from the Neolithic age. It speaks of the ancient association of silk with Chinese culture.

Producing silk is a lengthy process and demands close and constant attention. To produce high quality silk, there are two conditions which need to be fulfilled – preventing the moth from hatching, and secondly, perfecting the diet on which the silkworms should feed. The Chinese developed their own indigenous ways for both.

The idea of manufacturing silk came to Lei-Tsu when she was closely watching a silk worm spin its thread. She figured out how best to treat the silk worm and its thread, thereby ensuring that the resultant tissue surpassed all the other materials of the orient.[15] This process was developed in the north of China in Shantung. The province is still a great producer of wild silk.

Confucius compiled catalogues of the principal products of the various Chinese provinces during the reign of Emperor Yu of fifth century BC, in his book "Shu-Ching", a collection of ancient documents relating to the history of China. The tributes made to Yu indicate that there were six provinces producing silk and that they paid silk as a tribute to the emperor. Silk was used only for the ruling class. Silk was permitted only for the emperor, his close relations and the very highest of his dignitaries. Within the palace, the emperor is believed to have worn a robe of white silk; outside, he, along with his principal wife, and the heir to the throne wore yellow, the color of the earth.

More rapid methods of silk manufacturing began to exceed the demands of the aristocracy and silk came into general use. Gradually all the various classes of society began wearing tunics of silk, and silk became popular among each class.[16] Along with being used for clothing and decoration, silk was quite quickly put to industrial use by the Chinese. This was something which happened in the West only in modern times. Silk, indeed, rapidly became one of the principal elements of the Chinese economy. Silk was used for musical instruments, fishing-lines, bowstrings, bonds of all kinds, and even rag paper, the world's first luxury paper. Eventually even the common people were able to wear garments of silk.

During the rule of the Han Dynasty, silk ceased to be a mere industrial material and became a value in itself. Farmers paid their taxes in grain and silk. Silk began to be used for paying civil servants and rewarding subjects for outstanding services.[17] Values were calculated in lengths of silk in lieu of pounds of gold. Before long silk was to become a currency used in trade with foreign countries. This use of silk continued during the Tang era as well. It is possible that this added importance was the result of a major increase in production.

In spite of their secrecy, however, the Chinese were destined to lose their monopoly on silk production. Sericulture reached Korea around 200 BC, when waves of Chinese immigrants arrived there. Silk reached the West through a number of different channels. Shortly after AD 300, sericulture traveled westward and the cultivation of the silkworm was established in India.

From about the first century BC, the Greeks and Romans began talking of Seres, the Kingdom of Silk. Some historians believe that the first Romans to set eyes upon the fabulous fabric were the legions of Marcus Licinius Crassus, Governor of Syria.[18] At the fateful battle of Carrhae near the Euphrates River in 53 BC, the Syrian soldiers were so startled by the bright silken banners of the Persian troops that they fled in panic.[19] Within decades Chinese silks became widely worn by the rich and noble families of Rome. The Roman Emperor Heliogabalus (AD 218-222) wore nothing but silk.[20] By 380 AD, Marcellinus Ammianus reported, "The use of silk which was once confined to the nobility has now spread to all classes without distinction, even to the lowest." The craving for silk continued to increase over the centuries. The price of silk was very high in Rome. The best Chinese bark (a particular kind of silk) cost as much as 300 denarii (a Roman soldier's salary for an entire year).[21] Among Roman citizens demand for imported silks was so high as to be damaging to the Roman economy.[22]

Great Silk Route: Formation and Development

The Trans-Asian overland trade linked the West with China much earlier than the Han times (silk has been found in Egypt from around 1000 BCE and in Europe from around 300 years later)[23] but Han efforts helped make the long and dangerous trans-continental journey a single trip. Along this route silk and other high value goods were transported to contiguous states under the control of various political and economic systems. The western end of the Silk Route appears to have developed earlier than the eastern end. The Persian empire controlled a large swathe of the Middle East, extending as far as the Indian kingdoms to the east. Trade between the different parts of the empire was already starting to influence the cultures of these regions when Alexander the Great conquered this area as far as Ferghana on the border of modern day region of Xinjiang of China.[24] Here, in 329 BC, he founded the city of Alexandria.

For the next three centuries, the Greeks remained in central Asia, always expanding eastward. In fact, the Greek historian Strabo, writing in 1st century BC, stated that 'they extended their empire even as far as the Seres [China].' Some historians think that Euthydemus (r. 230-200 BC) of Bactria, which had been Persia's eastern-most province, may have led expeditions as far as Kashgar in Chinese Turkestan, resulting in the first official contacts between China and the West.[25]

The process of the Silk Route thrust towards the West started with a marital alliance. A princess of the Han dynasty (206 BCE-CE 220) was sent to marry the Shanyu or ruler of a pastoral nomadic people known in Chinese sources as the Hsiung-nu (the predecessors to the Huns) who tended their animals in the area of modern Mongolia and southern Siberia.[26] This group, which needed trade with China, became increasingly bellicose when denied such commerce. Ecological crises also could have prompted them to raid Chinese settlements to obtain the goods they required. The Han ruler, who professed to be economically self sufficient, tried to limit commercial and diplomatic relations with these peoples, whom they perceived as "barbarians". Yet the awareness of the threat posed by the Hsiung-nu cavalry and armies compelled the Chinese dynasty to seek peace. One of their tactics was marital alliances, and thus the dispatch of the Princess.[27]

Despite the marital alliances, the Han-Hsiung nu association remained fraught with conflict and the Chinese were denied badly needed trade to the pastoral nomads. Simultaneously, economic difficulties, on occasion, compelled the Hsiung-nu to raid the

Chinese border settlements. Deciding to seek assistance against its bellicose neighbours, around 139 BCE the Han emperor of China, Wu-ti, sent Chang-Chien to Central Asia to forge an alliance with the ruling sections there.[28] Chang traveled through the oases and towns that would eventually constitute the Silk Roads and reached Central Asia but was rebuffed in his efforts to secure allies. The Chang mission failed but Chang himself learned quite a bit from his travels on which he spent around thirteen years. He was captured and imprisoned by the Hsiung-nu. He escaped from prison and was imprisoned again on his way back home but finally he managed to return and make his report to the emperor.

Chang's mission was less an official embassy than "an intelligence mission staffed with expendable personnel".[29] Chang gave to Wu-ti tempting opportunities for trade with western lands. Within a few years Chinese merchants were regularly braving the difficult journey west through the Gansu corridor, around the Takla Makan desert, and into Central Asia. Trade seems to have thrived in the coming years. Wu-ti was particularly keen on obtaining horses from Ta-yuan, probably the Farghana Valley, which Chang had visited. The Chinese referred to these mounts as "heavenly horses".[30] The people of Ta-yuan were reluctant to part with these horses, but, in 104 BC the Han emperor sent his general Li Kuang-li as the head of a large army with instructions to acquire the horses by force. Wu-ti reinforced on massive and finally succeeded in forcing the inhabitants of Ta-yuan to capitulate. The Chinese managed to bring home only thirty "heavenly horses", but the trade route had been definitively opened and its eastern part put under control of the Han Empire.

Silk Route under the Han Empire (206BC–200AD)

The process of the Silk Route formation began during the Han empire, when Emperor Wu-ti sent missions against southern Siberia, known as Yuezhi. The Han emperors pushed China's frontiers further westwards. In order to maintain the free flow of goods along the newly opened route, the Chinese policed it with garrisons and watch-towers. Despite many hazards and interruptions, the Silk Route continued to flourish for a long time.

The development of Central Asian trade routes caused some problems for the Han rulers in China. Bandits took advantage of the terrain to plunder trade caravans along the Gansu corridor. As a result, trade began to suffer great losses at the expense of merchants at either end of the route. Han rulers answered the bandit threat by constructing forts and defensive walls along part of the route. These sections were later combined to form the 'Great Wall' which still stands today as a testament to human achievement.[31] It became apparent to later Han rulers that in order to control the route, especially the Takla Makan region, a permanent local government had to be established. Once a local government in the Takla Makan region was secure, the growth of settlements along the routes really began to take off. Under the protection of the Han Empire, the settlements were able to reap the benefits of secure and reliable trade. They also absorbed a lot of the local culture, and the cultures that passed along the silk route.

During the Han dynasty (206 BC-AD 220), many settlements were set up along the Silk Route, mostly in the oasis areas. The settlers profited from the passing trade, and also absorbed much of the local culture in addition to the alien cultures they encountered through commerce. Local guider accompanied the caravans over the markedly dangerous sections of the route.

The Han Empire set up the local government at Wutei, not far from Kuqa on the northern border of the Taklimakan, in order to protect the states in this area, which numbering about fifty.[32] At the same time the city of Gaochang was constructed in the Turfan basin. This city was developed into the center of the Huihe Kingdom; the people later became the Uygur minority of this region. Many settlements were set up along the way, mostly in the oases areas, and profited from the passing trade. They also absorbed a lot of the local culture and the cultures that passed them by along the route. In 115 BC, Wudi sent the first Chinese embassy to Anxi (Persia), to the court of the Parthian King Mithridates II.[33] Its aims were commercial and the Parthian sovereign responded courteously. According to historians this mission started the trade relations between China and Persia and the latters purchasing of Chinese silk. A few years later the Parthian was able to dazzle the Romans with banners of embroidered silk imported from China.

In 104 BC, 102BC and 42 BC, Han armies conducted campaigns across the Pamirs as far west as Sogdiana and Ferghana in Central Asia opening up the Silk Road even farther.[34] At the campaign of

42 BC they laid siege to a walled settlement in Sogdiana, near the Talas river. The defenders were the Xiongnu tribe, but the settlement was protected by wooden railings, a structure favoured by the Romans and unknown in the East till this event. The sinologist Homer Dubs (Dubs, 1957) explained that the Xiongnu defenders were assisted by Roman soldiers, captives taken at the Battle of Carrhae and sent East as slaves. The Chinese were victorious and captured 145 of the Roman soldiers. The captives were taken back to China as this was the first contact of China with the Romans.[35]

The expansion of commerce with the west set in with the arrival of some foreigners at Xian and this was also the cause of foreign influence on Han art. As China expanded its borders into Central Asia merchants and envoys started to arrive in China to swear allegiance to the Han court and bring exotic goods as tribute. Chinese merchants joined many of the expeditions to the west and developed a process of trade and cultural interchange. The Han dynasty acquired technical know-how from neighbouring countries through the Silk Road. This acquisition was critical in the development of Chinese civilization and it was procured through early trade and military contacts via the Silk Road. Construction methods for bridges and mountain roads, knowledge of medicinal plants and poisons, the cultivation of cotton, and techniques of navigation and seafaring (from India) were some features of the know-how acquired.[36]

Merchants frequently went as emissaries to the Han court to ensure favourable receptions for their goods. During the reign of Chengdi (33-7 BC) all the delegations that had come to pay tribute to the Hans belonged to merchant groups from various places. From AD 73 Er onwards General Ban Chao (31-103 AD) of the Hans began the process of restoring Han rule in Central Asia. The various states of the Tarim Basin had submitted to Han rule till 91 AD. The restoration happened through a process devised by Ban Chao at minimal expense and by the use of local troops. This enabled China to reoccupy its control of the Silk Road. In the same period he was appointed "Protector General of the Western Region"[37] and led an expedition across Central Asia as far as the Caspian Sea. Ban Chao dispatched an emissary called Gan Xing to Da Qin (Rome) in 97 AD. Gan Xing was deterred from continuing his journey and he preserved the lucrative role of the Parthians as middlemen in the silk trade between China and Rome. The Romans refer repeatedly to China as the "Land of Seres",[38] a country where silk was produced by combing it from trees, and the Chinese believed that the Romans were physically similar to the Chinese and they called the country 'Great Qin' after China.

The first century (AD) of Han rule was a period of increasing trade between China and the West. Hou Han Shou (Han historian) has noted that peasant colonies were founded in the fertile land areas inns and posts for changing horses established along the main routes. Messengers and couriers traveled in every season of the year and merchant strangers knocked daily on the gates.[39]

The growing trade and commerce influenced art. Dominant themes of Steppe art, such as aggressive animals or openwork narratives and landscapes are to be found on Chinese bronze belt plaques and harness fittings. These were absorbed via trade with the Xiongnu. A silver box and a jade rhyton (drinking pot) found in the settlements of Central Asia reflect contacts with Western and Central Asia. When the region was absorbed into the Chinese empire in 111 BC, the new Han rulers of the South introduced Chinese culture and craftsmanship but indigenous styles were not entirely displaced. A lot of examples of Han dynasty art reveal contacts with and influences of Southeast and Central Asia. The naked cherub motif appears on a liquer plate unearthed at the tomb of General Zhu Ran (d. 249 AD) in Ma'anshan, Anhui province. The plate dates back to the Eastern Han dynasty (25-220 AD) and contains an inscription that suggests it was manufactured in Chengdu, Sichuan province. This motif occurs many times in Roman mosaic and on silver vessels and has traveled so far with unchanged form.[40] Such motifs reached China through the intermediacy of nomadic art.[41] New metallurgical techniques such as granulation, loop in loop chains and an early form of cloisonné were acquired from the West by the Chinese through contact with the nomads during the Eastern Zhoa dynasty, and perfected during the Qin and Han dynasties.[42]

Artistic styles such as the carving of narrative scenes on stone and making stone sculpture in the round have no precedents in previous dynasties. Their origins may be traced to the sculpture and bar reliefs of the Greco-Roman world and Assyria, by a process of gradual dissemination along the Silk Road.[43] This is also the case with the more naturalistic style of Han art. In the feudal setups of the earlier dynasties art was produced almost exclusively for ritual use, but during the affluent years of the Han dynasty it was created to beautify the home. The new qualities of dynamism, naturalism and the very inclination must have been due to ideas imported from the outer world.

Silk Route during the Tang Dynasty (618 AD–907 AD)

Silk Route reached its height of importance during the Tang dynasty, with relative internal stability in China after the division of the earlier dynasties that succeeded the Han. The individual states had mostly been assimilated and the threats from marauding peoples were rather less. In the seventh century, the Chinese traveler Xuan Zhuang crossed the region while on his way to India to obtain Buddhist scriptures from there. He followed the northern branch of the Silk Road round the Taklamakan on his outward journey, and he returned to the Tang capital at Xian via the southern route. He is still seen by the Chinese as an important influence in the development of Buddhism in China and his travels were dramatized by the popular classic "Tales of the Journey to the West".[44]

When the Silk Road was first established, silk was not its chief commodity of trade. The Han dynasty made very little profit from it and it was not until the Romans became fanatic about silk that the large profits came in. The Romans loved silk so much that they even exchanged silk for its weight in gold. During the Tang dynasty, thirty percent of the trade on the Silk Road comprised silk.

The civilization and art of the Silk Road reached their climax during the Tang Dynasty. Xian, as the starting point of the route, as well as the capital of the dynasty, developed into one of the largest and most cosmopolitan cities of the time. By 742 AD, the population had reached about two million and the city itself covered almost the same area as present day Xian, considerably more than the area within the present walls of the city.[45] The census of 754 AD showed that five thousand foreigners lived in Xian, Turks, Iranians, Indians and others from along the Road, as well as Japanese, Koreans and Malyas from the east.[46] Among these foreigners many were missionaries, merchants and pilgrims but all other occupations were also represented. Rare plants, medicines, spices and other goods from the west were to be found in the markets of the city. It is quite clear, however, that despite the exotic imports, the Chinese regarded all foreigners as barbarians; the gifts provided for the Emperors by foreign rulers were simply considered as tributes from vassal states.

The Tang Emperors of China welcomed foreigners and foreign trade. A Persian merchant and a Central Asian dancer represented the travelers of this time. The Persian merchant could have been used to spread Islam, Zoroastrianism and Nestorianism throughout Asia along the Silk Roads.[47] Accounts based on the travels of such traders yield descriptions of the lively markets in the Central Asian towns and in the great Chinese capital of Xian, of the products exchanged, and of the state of commerce. The Central Asian dancer, who can be visualized through the Tang tricolored ceramic figurines of foreign entertainers (examples of which may be found in almost any museum with a significant collection of Chinese art), could have been used to project cultural diffusion in music and dance, and to show the activities of the court.

The Nestorians, persecuted by the Council of Ephesus in 432 AD fled eastward to Central Asia and from there to Xian via the Silk Road where their first church was established in 638 AD during the Tang Dynasty.[48] Nestorian books have been found in ancient oases like Turfan and Dun Huang.[49] The advent of Islam in Western China via the Silk Road makes fascinating study. According to Tang Dynasty records two emissaries, one from Yezdgerd III, the grandson of Khosro, and the other from the Roman empire came to the court of Tai Tsung, the second Tang Emperor (627-650 AD), in 638 and 643 respectively and both reported their defeat by the Arabs.[50] Yezdgerd, the last of the Sassanian kings of Iran had sought refuge with the Turkish tribes of Ferghana and had also sought friendship with emperor Tai Tsung. The Chinese were at the height of their power and had frontiers with the Persian Empire.[51] In AD 650, Tai Tsug died and his son Emperor Kao Tsung received an appeal for help from Firoz, the son of Yezdgerd. Kao Tsung sent an emissary to Caliph Osman to plead for Firoz and the Caliph in return sent one of his generals to Xian in 651 AD and thus the first Muslim Embassy was established in Western China.[52]

Contacts with China and the states of the Korean peninsula gained greater intensity at the beginning of the sixth century when Japan experienced a wave of immigration. The Japanese sent students, officials and Buddhist monks to China for training. The

Yellow and Eastern Seas became a continuation of the Great Silk Road. From the sixth century on, Japan's path to the West began in Osaka the sea route to Japan. The two largest collection of silk fabrics in the world brought to Japan from China in the Tang epoch testified to the importance of the Silk Road in Japanese civilization. These are found in the monastery of Horyuji and in the imperial treasure-trove of Shosian (in the City of Nara).[53]

The art and civilization of the Silk Route, in common with that of the rest of China achieved its greatest glory during the Tang Dynasty which is generally regarded as China's 'Golden Age'.[54] At the same time, with the spreading of various religions in the world range, more and more missionaries reached the east in succession by this road. With the Silk Road acting as an information superhighway, the exchange of ideas grew on a larger scale than ever before. And as a result, the Tang dynasty experienced the best periods of the Road. During the long period of peace and stability which characterize this era, prosperity reigned throughout the empire. Its capital Chang-an, the 'Rome of Asia'[55] and the point of departure for travelers using the Silk Road, was one of the most splendid and cosmopolitan city in the world.

The height of the importance of the Silk Route was during the Tang dynasty, when a relative internal stability prevailed in China. Individual states had mostly been assimilated, and the threat from marauding peoples was rather less. During this period, in the seventh century, the Chinese traveler Xuanzang crossed the region on his way to India to obtain Buddhist scriptures. His journey took him along the Northern Silk Road to Turfan and Kuqa, then across the Tianshan Mountains to Tashkent, Samarkand and Bactria; over the Hindu Kush to the Gandhara kingdom in a vast circuit of India and finally back to China through the Pamirs and along the Southern Silk Route. He is still seen by the Chinese as an important influence in the development of Buddhism in China. The Tang regime was the golden period of the art and civilization of the Silk Road.

Spread of Buddhism along the Silk Route

Besides silk, paper and other goods, the Silk Route carried Buddhist ideology which has great significance in world history.[56] Along with trade and migration this oldest highway of the world was the carrier of Buddhism through Central Asia. Buddhism came to

China from India as early as the first century AD, and changed the face of the Silk Route towns with monasteries and pagodas. The transmission was launched from north-western India to modern Pakistan, Afghanistan, Central Asia, Xinjiang, China, Korea and Japan. Buddhism not only affected the lives and cultures of these regions but also left us a world of wonders in arts and literature. Buddhist influence was seen in the art of the era, as more artists began using the image of the Buddha in their work.

It is not certain when Buddhism reached China, but with the Silk Route in operation, missionaries and pilgrims began to travel between China, Central Asia and India. Records say that Chang Chien, on his return from Ta-hsia (Ferghana) in the 2nd century BC, heard of a country named Tien-Chu (India) and their Buddhist teaching.[57] This is probably the first time a Chinese heard about Buddhism. A century later, a Buddhist community at the court of a Han prince is mentioned in a record. However the most famous story is that of the Han emperor Mingdi's dream about Buddha. In 68 AD, Mingdi sent his official Cai Yin to Central Asia to learn more about Buddhism after a vision of a golden figure appeared to him in a dream.[58] The next morning he asked his ministers what the dream meant and was told that he had seen the Buddha— the god of the West. Cai Yin returned after 3 years in India and brought back with him not only the image of Buddha and Buddhist scriptures but also two Buddhist monks named She-mo-teng and Chu-fa-lan to preach in China.[59] This was the first time that China had Buddhist monks and their ways of worship. A few years later, a Buddhist community was established in Loyang, the capital. From this time, Buddhism grew uninterruptedly. In 148 AD, a Parthian missionary, Shih-kao arrived in China. He set up a Buddhist temple at Loyang and began the long work of translating Buddhist scriptures into the Chinese language. The work of scripture translation continued until the 8th century when the Arabs accessed Central Asia and India.

During the 4th Century, Kumarajiva, a Buddhist from Central Asia organised the first translation bureau, better than anything that had existed before in China. He and his team translated some 98 works from many languages into Chinese of which 52 survive and are included in Buddhist literature.[60] By around 514 AD there were 2 million Buddhists in China,[61] Buddhism (Mahayan) in China reached its highest point during the Sui and Tang dynasties (581-

907 AD). Popular forms of Buddhism filtered down to the common people.[62]

While numerous pilgrims came to China from the West, Chinese Buddhist pilgrims were sent to India at different times and the accounts which some of them have left of their travels in the Silk Road provide valuable evidence of the position of Buddhism in Central Asia and India from the 4th to the 7th centuries. Some of the more famous Chinese pilgrims were Fa-hian (399 to 414), Xuan-zang (629-645) and I.tsing (671-695). Buddhism produced a body of texts more vast than any other religion in human history, making the study of even one school a life-long task. In China today philosophy professors warn their students, "The serious study of Buddhism is a Black Hole – if you enter, you will never re-emerge".[63] Buddhist manuscripts and artwork continued to pour into China changing the look of the civilization as a whole. By 742 AD, Chang-an had become an exotic metropolis, boasting of a population of nearly two million, five thousand of which were foreigners from along the Road, as well as Japanese, Koreans, and Malays.

According to the records of Chinese monks both the Hinayana and Mahayana forms of Buddhism were practiced in India around the second century AD. Mahayana Buddhism which incorporates the idea of many Buddhas and Boddhisatvas, was established through the help of great monks, such as Nagarjuna, the two brothers Asanga and Vasubandhu, and support from various excellent doctrines, including those of "Bodhisatvas, Tathagata-Garbha and Sukhavati".[64] The Mahayana or "Great Vehicle" first gained influence in Central Asian regions such as Khotan, before displacing the Nikaya schools from the Silk Road altogether.[65] As one contemporary scholar has cautiously put it, "It is just possible that the popularisation of the Mahayana was a phenomenon which took place outside the Indian subcontinent, for reasons connected perhaps with the transmission of Buddhism to other cultures".[66] There was a branch of the Great Silk Route which ran over the Karakorum Range to the Gandhara kingdom of the Kushans and on to India. Buddhism certainly had a strong effect on some other lives in the steppes. Grousset has pointed out that once a nomadic tribe adopted the Buddhist faith, it no longer possessed tough barbaric and soldierly qualities. Eventually these bribes lost their nomadic identity and were absorbed by the non-nomadic neighbors. When the Mongols were in a controlling position on the Silk Road, Kublai Khan clearly showed his preference for Buddhism even though most of the Mongol kingdoms converted to Islam. Along this long and unpredictable highway came what Kipling calls a "river of life",[67] carrying exotic goods and conveying new ideas about the Buddhist-Philosophy.

Kushans and the Silk Route

During the rule of the Kushans, northwest India and the adjoining regions participated both in seagoing trade and in commerce along the Silk Route to China. The period of the 1st century AD introduced a new era in Indian history when Kushans belonging to the Yueh-chi tribe of Central Asia,[68] migrated into India from Central Asia. The Yueh-chi appear to have begun their migration in about 165 BC arriving in Bactria in about 140 BC, migrating over a distance of more than 4,000 km within a single generation. They extended their rule across Bactria and the Kabul region and during the first century AD into the Gandhara Kingdom in Punjab. Much of this was accomplished during the reign of Kujula-Kadphises (ca 30-80 AD) thereby ending Parthian rule in the area. The Kushans conquered large parts of Central Asia. Kushan kings issued coins that initiated the style of the Scythians and Parthians who preceded them.[69] Fascinatingly, some of these coins include depictions of the Roman Emperor, Augustus, with modifications of the coins the design.

In the second century AD the Kushan King Kanishka I ruled an empire that extended from the Gangetic Plain of northern India to Sogdiana. He administered from two capitals: Purushapura (now Peshawar) near the Khyber Pass, and Mathura in northern India.[70] Under Kanishka's rule, ruler the dynasty was at the peak of its power, the Kushans controlled a large area ranging from the Aral Sea through areas that include present-day Uzbekistan, Afghanistan, and Pakistan into northern India as far east as Benares and as far south as Sanchi. Kanishka was the greatest of all the Kushan rulers. His rule brought prosperity and security and led to an increase in trade throughout the region. Bactria was the original nucleus and center of the Kushan Kingdom.

The Great Silk Route, the first transcontinental trade and diplomatic road in the history of mankind was laid across the lands of the Kushans and the Parthians from China to the Mediterranean Roman empire. The principal trade route from India passed through Taxila, through the Khyber Pass to Bamiyan and across the Hindu Kush to Balkh. From Balkh, the highway led east along the Wakhan corridor and through the Pamirs to China or north to Termez and onward to Central Asia. Taxila was the meeting point on one side of the royal highway and the trade route running from the Ganga valley via the watershed and through the upper Doabs, and, on the other, the route from West Asia via the Khyber Pass as well as the recently discovered route from Central Asia through Gilgit and Chitral. Mountain passes promote communication and the Khyber Pass, with cities such as Taxila and Begram[71] has always been the route of migration, trade and invasion. Bamiyan was the approximate halfway point of an arduous journey across the country. At the eastern end of this part of the Silk Road is the Khyber pass, rising through the foothills of the Suleiman range from its starting point, about 16 km west of Peshawar. The 45 km long pass has provided access to India since the beginning of recorded history.[72]

It was in the empire of the great Kushan King Kanishka that the agents of Maes Titanius set out from the Stone Tower for the eastern deserts and the land of the Seres. The east part of this great Route was under China. It was undoubtedly the ascendancy of these two powers over the many small states in their area that enabled the caravans of this period to go about their business in peace and with a reasonable degree of security. There were garrisons everywhere. It was a highly favourable period for trade.

Three western oases fell within the sphere of influence of the Indo-Scythian Kingdom of the Kushans.[73] Isolated Chinese garrisons got together with the local population and representatives of the Kushans and formed a united front against the Huns to ensure the continuance of the trade. There existed an agreement between China and the empire of the Kushans; that was why Pan-Ch'ao could send an ambassador to Rome, who, with his whole suite could cross the Kushan territory from side to side with no trouble at all. Both empires needed to be on good terms with each other: the Chinese wanted an ally against the Tibetans and the Huns, while the Kushans were anticipating trouble with the Persians in the west.

History records that the Kushans and the Chinese had one serious disagreement: a rejected proposal of marriage. In AD 90 the king of the Kushans sent an ambassador to the court of China to ask for the hand of a Chinese princess.[74] The ambassador was stopped by the commander of the Western Territories, who had no intention of allowing the visitors to carry out such an audacious project.[75] The Chinese could sell their silk either to the Persians or the Kushans; and the offer of marriage may well have been made in the hope of securing the monopoly of silk purchase and resale, which would have been a serious blow for the Persians. By refusing the Kushan offer, China expressed her wish for an alliance with Persia. Eventually, Persia won in the tussle and got the profitable alliance with the Chinese.

The Gandhara[76] region, in the heart of the Kushan empire was home to a multiethnic society tolerant of religious differences. Desirable for its strategic location, with direct access to the overland silk routes and links to the ports on the Arabian Sea, Gandhara had suffered many conquests and had been ruled by the Mauryans, Alexander the Great (327/26–325/24 BC), his Indo-Greek successors (third–second centuries BC), and a combination of Scythians and Parthians (second–first centuries BC). The melding of peoples produced an eclectic culture, vividly expressed in the visual arts produced during the Kushan period. The Kushan King sent an embassy to Rome because of the said trade agreement between China and Persia. The Kushan kingdom was hoping to form an association with Rome, due to its differences with China. Thus Rome and the Kushans came on common platform and engaged in direct trade.

It was in the Kushan period that the peoples of the East began to appreciate as never before the benefits of cultural relations and contacts, and so they proceeded to evolve common cultural values and build a culture for everyone inhabiting the great empire. A most important feature of these cultural and economical contacts made through the Great Silk Route was that in the process of cooperation each culture retained its local tradition, original character and distinct identity.

Trade along the Silk Route

The Silk Route did not exist for the sole purpose of trading in silk. Although silk was the most attractive part of the Route for Westerners, it was only one of the many items that were traded throughout the history of the Route. Gold and other precious metals, ivory, precious stones, and glass went towards China, while fur, ceramics, gun powder, jade, bronze objects, lacquer, and iron went west. All these items went overland by caravans of camels numbering from a hundred to a thousand. These caravans were extremely valuable and vulnerable to bandits; they needed escorts and a secure place to camp each night.

To the countries of the West, China was synonymous with silk hence the name Seres. However, the process of producing this precious commodity was kept a well guarded secret. It was known only to master weavers at centres like Hangchow in East Central China.[77] There are many stories about how the art of silk manufacture spread. Han princess, married to a prince of Khotan, smuggled silk worm eggs in her elaborate wedding headdress and thus made Khotan a centre for silk weaving, famous for its Atlas silk.[78] There is the story of Nestorian monks smuggling silk worms and eggs to Byzantium by concealing them in their hollowed-out wooden staff. Earlier the Parathians had come to know of silk and when the material found its way to Rome it became the rage of the time not only with the ladies who found it soft and enticing but also with men who loved to wear silk togas. The fashion caught on to such an extent that it adversely affected the Roman economy. So much so that early in time Tiberius banned men from using silk.[79] However, apart from silk, China also exported ivory and precious stones, textiles and furs, ceramics and lacquer, cinnamon bark and a variety of spices. These goods were bartered or sold in the various oases on the way, in Central Asian cities like Samarkand and Bukhara, in Parthia and then in the Mediterranean lands. The goods were eventually shipped to Rome and Alexandria.

The Parthians, the Kushans as well as the Central Asian traders played the role of middlemen and reaped profits on the two-way traffic.[80] The returning carvans brought mainly gold from the Greek and Roman empires, jewels and pearls from India, rubies from Badakhshan.[81] According to annals in China, a carvan moved out of China every lunar month. Each camel carried about 140 kilograms of weight and walked 30 kilometers per day. Pack-animals were changed at regular staging posts along the 9000 miles long route, but many perished each year either in the deserts or on the high passes enroute. There were many instances of the mass migration of entire communities along the route. The migration of the Yuezhi, the founders of the Kushan Empire is well known.[82]

Markets for Silk and its Supply in Eurasia

Silk weaving began in the early centuries AD in West Asia, but the weavers depended on China for the supply of silk yarn. The technology of breeding silk worms was introduced a few centuries later. In India silk yarn was made from species other than the mulberry silk worm in early times. From the fourth century AD, many countries began to produce polycrome patterned silk, though the Chinese retained their monopoly on translucent and thin fabric.[83] Chinese patterned silk remained desired commodities in various countries but products from the Central Asian states, Sassianid Persia, India and Byzantium also reached foreign markets. Chinese patterned silk textile products were traded among these countries as luxury goods because they differed in weave technology and artistic design.[84] These differences, stemming from the different cultural backgrounds of the producers made them exotic in foreign countries and added to their appeal as luxury goods. Silk transactions took the form of diplomatic gestures because of their high transport costs and labour. Some special kinds of silk were reserved for very powerful and wealthy persons. The important silk markets at that time were the following:

China

Han-China tried to bar merchants from wearing embroidered and polychrome silk and this tradition of controlling the use and sale of luxury goods was also followed by later Chinese rulers. The Northern Wei (AD 386-534) rulers tried to register all goldsmiths and other artisans. They ruled that whoever – prince or commoner—hired these artisans at his home exposed his whole family to a death sentence. A special category of these artisans under government control was referred to as the 'Silk Weaving Households'.[85] The royal manufacturers monopolized the production of certain kinds of polychrome silk in the Tang regime. All Chinese emperors used large quantities of silk as gifts to foreigners for political reasons or in exchange for coveted foreign goods. They also tried to control its export. An edict of AD 714 forbade the sale to foreigners of choice silk products: polychrome patterned silks, damasks, gauzes, crepes, embroideries and other fine silks.[86]

The rulers tried to reserve certain luxury goods for themselves and the wealthy also followed suit. Traders were allured by the possibility of high profits to make and sell fine silks as the technology for producing luxury silk was available. In the era of Shen-kui (AD 519-20), towards the end of the reign of the Northern Wei, the government tried to revive the sumptuary law that forbade merchants and artisans to wear gold and silver ornaments, as well as embroidery and polychrome patterned silk, but it could not enforce the law at all.[87] There were so many centers of silk weaving that the government could not possibly control the production and export of silk to the Tang areas. A study of the silk samples found in Central Asia shows that it came from various parts of China.[88]

It is not known when foreign silk entered into China, but it is clear that the popularity of domestic went down because of it. In as early as the fourth century AD, there is a record of women in the west frontier region, Ho-hsi, wearing a five-coloured silk fabric made in foreign countries.[89] Later records show that the foreign produced silks that entered China were from the Central Asian countries, Persia, and Byzantium. These later Chinese documents are dated mid fifth century. One important kind of foreign silk was the Kucha polychrome patterned silk made in Turfan. This was referred to as a specific kind of silk fabric originating in Kucha. Another kind of Central Asian silk fabric, Zandaniji, was woven in a place near Bukhara, around the seventh century was also found in Tunhung.[90]

Envoys and traders presented the best foreign silk products to the emperor. From the 6th century, Sassanian polychrome silk became very famous, so that visitors from Central Asia and South Asia brought Persian silk as gift or tribute to the Chinese court. Hua (an unidentified state in Central Asia) sent Persian silk along with a yellow lion and white sable in 520 AD.[91] Envoys from Khuttal and Kapisa offered Persian polycrome silk to a Tang emperor.[92] The polychrome silk from the Roman empire has been mentioned in the biography of the late fourth century Buddhist preacher, Kumarajiva. It is said that the king of Kucha honoured Kumarajiva with silk from the Roman empire.[93] It is hard to accept the early date of the fourth century for Roman or Byzantine silk appearing in Central Asia because the silk from the Byzantine empire was known in China only by the sixth century. In his famous book, "The Golden Peaches of Samarkand", Edward Schafer identifies a sample from Astana, Turfan, with its octagonal design (Ast. vii. 1.06, National Museum, New Delhi) as representing a Byzantine Greek Style.[94]

Some changes in Chinese silk weaving, both in technology and design, were introduced when silk fabric was imported from other countries. "From Han to Tang, the weaving technology of patterned silk first underwent a transition from warp-faced compound tabby to wrap faced compound twill. While the wrap threads were still the carriers of patterned colours in compound twill weaving, the more complicated technology produced a more aesthetic effect than the simpler tabby weaving. The more fundamental transition in weaving technology was the change to weft faced compound twill. Weft faced technology was traditionally used for wool weaving in the West. When these countries developed silk weaving they naturally adopted this technology. Using weft-faced technology meant that weft threads were carriers of colours for designed patterns. The coloured weft threads were operated by hand and were thus more flexible in forming patterns than were the warp threads which were fixed on the loom. This flexibility gave high - Tang silk a wider breadth, with larger and more elaborate patterns than that (those) of previous periods".[95]

Many changes were taken place when Buddhism flourished in China. Foreign influence on designs made from the fifth century. Whereas auspicious animals such as the tiger, horse, deer and phoenix and other traditional Chinese sacred symbols dominated the designs on Han silk. After the Buddhist inroad, auspicious objects from India such as the peacock, the lion, elephant and Boddhi tree joined the menagerie of Chinese animals on textile design (e.g. Sinking Vighur Autonomous Region, Museum, 1972, pl. 23, 26, 27).[96] Central and Western Asian influence resulted in some designs showing stiff animal and plant motifs in contrast to the supple, floating Han motifs. One example is a fifth or sixth century piece of silk found in Astana with rows of birds and sheep facing each other, separated by rows of trees.[97] Iranian influence appears in the design of animal motifs in pearl roundels, where small circles form a larger circle with an animal motif inside.[98]

Weft-faced compound twill with typical Persian animal motifs and roundels had become very popular in China during the late seventh and the eighth centuries.

Chinese polychrome silks with foreign designs were produced for both foreign and domestic markets. Polychrome silks with Indian motifs were suitable for Buddhist pilgrims and Buddhist traders who carried that as donations westward to the land of Buddha. From the seventh century, Yang-Chou in South China specialized in making 'polychrome silk for the robs of foreigners'.[99] Traditional warp-faced technology was still adequate for export purposes. Meanwhile, the Chinese elite built up their taste for imported silk. If genuine imported silk was not available for Chinese requirements they brought domestic copies of it. They promoted western technology for Tang artisans not only for making authentic seeming foreign style silk, but also for absorbing foreign traditions in weaving domestic silks. Producing silk of high aesthetic value was the special feature of Chinese silks.

Central Asia

The silk trade began along the Central Asian routes in the second century BC. The Central Asian peoples were the earliest agents who carried silk products and transferred the technology of silk weaving and sericulture. However, these were not a homogeneous or stable population. While the sedentary communities who resided in the oases along the trade routes were relatively stable, who nomadic tribes were constantly on the move. The Scythians, Hephthalites, the various Turkic tribes and the Arabs controlled different parts of Central Asia after the retreat of Hsuing-nu. Thus, both nomadic and settled of groups in silk trade.

Some painted bricks excavated from the tombs of Chia-yu Gate, a border region between the interior of China and Central Asia, depict scenes of people cultivating mulberry trees and taking care of cocoons.[100] About a century later, literary sources referred to sericulture in the oases states of Turfan and Argi.[101] In Central Asian Kingdom used silk that did not endear them to their silk purchasing neighbours: capturing traders and commodities was not beneficial for long distance trade.

Its function as a medium of exchange, increased the flow of silk fabrics into Central Asia. There was no currency in politically unstable Central Asia like the copper coins of China. The flourishing trade along the silk routes required a common currency, and silk was the most popular commodity so it was a parallel currency to copper coins in China. Kharosthi documents dated late third or early fourth century AD from Central Asia say that silk fabric and garments were used as payment in transactions. The price of a woman was fortyone bolts of silk.[102] A Buddhist monastery listed fines in bolts of silk for monks who broke rules.[103] As a monastery was a station for pilgrims and traders they preserved silk as their property. The practice of using bolts of silk was like money in Central Asian regions.

India

During the Gupta era, the silk industry, from sericulture to weaving, was well established. The silk weaving guild of Mandasor testifies to the prosperity of the trade.[104] During the Kushan period Kashmir developed a high tradition in uni- and bi-voltine silk. Japanese authors have stated that the bi-voltine worm is the genus from which the univoltine evolved in colder climates and the multivoltines in warmer climates. The home of the original species had to be located in temperate zones and both the Indian Himalayan tracts and the South China zone could qualify for silk worm rearing (Bombyx-mori). Muga silk is woven in the eastern Himalayas, Nagaland, Assam, South Tripura and North Burma. Commercial exploitation is based on the semi domesticated warm in this region. The presence of this variety is also noted in the valleys of Kumaon and Kamgra.[105] Gold coloured muga, which was the most common in upper is Assam traded widely. Chapa silks are reputed to be stronger and more pleasing than the other, is the name given to the Bombys – mori silk (China).[106]

In eastern, central and south India, tasar silk is produced by the A. mylitta worm. In Assam the worm is A. Frithii while in north-western India it is A. Sivalika. In the sub-Himalayan belt the A. Roylei pre-dominates. In China tasar is woven by the A. Pernyi worm.[107] The tasar belt in India is divided into two, tropical and temperate. The Deccan plateau constitutes the home of the tropical tasar worm. Some of the tribal groups such as the Bhils of Bihar and Gonds of Madhya Pradesh, are involved in tasar production. The temperate tasar tract extends from Jammu and

Kashmir in the West to Manipur in the East, including Himachal Pradesh, the Kumaon and Garhwal divisions of Uttar Pradesh, Meghalaya and Nagaland.[108] Eri silk was also famous in Indian markets.

Indians imported both silk textiles and silk yarn from China, as India controlled part of the silk trade between China and Byzantinians. Before the Byzantine acquired the knowledge of sericulture, their silk industry was heavily dependent on Chinese yarn, which they obtained through the Persians. The Persians in turn bought silk yarn from the Central Asians and Indians.[109] If Persia bought silk from India, the Indians were obviously dealing in seric, i.e. Chinese silk yarn. Chinansuka, a type of Indian silk was used by the Indian elite and also exported outside India.[110]

Persia

Persian merchants traveled to China from an early period. Sources suggest that the Persians began to weave polychrome silk in the fourth century AD, but reliable literary records and material evidence come only later in the Sassanian period.[111] This silk woven with gold thread was famous in east and west both Gold brocade trimmed with precious stones was the material of royal robes.

Silk samples which have been identified as Sassanian are often found in European churches and Egyptian tombs and some places in Central Asia.[112] Sassanian silk clearly reached the territory of Byzantium and beyond. Sassanian silk fabrics were so popular that both westerners and eastern weavers tried to copy them. They probably had to import some of the silk yarn for their looms from China. Trade with China via the land routes began in the second century BC, mainly through the trading posts in Sogdiana. As the Sassanians bought whole cargoes of Chinese silk from the Indians, they had an upper hand over Byzantium until the latter developed its own sericulture. Because of this trade Persia became a strong mediator between China and Rome.

Byzantium

Around 150 BC the Hans who had brought the Hioung-nou insurgency under control, proceeded to establish colonies in Central Asia. The increased access of silk led to significant developments in Syrian weaving. The earliest examples of twill damask weave in silk are those of Syrian provinces, dated the year between the first and fourth centuries AD.

Roman weavers developed multiple heddle rod looms for weaving damask in eastern provinces in 250 AD.[113] After the establishment of the Eastern Roman Empire at Byzantium in 330 AD, a silk industry was developed at imperial workshops. Later, Greece and Egypt, as parts of the Byzantium Empire acquired their silk industries on a large scale. Till the time of Justinian (483-565), Byzantium depended on imported silk yarn.[114] Competition with Persia for access to silk yarn was very stiff.

The silk industry in Byzantium developed along with new fashions in clothing. Silk textiles as emblems of status became more and more elaborate in the year of the Roman-Byzantium empire. During Justinian's reign Byzantium started sericulture. Under the rule of Justinian the private silk industry in the territory was virtually extinguished and government monopoly on silks in purple with gold embroidery became effective. Purple dye-houses and silk workshops became key government departments, occupying the same level as the imperial treasury and came under the administration of the minister of finance.[115] The Romans used to be proud of their freedom to wear purple and silk according to their economic means. It is well known that Pliny blamed the drain of the Roman treasury on imported luxuries, including fine textiles such as cotton and silk, along with spices, pepper and gem stones.[116]

The Silk Route was a historical force that drove people to come to grips with cultural, national, and racial differences. Themes of cultural borrowing, interactions of civilizations, development of new economic institutions and technologies to facilitate commerce, together with the sheer excitement of travel and adventure are conveyed through historical descriptions of the Silk Route. Silk was more valuable than gold in early times, and the Silk Route emerged as a boon for the people of China, Central Asia, India, Persia and Rome. Just as the Gupta era is called the "Golden age of India", in Chinese History the Tang age is depicted in similar terms, made possible and that by the Silk Route and silk production. The Silk Route trade and commerce was truly global in nature because the commodities of the trade have been unearthed in distant corners of the earth, such as, "an Indian ivory mirror handle from the first century AD found in the ruins of

Pompeii, an Egyptian Pharaoh mask found in the thirteenth century grave of a Mongol Woman at Genghis Khan's capital of Karakorum in Mongolia, and a seventh century bronze Buddha from Pakistan's Swat Valley found in a Viking grave at Helgo in Sweden, and Chinese silk in the Roman Empire".[117]

The beginnings of land-based trade between Orient and Occident can be traced to around 105 BC, when the Chinese Emperor Wu-ti sent a group of Chinese emissaries to the court of Mithradates II, of the Parthian rulers of Persia. At different times and throughout history, trading centers grew and prospered along the highways of the Silk Route. Great cities like the Abbasid capital of Baghdad, the Sogdian town of Samarkand and the Bactrian metropolis of Merv became dynamic entrepots where goods were traded in both directions. This trade was driven by three basic factors: firstly, the obvious desire of profit; secondly, a fascination with the exotic and thirdly, as a means to enhance political power. The Silk Route was an early example of political and cultural integration due to inter-regional trade. In its heyday, it sustained an international culture that brought together groups as diverse as the Magyars, the Armenians and the Chinese and encouraged them to integrate, and helped spread new products and, even more importantly, new ideas.

Buddhism, Christianity, Manichaeism, Zorostrianism and Islam spread in Central Asia and China through the Silk Route. The Silk Route played the role of a connecting bridge between countries and civilizations. It served as a channel for trade, which became the catalyst for the development of the arts and the crafts. Travelers and explorers studied the countries and peoples of the lands along the Silk Route, thus making an enormous contribution to the growth of knowledge. The world came to know of the ideas and work of the great philosophers, scholars and statesmen. Mutual enrichment of cultures took place, and there was an active exchange of knowledge and of spiritual and philosophical concepts and views through the ancient Silk Route.

NOTES

1. Richard C. Foltz, *Religions of the Silk Road: Overland Trade and Cultural Exchange from Antiquity to the Fifteenth Century,* (London: Macmillan Press, 1999), p. 2.
2. Hsuan Tsang's description of his visit to India, *On Yuan Chwang's Travels in India,* ed. Watters (London, 1904-5), p. 427.
3. Kyotaro Nishikawa, *The Grand Exhibition of Silk Road Civilizations: The Route of Buddhist Art,* (Nara, 1988), p. 16.
4. Jonathan Tucker, *The Silk Road – Art and History,* (New Delhi: Timeless Books, 2003), p. 188.
5. Kyotaro Nishikawa, n. 2, p. 17.
6. *Ibid.,* p. 17.
7. Amalendu Guha (Ed.), *Central Asia—Movement of Peoples and Ideas from Times Prehistoric to Modern,* (ICCR New Delhi), 1970), p. 185-186.
8. Jonathan Tucker, n. 3, p. 24.
9. L. Boulnois, *The Silk Road,*(London, George Allen & Unwin Ltd., 1963), p. 56.
10. Marylin M. Rhie, n. 23, p. 6.
11. Iqbal M. Shafi, *Silk Road to Sin Kiang,* (Lahore: Wajidalis Pub., 1988), p. 14.
12. Jonathan Tucker, n. 3, p. 12.
13. Warikoo K, *Central Asia and Kashmir: A study in the Context of Anglo-Russian Rivalry,* New Delhi, p. 1.
14. L. Boulnois, n. 6 , p. 59.
15. S.K. Pathak, 'Sanskritism had Moved Forward the Silk Routes when Xuanzang Traversed', Paper presented in international seminar on, *Xuanzang and the Silk Route,* (IGNCA, New Delhi, January 17–19 2003). p. 27-30.
16. J. Eggline, Tr., *The Satapatha-Brahamana,* III, Delhi. Varanasi, Patna reprint, 1894. p. 89.
17. Fa Xian, *A Record of Buddhistic Kingdoms, Being an Account of the Chinese Monk Fa-Hien.* Trans by James Legge, Oxford: Clarendon Press, 1986. p. 129.
18. Jonathan Tucker, n. 3, p. 15.
19. *Ibid,* p. 15
20. Herodotus, *The Histories,* Tr. Aubery de Selincourt, Penguin Books, 1954. p. 229.
21. W.W. Tarn, *Hellenistic Civilization* (London, 1930), p.217. Also in Pliny's *Natural History.*
22. Jonathan Tucker, n. 3, p. 15.
23. Johan Noble Wilford, 'New Finds Suggest Even Earlier Trade on Fabled Silk Road', *New York Times,* March 16, 1993, pp. C1, C8.

24. Greek accounts both of visitors and others have been collated and translated by J.W. MeCrindle in a series of books – *Ancient India as described by Ktesias the Knidian* (Calcutta, 1882), p. 139.
25. L. Boulnois, *The Silk Road,* (London, George Allen & Unwin Ltd., 1963), p. 116.
26. Garnet Jacques, *A History of Chinese Civilization,* [Translated by J.R. Foster], (Cambridge: C.P.U., 1982), p. 86.
27. *Ibid.*, p. 88.
28. Richard C. Foltz, n. 1, p. 2.
29. Laszlo Tordy, *Mounted Archers: The Beginning of Central Asian History,* (Durham: Durham Academic Press, 1997), p. 91.
30. Richard C. Foltz, n. 10, p. 3.
31. Sima. Qian, *Records of the Grand Historian: Shij. 2 vols.*, trans. by Burton Watson, New York: Columbia University Press, 1993, p. 238.
32. *Si-yu-ki*: Buddhist Records of the Western World, by Hiuen Tsiang. Trans. by Samuel Beal, 2 vols. in 1, London: Kegan Paul et al, 1884, p. 94.
33. Jonathan Tucker, n-6, p. 82.
34. *Ibid.*, p. 82.
35. *Ibid.*, p. 82.
36. Garnet Jacques, *A History of Chinese Civilization,* [Translated by J.R. Foster], (Cambridge: C.P.U., 1982), p. 186.
37. Jonathan Tucker, n-6, p. 83.
38. Xinru Liu, n-9, p. 11.
39. Sima. Qian, *Records of the Grand Historian: Shij. 2 vols.*, trans. by Burton Watson, New York: Columbia University Press, 1993, p. 129.
40. Jonathan Tucker, n-6, p. 85.
41. White J. & Bunker, E., *Adornments for Eternity: Status and Rank in Chinese Ornament*. (Exhibition Catalogue, Denver, Denver Art Museum, 1994).
42. *Ibid.*, p. 49.
43. Jonathan Tucker, n-6, p. 86.
44. Marylin M. Rhie, 'Aspects of the two Colossal Budhas at Bamiyan' Paper Presented in International Seminar on *Xuanzang and the Silk Route,* (Indira Gandhi National Centre for the Arts, New Delhi, January 17-19, 2003), pp. 2-3.
45. Oliver Wild, 'The Silk Road', (web on line) www.ess.uci.edu/silkhtml., page 5 of 9.
46. *Ibid.*, p. 6 of 9.
47. Morris Rossabi, 'The Silk Road', *Education About Asia,* (Vol. 4, November 1, Spring, 1999), p. 6.
48. Iqbal M. Shafi, n-9, p. 16.
49. *Ibid.*, p. 16.
50. Ibn Battuta, *Travels in Asia and Africa* 1325-1354. Trans. by H.A.R.

Gibb, London: The Broadway Travellers, George Routledge and Sons, 1929, p. 341.
51. *Ibid.*, p. 16.
52. *Ibid.*, p. 17.
53. Kyotaro Nishikawa, n-2, p. 25
54. Peter Hopkirk, *Foreign Devils on the Silk Road: The Search for the Lost Cities and Treasurer of Chinese Central Asia*, (Oxford University Press, John Murry, 1980), p. 28.
55. *Ibid.*, pp. 28-30.
56. Ho Chang Chun, "Fa-hsien's Pilgrimage to Buddhist Countries", *Chinese Literature*, No. 3. 1956, p. 642.
57. Marylin M. Rhie, n-23, p. 6.
58. Chen, Yu, *Tales from Dunhuang*. Trans. By Li Guishan, Beijing: New Work Press, 1989, p. 29.
59. Xinru Liu, n-9, p. 67.
60. B.N. Puri, *Buddhism in Central Asia*, (Delhi: Motilal Banarsi Das 1987), p. 169.
61. S.K. Pathak, 'Sanskritism had Moved Forward the Silk Routes when Xuanzang Traversed', Paper presented in international seminar on, *Xuanzang and the Silk Route*, (IGNCA, New Delhi, January 17–19 2003).
62. F.A. von Schiefer has translated a history of Buddhism in India written by a Tibetan monk Taranatha, *Geschichte des Buddhismum* in Indien (St. Petersburg, 1869), p. 187.
63. A.L. Basham, *A Cultural History of India*, (Delhi: Oxford University Press 1984), p. 273.
64. Kyotaro Nishikawa, n-2, p. 157.
65. Richard C. Foltz, n-1, p. 39.
66. Paul Williams, *Mahayana Buddhism: The Doctrinal Foundation*, (London: Rutledge Pub., 1989), pp. 277-278.
67. Jonathan Tucker, n-6, p. 66.
68. V. Trenckner, ed., *Milindapanho*, 1928, Tr. T.W. Rhys Davids, SBE, Oxford, 1890 p. 254.
69. James Legge, Tr. *A Record of Buddhistic Kingdoms* (being an account of the Chinese monk Fa-hian's Travels), Oxford, 1886, p. 342.
70. A.S. Altekar, *Corpus of Indian Coins*, Vol. IV, *The Coinage of the Gupta Empire*, Banaras, 1957, p. 342.
71. Romila Thapar, *Cultural Pasts: Essays in Early Indian History*, (New Delhi: Oxford University, 2000). p. 100.
72. Jonathan Tucker, n-6, p. 57.
73. L. Boulnois, n-5, p. 67.
74. Sima. Qian, *Records of the Grand Historian: Shij. 2 vols.*, trans. by Burton Watson, New York: Columbia University Press, 1993, p. 327 *et. al.* Studies in New China, *Xin Zhongguode kaogu Faxian he yanjiu/*

Archaeological discoveries and studies in new China, Institute of Archaeological Studies of the Chinese Academy of Social Science, Beijing, 1984.
75. *Ibid.*, pp. 67-68.
76. *Kautalya's Arthashastra* edited by T. Ganapati Sastri and translated by R. Shamasastri (Mysore, 1958), p. 27.
77. Xinru Liu, n-9. p. 11.
78. Iqbal M. Shafi, n-27, p. 15.
79. Richard C. Foltz, n-1, p. 7.
80. Marco Polo, *The Travels of Marco Polo The Venetian*. Trans. by William Marsden, New York: Doubleday and Co., 1948, p. 473.
81. Jonathan Tucker, n. 6, p. 16-17.
82. *Ibid.* p. 19.
83. Xinru Liu, n. 9, p. 15.
84. S.K. Pathak, n. 52, p. 87.
85. Wang Chung-Lo, *History of the Wei, Chin and Northern and Southern Dynasties*, (Shanghai: People's Publisher, 1979), p. 536.
86. Schafer, Edward, *The Golden Peaches of Samarkand*, (California, CUP, 1963), p. 24.
87. Yang Hsuan-Chih, *Memories of Holy Places in Loyang*, (Shanghai: Ku-chi Ch'u-pan She, 1978), p. 205.
88. Liu, Man-ch'un, *Silk Trade Along the Silk Route from the Han to Tang*, (Lan Chou: People's Publisher, 1982), p. 88.
89. Hsi-ho. Chi, *Record of Hs - ho region*, (Shanghai: Commercial Press, 1936), p. 1.
90. Shepherd, D.C. & W.B. Henning, *Zandaniji Identified*, (Berlin: Fertschrift Ernst Kuhnel, 1959), pp. 22-4, 35.
91. Chang, Hsing-lang, *Historical Sources of Communications between the West and China*, (Beijing: 1930), p. 71.
92. Schafer, Edward, n-54, p. 202.
93. Kao-seng-chuan, 'Biographies of Outstanding Monks', compiled by Hui Chiao, *Tripitaka*, Vol. 50, p. 331.
94. Shafer, Edward, n-54, p. 202.
95. Meister Michael, 'The Pearl Roundel in Chinese Textile Design', *Arts Orientalis*, Vol. VIII, 1970, pp. 255-67.
96. Xinru, Liu, n-9, p. 18.
97. *Ibid.*, p. 18.
98. Meister Michael, n-63, p. 261, fig. 26.
99. Liu Man-Ch'um, n-56, p. 88.
100. Liu, Xinru, n-9, p. 19.
101. *Ibid.*, p. 19.
102. Burrow, Thomas, *A Translation of Kharosti Documents from Chinese Turkistan*, (London: The Royal Asiatic Society, 1940), no. 3, p. 1.

103. *Ibid.*, n-485, p. 95.
104. Habib Irfan,Tapan Raychaudhuri, Dharma Kumar, *The Cambridge Economic History of India: c. 1200-c. 1750,* Cambridge University Press, 1982. P. 224 *et. al., Corpus Inscriptionum Indicarum,* Vol. III, rev. ed, (Varanasi: Indological Book House, 1970), 322 ff.
105. S.N. Chowdhury, *Muga Silk Industry,* (Gauhati: Peoples Pub., 1981), p. 4.7.
106. *Ibid.*, p. 19.
107. D.C. Sarkar, *Sericulture and Silk Industry in India,* (Indian Museum, Bulletin XII, 1977), pp. 7-75.
108. *Ibid.*, p. 56.
109. S.K. Maity, *Economic Life of Northern India,* (Calcutta: The World Press Private Ltd., 1957), p. 178.
110. *Ibid.*, p. 189.
111. *The Cambridge History of Iran,* (Cambridge: Cambridge University Press, 1983), III, 1108.
112. *Ibid.*, p. 1109.
113. H. Granger Taylor, *Two Silk Textiles from Rome and Some Thoughts on Roman Silk Weaving,* (Lyon, 1987), pp. 13-30.
114. Day, Florence, *Silk of the Near East,* (Metro Political Museum of Art Bulletin, 1950), p. 108.
115. Starensier, Actele La Barre, *An Art Historical Study of the Byzantine Silk Industry,* (Columbia: Columbia University, 1982), p. 76.
116. Pliny, *Natural History,* [trans. H. Rackham], (Cambridge, Mass: Harvard University Press), 1956-62, XII, 41, 18.
117. Lotika Varadarajan, "Silk-The extra Silk Route Story" [paper presented in International Seminar on 'Xuanzang and the Silk Route' on January 17-19, 2003, at Indira Gandhi National Centre for the Arts, New Delhi, Department of Culture, New Delhi, pp. 15-17.

2

Decline of the Silk Route

The downfall of the Tang Empire in the early 10th century gave a deathblow to the trade along the Silk Route. The trade on the route declined sharply till in the 13th century, when the conquests of the Mongols ushered in an era of frequent and extended contacts between East and West. This increased contact created a demand for Asian goods in Europe, a demand that eventually inspired the search for a sea route to Asia.

After the Tang rule, traffic along the Silk Route subsided. The successors of the Tangs could not maintain internal stability in China, and again, the neighboring states started to attaching and plundering the caravans. China was partially unified again during the Sung dynasty (960–1279 AD), but the Silk Route was not as important as it had been in the Tang era. With the decline of Tang power and the rise of Islam between the eighth and tenth centuries, central Asian region again slipped out of China's control.[1] The area remained under the actual influence or control of Imperial China only intermittently, for less than five centuries in a period of two thousand years.[2] The decline of the Silk Route mainly started with the crumbling of the Mongol Empire due to the internecine feuds among the various Mongol Khans. Chinese nationalism and isolationalism was emphasized with the revival of Islam in the West and the rise of the Mings in China. Land route communication suffered a setback. With the development of easy and profitable sea routes, the long and arduous land route was side lined. There were many more factors behind the decline of the Silk Route.

Downfall of the Tang Dynasty

The fall of the Tang dynasty led to political chaos, an unstable economy and less support to extravagant foreign imports. At the same time, entire communities, active oases towns, thriving monasteries and grottoes along the Silk Route were appearing in the space as frail, the glacier-fed streams ran dry or changed course. The Great Tang dynasty came to its end in the year 907 AD. The Tang period, was one however, during which the Chinese people greatly extended the areas of their demographic dominance by migration towards the west, where no such ecological barriers existed. Armed conflicts were the constant feature on the northern borders with Inner Asia, where the non-Chinese peoples possessed the means to sorely test Chinese military capacities.[3] Their striking force enabled the northern peoples to take active part in Tang China's internal power struggles. Inner Asian military power became a component of Tang internal politics from the mid-eighth century onward.[4]

During the time of Emperor Su Tsung (756-762) military generals in the northern regions were worked like dictators. He sought aid from Central Asia against the An Lu-Shan and his capable general Shih-Ssu-Ming (himself a Turk).[5] A small contingent of Arab troops sent by the Caliph Abu-Jafar, and an important Uighur cavalry force arrived from Turkistan in substantial strength. At the end of 757 AD there was a great battle in the neighborhood of the capital, in which An Lu-Shan was defeated by the Uighurs. Shortly afterwards he was murdered by one of his eunuchs. The victorious Uighurs further received 10,000 rolls of silk in payment from the Tang government with a promise of 20,000 rolls per year.[6] The Turk Shih Ssu-Ming entered into An Lu-Shan's heritage and dominated so large a part of eastern China that the Chinese once more made use of the Uighurs to bring him down.

The later Tang emperors never regained full control over their country. The character of governing changed. The holders of real power who were Chinese, came from either the defeated forces of Huang- Chao or from other bandit uprisings. The great families of the Tang civil and bureaucratic elite played almost no part in the final struggles of the Tang to survive. As sectors of elite society they had been largely nullified if not eliminated.[7]

The later Tang emperors were like pawns in the hands contesting military leaders. One such leader, a Chinese named Zhu Wen, a former captain in Huang Chao's rebel armies, seized the capital in 901 AD.[8] In 905 AD he killed the emperor and most of the Tang imperial family and placed a teenage imperial prince on the throne as his puppet. Finally, in 907 AD he abandoned all pretense and declared himself the founding emperor of a new dynasty. In 908 he killed the deposed last Tang emperor, a boy of sixteen.[9] A cycle of violence set in during the Liang era, the first of the Five Dynasties. By sheer maladministration, ultimately, the Tang Empire was brought to its end.

Obviously, the collapse of the Tang Empire was the important factor in the decline of the Silk Route. Imports and exports by China with the western world through the Silk Route were almost over at the end of the ninth century. Businessmen were engaged in the uprisings against Tang power. The later Tang emperors had not decided about the state of commerce in any proper way. The peasantry and businessmen stood against the Tangs. Wang-Hsien-Chih e.g. was a peasant and Huang-Chao a merchant, leading the uprisings. In these circumstances the Silk Route could not survive and function as in its golden age.

Chaos of Five Dynasties

After the collapse of the Tang dynasty in 907AD, China followed fifty years of black chaos, known as the period of 'Five Dynasties and Ten Kingdoms', when local military governors declared themselves rulers or even emperors of territories they happened to hold.[10] None of the Five Dynasties, based in north China, was able to reunify China. The political instability was reflected in the short lives of the Five Dynasties. The regional power bases that produced the ten states were direct outgrowths of the decentralization of political and military power. The military governors of the provinces enhanced their prospects of survival in the competition among themselves.

In these territories there was comparative peace and economic progress, since they were able to control their own affairs and were no longer dependent on a corrupt central government. "As an example of these states, in Chu state, Ma Yin, a carpenter had declared himself king. He controlled some of the main trade routes, set up a clean administration, bought all merchandise which the merchants brought, but allowed them only local products, mainly tea, iron and lead. This regulation gave him a personal income of several millions every year".[11]

There had been certain other changes too in this period. The north west of China, the region of the old capital, Changan, had been so ruined by the fighting that had been going on farther north, that it was eliminated as a centre of power for a hundred years; it became largely depopulated. The north was under the Kitans' rule; its trade, which in past had been with the Huang-ho basin, was now perforce diverted to Peking, which soon became the centre of power of the Kitans. One important event of this period – 955 AD – was the great persecution of Buddhism, which affected the trade along the Silk Route. Not only because 30,336 temples and monasteries were secularized, but because some 2,700 of these, were left.[12] The immediate reason for this action was the conscription of the monks of the monasteries as soldiers.

The political chaos of the Five Dynasties accomplished the decline of the silk route. The decentralisation of power in China finished the economic relations with neighbour states. Government of Five Dynasties was not interested in the silk trade with the Roman Empire.[13] Central Asians and Persian middle men were not pursuing the exchange of silk with other products because border states were fighting with each other. In these circumstances, the rule of Five Dynasties constituted a major factor in the decline of the Silk Route.

The attitude of the later Chinese dynasties was the final blow to the trade route. The isolationist policies of the Ming (1368-1644) and Qing (1644-1912 AD) dynasties did nothing to encourage trade between China and the rapidly developing West.

Coming of Islam in Central Asia

The arrival of Islam in Central Asia led to the destruction of non-Islamic artwork and architecture in key cities. In China it raised the barriers on the land route once again for some time. After the defeat of the Sassanian Empire in 651 AD, Arabian armies sought to bring Islam to the land beyond the Oxus and Transoxiana. The Arabian army from Basra (today's Iraq), succeeded in taking the great oasis city of Merv in 651 AD.[14] During their early years the Arabs lacked a power base in Central Asia, and were compelled to rule through the nobles and administrators of the former

Sassanian regime. But by the end of the seventh century some 50,000 families from Kufa and Basra joined their men in Merv and the city became the base for the Muslim conquest of Central Asia.[15]

During the Umayyad Caliphate (661-750 AD) and the earlier time of the Abbasid Caliphate (749-1258 AD), Merv was the capital of the eastern Islamic territories.[16] This prevailed until the transfer of the capital to Nishapur during the Tahirid dynasty (821-73). The first military incursion in the Oxus region began in 673 AD, led by Ubaidullah Ziyad, governor of Khurasan. Termez was taken in 676 AD and attacks were launched against the great carvan cities of Bukhara and Samarkand, ruled by the Khorezm dynasty.[17] General Qutabia ibn Muslim, appointed governor of Khurasan in 704 AD, consolidated Arab control of the region. Bukhara fell to the Arabs in 709 AD, followed by Samarkand in 712 AD. Qutabia systematically killed off all the scholars of Khorezm in an attempt to erase the country's culture.[18] He established a large Arab garrison at Samarkand and rampaged Chach (Tashkent), Khujand and Ferghana. Qutabia swept all before him, brushing aside all opposition, including attempts by the surviving relative of the last Sassanian ruler, Yezdegard III who raised an army against him and elicited Chinese support. The advance of Qutabia was finally checked when his patron Hajjaj ibn Yusuf, governor of Iraq died.[19] After the death of Qutabia the Arab tribes of Khurasan were riven by internal disputes and few territorial gains were made. Abbasid soldiers worked to bring about the overthrow of the Umayyad Caliphate: north of the Syr Darya River, the Turgesh Turks rallied to the cause of the beleaguared Sogdian armies who had fled to the Ferghana valley in 721 AD.[20] In 724 AD the Turgesh Turks heavily defeated a Muslim expeditionary force sent into the Ferghana Valley. Turks controlled almost all the territory north of the Amu Darya (the Oxus river). It appeared as if the Arabs would be ousted loch, stock and barrel from Transoxania. The Sogdian chieftain Divastich, the last ruler of Penjikent, fled to the mountain citadel of Mugh after the fall of Penjikent.[21]

The death of Turgesh Khagan Su-Lu brought about the disintegration of the Turk state. With the threat to their rule removed, the Arabs were able to set in force a process of reconcilation and pacification in Central Asia. The last Umayyad governor, Nasr-ibn-Sayyar, came to power in 737 AD and pursued a strategy of amnesty and tax reform among his subjects and

Sogadian landowners. Many people voluntarily converted to Islam and Sogadian merchants financed many of the Arabs' expeditions.

Trade along the silk route was profoundly affected with the rise of Islam for some time because the system of trade changed. Its followers had conquered Byzantine, Syria, the whole of the North Africa, Sassanian Persia and much of Central Asia. The power of Islam held sway from Spain to the Ferghana Valley.[22] Arab traders controlled both maritime and land routes and Muslim Persia developed a domestic silk industry that rivaled China's.

Islam spread through Central Asia at three levels:[23]

(i) At the political level, as an instrument of foreign policy,
(ii) At the commercial level: followers an converts enjoyed greater opportunities for trade, and
(iii) At the level of assimilation by which successive generations would forget the ways of the past.

Islamic rule over the western half of the silk route came fairly early and was established by mid-eighth century. Muslims thereafter controlled much of Asian trade, and this became the major factor for the decline of the Silk Route.[24] The presence of Muslim rule and the increasing Muslim dominance of trade meant that the spred advancement of Islam took place first in the urban areas along the Silk Route. The gradual Islamisation of the nomadic Turkic peoples of Central Asia at first directly led to their increasing participation in the oases-based Silk Route trade in the tenth century.[25] It gained greater momentum by the political activities of three Turkic Muslim dynasties, the Qara Khanids, the Ghaznavids and the Seljuks, supplemented by the proselytizing efforts of Muslim missionaries.[26]

The government of China attempted to regain control of the lucrative trade routes across Central Asia in the eighth century. Arab and Chinese armies finally clashed in 751 AD, at the river Talas.[27] The Chinese army fought but was eventually defeated by the Arab troops of Ziyad ibn-Salih. Many Chinese were captured and sent to work in Samarkand and Damascus where they taught their skills to the native craftsmen. Among them were the techniques of paper and silk manufacture. A more important consequence of the battle was that Chinese control of Central Asia was lost for the next thousand years. Although the Arabs did not pursue the fleeing Chinese troops and the battle marked the limit of their territorial expansion, they remained the dominant force in the Silk Route trade until the coming of the Mongols in the thirteenth century.

After the end of the Umayyad dynasty the Caliphate was moved from Damascus to Baghdad. The demise of the Umayyad Caliphate was coupled with the ascendancy of Persian culture and language in Central Asia. The old culture and language of Bactria, Khorezm and Sogdiana disappeared and were replaced by all things Persian.[28] The reasons for the Persianisation of Central Asia were complex but they included the fact that the merchants of Central Asia were prepared to embrace Islam and accept foreign rule as long as the trade routes and the commerce they conducted along them were safeguarded. Persian quickly became the language of choice among the Arab soldiers and Sogdian merchants of Central Asia.

The period of Abbasid rule (749-1258 AD) gave rise to many technological and cultural developments, many of which reached the West via the Silk Route. Arab soldiers who got the chance of looting the prosperous towns of Central Asia that lay on the Silk Route were naturally ever ready for battle. After the disintegration of the Abbasid Caliphate, the adjustments in Islamic institutions and the reorganization of state and society affected long distance trade in general, and the silk trade in particular. The Islamic empire bifurcated into two major linguistic domains.[29] Arabic became the official language of the western sphere and Persian was the lingua franca of the combined regions of Central and South Asia a region much larger than any earlier Persian empire. There were many regional states. While the Ghaznavids and Saljuks still sought legitimacy from the caliphate in Baghadad, Shi'ite regimes, such as the Buwahids, Hamdianids, Qurmatians and Fatimids threatened the dominance of Sunni orthodoxy. The Buwahids even claimed glory by establishing a link with ancient Iranian Kings.[30] During the ninth century a number of semi-autonomous Islamic states began to emerge in Central Asia. The Tahirids (AD 821-73) and Saphavids (AD 867-908) were quickly followed by the empire of the Samanids, a dynasty founded by the empire of the Samanids, a dynasty founded by an Iranian noble, Samon, from northern Afghanistan. Samon's four grandsons became governors of Herat, Samarkand, Ferghana and Tashkand. Nasr-ibn Ahmad, son of the

Ferghana governor, eventually assumed control of all Transoxiana. Samanid territory reached its largest extent during the reign of Nasr II ibn Ahmad (AD 914-43) from Tashkend (Chach) in the north and Ferghana in the northeast to Ray (South of Tehran) in the southwest.

Under Samanid rule trade along the Silk Route, both east and west, became safe again and commerce flourished. The massive brick-built caravanserai at Rabat-I Malik, midway between Samarkand and Bukhara attests to the high level of commercial activity along the Silk Road during the tenth and eleventh centuries.[31] A list of trade goods compiled by the tenth century Arab geographer Mukadisi are rugs and prayer mats from Bukhara and Samarkand; woolen cloth and fine weavings; cotton, silk, soap, cosmetics; bows and other weapons; armour; horse-fittings; tents, food stuffs (including raisins, nuts, sesame and honey); livestock (including horses, sheep and cattle); hawks for hunting; gold, silver, sulphur and iron—all this and more were exported to China and the West. The tens of thousands of Samanid coins found in Scandinavia and smaller numbers of the same that were unearthed in Central Europe, are a testament to the commercial reach of the Silk Route traders of Central Asia.[32] Silk cloth was the Silk Road's staple currency and patterned silks (known as Zandaniji) were more valuable than almost any other commodity. "St. Josse Silk", produced in Khurasan around AD 960 for the Samanid amir Abu Mansur Bakhtgin, was formerly in the church of St. Josse sur Mer in the Palais de Calasis. Its motifs are an extraordinary mix of styles from the countries of the Silk Route.[33]

Samanids were being burnt by Sunni Muslims who embarked upon a concerted campaign to first convert and then provide military training to the region's Turkish tribesmen. These Turkish military slaves embraced Islam but retained their own traditions, language and culture. In 961 AD a Turkish slave-soldier named Alptigin, successfully engineered his own appointment as governor of Khurashan. He was promptly divested of his post, however, and be sought refuge in the town of Ghazni. After his death in 963 AD he was succeeded by another ex-slave named Sebuktgin, founder of the Ghaznavid Empire and considered himself a loyal vassal of the Samanids. To the north another Turkish dynasty, the Kharakhanids displaced the Karluks of the region east of Ferghana and established themselves in the town of Uzgen on the banks of a tributary of the Syr Darya.[34] The first Turkish tribes to adopt Islam appear to have emerged in the area around Balasagun. During the tenth century their territories were extended eastwards a far as Kashgar where they established their capital under Satuk Boghra Khan. In the final years of their rule the Samanids were sandwiched precariously between the Ghaznavids and the Kharakhanids. In 999 AD fighting erupted between the last Samanid ruler, Abd-al-Malik II and Mahmud of Ghazni. Abd-al-Malik was defeated by Mahmud and the Samanids abandoned Khurasan to the victors. The Kharakhanid ruler Arslan Ilk Nasr grasped the opportunity and seized Bukhara and annexed the whole of Transoxana. The fall of the Samanid dynasty marked the end of the Persian domination of Central Asia. The Samanid empire was divided between the Ghazanavids and the Kharakhanids, both Turkish dynasties.

In 1006 AD, while Mahmud was campaigning in India, Arslan, of the Saljuk bribe invaded Khurasan and seized Balkh and Nishapur. Mahmud drove him out of Khurasan in 1008 AD. The Ghazanavids further extended their empire, and by 1025 AD it extended as far as Iraq in the west and the Ganges in the South. The same year Mahmud attacked the Kharakhamid ruler Alitigin and advanced briefly as far as Samarkand. The Ghaznavids were defeated by the Saljuks – another Turkish tribe who lived around the mouth of the Syr Darya River. After their defeat by the Seljuks in 1140 AD, the Ghaznavids were expelled from Khurasan and confined to their domains in Northern India and Afghanistan. In 1055 AD the Seljuks entered Baghdad, where the Abbasid caliph handed over control of all of Central Asia to them. The Seljuk Empire was extended eastward and west until it extended from the Mediterranean to the Oxus. In 1071, the Byzantine Emperor Romanus Diogenes was taken captive by the Sultan Alp-Arslan.[35] After Diogenes's defeat the Seljuks established the Sultanate of "Rum" (i.e., 'eastern Rome') in present day Turkey, thereby laying the foundation for the emergence of the Ottoman Empire some two centuries later.[36] After a short time they took over a large territory of Kharakhanids in Central Asia. In 1129 AD, the Seljuk Empire fractured from nepotism and feuds among the ruling clans. Sultan Sanjar the last ruler of the Seljuks sustained the Empire for a while, until 1141 AD when a new threat emerged in the shape of the Kharakhitai. It was a non-Muslim tribe of Mongolian descent.

In about 1128 AD they entered Kashgaria with an army and attacked the Kharakhanids from the rear. The Kharakhitai wrested town after town from the Muslims and the defeat of Sanjar gave them the great Silk Route cities of Samarkand and Bukhara. Later on the Kharakhitais invaded Kharezm, and the extent of their empire after this was Hami in China's Xinjiang province and the Aral Sea.[37]

The decline of the Seljuks gave a chance to the Khorezmshahs, the vassals of the Seljuks, to found a new ruling house. The Khorezmshahs were Muslim Turks who saw themselves as defenders of the faith against the pagan Kharakhitai.[38] During the region of Muhammad, the Khorezmian territories were extended to include the Ghurid lands in Afghanistan. It was inevitable for Shah Muhammad of Khorezm and Muhammad of Ghur to come to blows. The first battle occurred in 1204 AD and the Khorezmian ruler lost. Later on, the Khorezm territory came under the control of the Mongol sweep.[39] However, the fanatical spread of Islam in Central Asia was one of the most critical factors in the decline of the Silk Route. The Buddhist civilization disappeared along the silk road and the most destructive aspect of it was the loss of Seridian art. Only those caves and monastries that had been buried under the sands centuries before were able to survive unmutilated by the followers of Islam. The entire Taklamakan region was thoroughly overcome by Islam; Buddhist stupas and temples were either destroyed or left to crumble.

Spread of Islam in China

The coming of Islam in China was a major factor in the decline of the Silk Road. The advent of Islam in Western China via the Silk Route was a fascinating event. According to the records of the Tang dynasty, two embassies, one from Yezdgard, the grandson of Khusro, and the other from the Roman Empire came to the court of Tai-Tsung, the second emperor of Tangs. Both reported their defeat by the Arabs.[40] Yezdgard, the last of the Sassanian Kings of Iran, had sought refuge with the Turkish tribes of Farghana and had also sought friendship with the emperor Tai Tsung whose capital was at Changan. The Chinese were at the height of their power, and had frontiers with the Persian Empire. In 650 AD, Tai Tsung died and his son Emperor Kao Tsung received an appeal for help from Firoz, the son of Yezdgerd. Kao Tsung sent an emissary to Caliph Osman to plead for Firoz and the Caliph in return sent one of his generals to Xian in 651 AD and thus the first Muslim embassy was established in Western China.

At the time when Mohammad Bin Qasim landed in Sind, Kutaiba Bin Muslim was making inroads into Central Asia. Emperor Hsuan Tsung of the Tang dynasty sent 200,000 men under his nephew to stem the tide but the nephew was defeated at the battle of Talas in 751 AD by Kutaiba Bin Muslim and many Chinese were taken prisoners.[41] A more enduring consequence of the battle was that the Chinese lost control over Central Asia for the next thousand years. A Turk named An Lu-Shan led a rebellion in China. Emperor Husan Tsang was driven from the capital and he abdicated in favour of his son Tsu Tsung who appealed to the Arabs for help. Abu Jaffar, the third Caliph sent 4,000 Arabs who recovered Xian and Honanfu for the emperor. These Arabian soldiers married and settled down in China and formed the nucleus of the naturalised Chinese Muslims in Western China.

As a result of contact with Muslims, many Chinese accepted Islam. The person responsible for converting the whole of South Xinjiang to Islam was the Satuk Bogra Khan of Karakhanid Kingdom.[42] The advent of Islam in Western China had a profound effect on trade along the silk routs.

Collapse of the Mongol Empire

There was one unforeseen consequence of the rise of the marauders along the Silk Route, attracted by the riches passing through. Some of the nomadic tribes became skilled warriors, able to conquer rich cities and fertile lands and build strong military empires.

The collapse of the Mongol empire in the fifteenth-century led to a precipitous decline of the Silk Route trade in Central Asia. The flourishing towns and oases sank into poverty, and nomad empires of namods such as the Mongols', could no longer match advanced military technology (gun, rifles, cannons, etc.). In fact Qing China and Tsarist Russia gained control over these regions and ruled what was by then a mostly Turkish Muslim population.[43] Central Asia and the Silk Route seemed to disappear from the stage of history.

The Mongol Empire according to Chinese and Central Asian histories was created by Temochin, who later, in 1206 became famous as Chengiz Khan or "Universal Ruler".[44] The Mongols created an empire that ultimately included all of Mongolia, China, Korea, Russia, Iran, Iraq, Afghanistan, Transoxania, Syria and the Caucasus.[45] They were purely nomadic tribes. The Kin dynasty was then ruling over North China, but even at that period, the Mongols were strong enough to merit the status of allies of the Chinese, and towards the end of the 12th century the Chinese government incited them against the Tartars. By 1206 AD, Chengiz Khan defeated the Naimun tribe, killed their ruler Jamuka, and brought the whole of Mongolia under his sway. He now proclaimed himself King of Mongolia. Chengiz maintained strict discipline in his army. After some years of preparation, the Mongol army began to advance towards China. In 1215, after the fall of Peking, the whole of North China came under his control. Khwarizm was the first Islamic state in Central Asia to face the Mongols, Chengiz Khan sought to open trade relations with the Khwarizmshahs. Envoys were sent to their kind Muhammad, in his capital at Kung Urgench with the following message:

"I am master of the rising sun while you rule those of the setting sun. Let us conclude a firm treaty of friendship and peace. Merchants and their caravans should come and go in both directions, carrying the valuable products and ordinary goods from my land to yours, just as they do from your land to mine".[46]

After some time, a trading caravan with Mongol envoys reached the Central Asian city of Otrar. The local governor, a relative of the Shah, ignored their diplomatic status and ordered them all killed. This was a declaration of war. The conflict that followed drew the Mongols into Western Asia and generated the three great campaigns that over the next forty years led to the establishment of the Mongol Khanates in Central Asia, Persia and Russia.

Muhammad's fragile and newly fledged empire, riven by hatred between its Iranian and Turkish peoples, was no match for the well-organized legions of Chengiz Khan. He launched his campaign against Khwarezm with a force of 150,000 to 200,000 men.[47] Otrar was the first to fall. The beleaguered governor Inal-Khan who had ordered the killing of the merchants was captured and tortured to death.

The next campaign was against Bukhara, this time by a force led by Chengiz himself. Most of the people fled the city and were spared but some Turkish soldiers who bought to defend the city were annihilated. Samarkand was attacked in 1220, again by an army led by Chengiz Khan. In 1221, the Mongols captured the Khorezmian capital, Kunya Urgench and Chengiz occupied Balkh in the same year.[48] Bamyan, Ghazni and the hilly areas of Afghanistan were taken over by the Mongols in their quick march to victory.

The Mongols then advanced towards the Caucasusnes and attacked Georgia. Their next step was to invade Russia and by 1241 they had seized the southern area of Russia and advanced as far as Hungary, Poland and Romania.[49] Also in 1241, Mongol troops under an army led by Batu Khan were at the gates of Vienna and the whole of Western Europe lay supine before them. Baghdad was attacked and destroyed in 1258 by the army of the Mongol Khan Hulagu. The last Abbasid ealiph was sewn into a sack and trampled to death by horses. Syria was next and many of its cities, including Aleppo and Damascus were sacked.

The limits of the Mongols' westward expansion were reached in 1260 when they attacked Egypt.[50] They were pushed out of Egypt and Syria. Hulagu settled down in Persia as the II-Khan and remained there not returning to Mongolia. Thus ended the last great Mongol campaign from Mongolia to Western Asia and Europe.

To the east, the Mongol advance continued. In 1259 AD Khublai Khan, the grandson of Chengiz Khan became the Great khan and during his long rule (from 1259-1294), the Song rulers of China were defeated and the country fell under Mongol control. Kublai and his descendents, with their capital at Beijing, ruled China as the Yuan dynasty until 1368 AD.

Under the reign of Chengiz Khan, all the land between Iran and Turan (the land of the Turks) enjoyed such peace that a man could journey journeyed "from the land of sunrise to the land of sunset with a golden platter upon his head without suffering the least violence from anyone".[51] Crime – especially theft – was ruthlessly stamped out: anarchy and strife among the countries along the Silk Route came to an end. With their safety guaranteed merchants carried on their business as never before. An interesting practice introduced by the Mongols was that of the use of the passport, known as paizi.[52] Posts were setup at intervals of about 40-50 km and travellers carrying paizi were able to traverse the empire unimpeded, a system which greatly facilitated trade and diplomatic contacts.

Among the many Europeans to travel the Silk Road at the time of Mongols were Marco Polo, Johannes Di Plano Carpini and William of Rubric. Once, a French woman named Paquette accompanied her Russian husband who served the Khan as an architect.[53] In the fourteenth century, trade was so well developed that European merchants began to compile guides for travellers. Pegolotti, a mercantile agent in the employ of the powerful Bardi family of Florence, even travelled to China. He was a chronicles of information and stories from travellers. Ibn Battuta set out in 1325 AD on a journey through Egypt, Iran, Central Asia and Northern India. After residing in Delhi for eight years he took a ship to China. Ibn Battuta was regarded by both within and without the Islamic world, as one of the greatest travelers in history.

Merchandise from all the Mongol domains flowed into Karakorum city. Excavations of graves in and around the site have unearthed large numbers of coins from the Arab world and China, fabrics from China and Persia, furs from Russia and Eastern Europe and the remains of slaves from every province of the Mongol Empire. In the arts, the forced deflection of artists to cater to the Mongols resulted in a wide dissemination of new styles and ideas. Islamic art was revitalized by influences from China that travelled westwards during the years of Pax Mongolia. The emergence of Persian miniature painting during the 14th century was undoubtly a result of patronage by Il-Khans, who also encouraged the writing of poetry and history.

Of the merchants from abroad, those belonging to peoples allied to the Mongols had in every respect a privileged position in the Mongol Empire. They were free of taxation, free to travel all over the country and received privileged treatment in the use of transport.[54] The impoverishment of China began with the flow abroad of her metallic currency.

Trade along the ancient Silk Route was safe and good during the Mongol period. As a result of such imperial approval, a large number of people of different nationalities and creeds took part in the trade across Asia and settled in China.[55] Following the collapse of the Mongol empire, the region came under the control of Turkic Muslims. The Yuan dynasty was finally replaced by the Ming dynasty in 1368. With the disintegration of the Mongol empire, the revival of Islam and the isolationist policies of the Ming dynasty caused the rise of barriers again on the land route between East and West. The steady advance of Islam, temporarily halted by the Mongols continued until it became a major force across Central Asia. The end of the Timurid Empire which succeeded the Mongols in Central Asia was one of a number of events that brought about the final decline of the Silk Route trade. After Ulugh Beg's passing away in 1449 the Timurid Empire finally disintegrated as town after town fell to the Uzbeks, and the absence of centralized control in Central Asia meant that the safety of merchants along the trade routes could no longer be guaranteed. Caravans were forced to hire armed escorts, resulting in higher costs.[56] All East-West trade was now compelled to pass through Ottoman territory bringing the Byzantine Empire to an end and the eastern Mediterranean under Muslim control. This resulted in an additional financial burden on merchants in the form of tolls and taxes. Because of these factors the decline of the Silk Route because irreversible.

Opening of the Sea Route

The discovery of the sea route from Europe to Asia in the late 15th century dealt a damaging below to the Silk Route trade. It was easier and safer to transport goods by water than overland, where problems with the politics between the different peoples along the route, with intermediaries, all taking their cuts, took their toll. The European trading powers began to seek ways to evade the Ottoman monopoly and reduce their costs, ushering in an era of maritime exploration that transformed the way in which trade would be conducted during the coming centuries.[57] The first voyages began during the early part of the 15th century, sponsored by Prince Henry, "The Navigator" of Portugal, to seek ivory, gold and slaves.[58] In 1498 AD Vasco-Da-Gama discovered the maritime route to India and in 1510 AD the Portuguese discovered Goa, quickly followed in 1511 AD by the Malay port of Malacca—both becoming important bases for trade with the East. Under the newly founded Mughal Empire the Portuguese were granted trading rights and by 1540 they were engaged in commerce with Thailand,

Burma, Cambodia and Japan. For more than a century the Portuguese dominated trade with Africa and India.

China was a maritime power during the Ming Empire in the 15th century. The Chinese state became directly involved in promoting and expanding its maritime activities. During the early years of the Ming dynasty. (1368-1644 AD) Chinese emperors launched a number of expeditions led by Admiral Zheng He. He distinguished himself in a number of military posts and became a favorite of Emperor Yongle. He restored China to a position of economic and military strength and selected Zheng to lead a series of maritime expeditions to unite the countries of South and Southeast Asia under Chinese hegemony. Zheng led seven different voyages under the Emperors Yongle and Xuande.[59] The first of these expeditions involved more than sixty ships—the largest 130 meters in length, carrying 27,00 men, in 1405 AD.[60] The flotilla left Suzhou and travelled for two years exploring the coastline of Vietnam, Java, Sumatra, Sri Lanka, Malacca and Southwestern India. Zheng's fourth expedition from 1413-15 was a round trip of 12,000 km stopping at Hormuz on the Persian Gulf.[61] The fleet than sailed down the Arabian cost as far as Dholar and Aden and went on to explore the east coast of Africa. A part of the expedition made a detour by land to visit Mecca and Egypt. When this fleet return to China in 1415 they brought envoys from more than thirty countries to pay homage to the Chinese court and a rich cargo that included a giraffe.[62] The final official expedition was sent after the death of Chengzu in 1431-1433[63] Zheng He died in 1433 and was buried at Nanjing, near the great shipyards where the ships were built.[64] This final expedition revisited the Persian Gulf and the East African coastline even though the voyages did not result in the establishment of permanent settlements in the places they sailed to.

These maritime expeditions of Zheng He sought to advance China's commercial interests. He ships carried cargo that included raw and embroidered silks, camphor, musk, pearls, precious metals, rice, millet and beans.[65] He returned to China with spices, gems, medicines, pigments and exotic animals, both as tribute and as the proceeds of barter with the countries along the route.[66]

More voyages west were not sent. The officials of the court objected that they were too expensive and produced nothing of value.[67] The state ceased its building of large ships and thereafter built only smaller war and transport vessels needed for its coastal and inland waterways naval operations. Chinese merchants continued to trade but without official approval.

The Portuguese arrived on the coast of Southern China in 1557 and were regarded with undisguised contempt by the Chinese. They established a trading past at Macau. They controlled most of the maritime trade with the East from their bases at Goa and Macau. The Portuguese continued to dominate trade across the Indian Ocean. Chinese merchants also traded with the Dutch in Taiwan. The Portuguese continued to seek out other ports on the southeast coast and tried other devices for being granted-permission to trade. They found a small peninsula on the southwest side of the estuary and there conducted trade fairs when their ships arrived, haden with buying rich Chinese goods, mainly silk, to trade in throughout the region or to take back to Europe.[68]

The Dutch, the English, the Spanish and other Europeans had joined the Portuguese in building mercantile empires in Asia after the end of the Ming dynasty.[69] Long a participant in international maritime trade, China at this time experienced the consequences of the greatly enlarged patterns in world trade. The southern coast of China was visited during the eighteenth century by the British. England was the principal client of China at this time. She paid for her tea and silk in coins. Silk, like tea was a highly profitable cargo—with high value for a relatively low weight—for England.[70]

Start of Maritime Trade through Astrakhan

In1554 AD the Russians annexed Astrakhan from the Ottoman Empire.[71] This area was in dispute until 1569 when after an abortive campaign to regain the lost region the Ottoman Empire relinquished claims to Astrakhan. The port of Azov in Astrakhan was a centre of Venetian merchant activity.[72] Azov was a major port on the Black Sea that had been a trading site for European and Asian merchants for hundreds of years. The opening of the Astrakhan port open to European merchants drastically changed the dynamics of Persian trade. The Ottoman Empire no longer had a stranglehold on Persia's finances.

The road from the Persian land to Astrakhan that leads through Julfa was the major reason for the decline of the old Silk Route. From Tabriz there were two main trade routes for silk in the sixteenth century. The eastern route went through Khuy to Erzurum and the northern route through Julfa to Erzurum.[73] Julfa experienced an economic boom out of proportion to its earlier role in the scheme of the silk trade.

The Crimean port Azov in Astrakhan was frequented by European and Asian merchants during the sixteenth century. And old silk routes went into disuse because of tribals' troublesome activities in that region. The Chinese and other Asian merchants selected the port of Astrakhan to trade with western world.[74]

Throughout this period the cities of the Silk Route were starved of revenue from land-based commerce. They began to wither and die. The decline was in terms of trade volume, the number of trading centers, transmission channels and the composition of the trading community. The impact of the revolution in commerce and the shift from commodity to cash transactions in Europe and Asia was also an important cause of the decline of the Silk Route. The political powers along the Silk Route drew frontiers between themselves and became economically and culturally cut off from each other. Land route remained more or less in its original state, with the same terrain of deserts and mountains that had been traversed by Marco Polo. Merchants, missionaries and diplomats followed its trails no longer. Up to the time of the First World War it was frequented only by short-distance caravans, trading between neighboring peoples.

The heirs of the Tangs could not maintain the internal stability of China, and the neighboring states started plundering the caravans. The rise of Islam at the same time started to affect Asia and a curtain came down between east and west. However, trade relations soon resumed with the Muslims playing the part of middlemen. The advancement of Islam along the Silk Road dealt a death below to figurative art and portrayals of the human form. Many statues and wall paintings were damaged or destroyed by these iconoclasts. By the fifteenth century, Islam had become the religion of the entire Takla Makan region. Under the Ming dynasty (1368-1644 AD) the Silk Route was finally abandoned when China shut herself off from all contacts with the West. The decline of the Silk Route started with the crumbling of the Mongol empire due to the internecine feuds among various Mongol Khans. With the revival of Islam in the West and the rise of the Mings in China which emphasized Chinese nationalism and isolationalism, the land route communication suffered a setback. With the development of easy and profitable sea routes, the long and arduous land route was sidelined.

NOTES

1. M. Hussain has translated relevant sections of the *Rehla* of Ibn Batutah (GOS, cxxii, 1953), p. 95.
2. K. Warikoo, 'Central Asia and China: The Geopolitical Imperatives', in Shams-Ud-Din, (ed.) *Geopolitics and Energy Resources in Central Asia and Caspian Sea Region,* (New Delhi: Lancer Books, 2000), p. 254.
3. Nizami of Ganja, *The Haft Paikar (The Seven Beauties).* Trans. by C.E. Wilson, 2 vols., London: Probsthain & Co., 1924, p. 266.
4. F.W. Mote, *Imperial China: 900–1800 AD,* (London: Harvard University Press, 1999), p. 6.
5. Wolfram Eberhard, *A History of China,* (Berkeley and Los Angeles: University of California Press, 1969), p. 185.
6. *Ibid.*, p. 185.
7. Sima. Qian, *Records of the Grand Historian: Shij.* 2 vols., trans. by Burton Watson, New York: Columbia University Press, 1993, p. 285.
8. L. Carrington Goodrich, *A Short History of the Chinese People,* (London: George Allen and Unwin Ltd., 1972), p. 125.
9. F.W. Mote, n. 2, p. 7.
10. Jonathan Tucker, *The Silk Road- Art and History,* (New Delhi: Timeless Books, 2003), p. 133.
11. Wolfram Eberhard, *A History of China,* (Berkeley and Los Angeles: University of California Press, 1969), p. 199-200.
12. *Ibid.*, p. 207.
13. Marco Polo, *The Travels of Marco Polo The Venetian*. Trans. by William Marsden, New York: Doubleday and Co., 1948, p. 196.
14. Richard, C. Foltz, *Religions of the Silk Road: Overland Trade and Cultural Exchange from Antiquity to the Fifteenth Century,* (London: Macmillan Press Ltd. 1999), p. 91.
15. Jonathan Tucker, n. 5, p. 212.
16. M. Hussain has translated relevant sections of the *Rehla* of Ibn Batutah (GOS, cxxii, 1953). p. 27.
17. *Ibid.*, p. 35.
18. UNESCO, *Amir Temur in World History,* Paris, 1996, p. 397.
19. Babur, Zahiru'din Muhammad. *The Babur-nama* in English (Memoirs of Babur). Trans. by A.S. Bereridge, London: Luzac and co., 1921. p. 279.
20. Mahapandita Rahula Sankrityayana, *History of Central-Asia: Bronze*

Age [200 BC] to Chengiz Khan [1227 AD], (New Delhi: New Age Pub. Ltd., Sep. 1964), p. 144.
21. Jonathan Tucker, n. 5, p. 268.
22. *Ibid.*, p. 213.
23. Richard C. Foltz, n. 10, p. 95.
24. UNESCO, *Mongolia's Tentative List: Cultural and Natural heritage*, 1996, p. 176.
25. *Ibid.*, p. 97.
26. *Ibid.*, p. 97.
27. Zhou, Xuejun and Song, Weimin (ed.), *Archaeological Treasures of the Silk Road in Xinjaang Uygur Autonomous Region*. Exhibition catalogue, Shanghai Museum, Shanghai: Shanghai Translation Publishing House, 1998, p. 432.
28. Mahapandita Rahula Sankrityayana, n. 12, p. 151.
29. Xinru, Liu, *Silk and Religion: An exploration of Material Life and the Thought of People, AD 600-1200*, (Delhi, Bombay, Calcutta, Madras: Oxford University Press, 1996), p. 171.
30. M. Ira, Lapidus, *A History of Islamic Societies*, (Cambridge: Cambridge University Press, 1988), p. 147.
31. Kalter, Johannes, *The Arts and Crafts of Turkistan* (London: Thames and Hudson, 1984), p. 19.
32. *Ibid.*, p. 20.
33. Jonathan Tucker, n. 5, p. 216.
34. Erik Hildinger, *Warriors of the Steppe: A Military History of Central Asia- 500 BC to 1700 AD*, (USA: Da Capo Press, 2001), p. 98.
35. Jonathan Tucker, n. 5, p. 218.
36. *Ibid.*, p. 218.
37. Mahapandita Rahula Sankrityayana, n. 12, p. 229.
38. Jonathan Tucker, n. 5, p. 238.
39. Babur, Zahiru'din Muhammad. *The Badur-nama* in English (Memoirs of Babur). Trans. by A.S. Bereridge, London: Luzac and Co., 1921, p. 167.
40. Iqbal M. Shafi, *Silk Road to Sinkiang*, (Lahore-Pakistan: Wajidalis Pub., 1988), p. 17.
41. Jonathan, Tucker, n. 5, p. 213.
42. Iqbal M. Shafi, n. 29, p. 18.
43. Babur, Zahiru'din Muhammad. *The Badur-nama* in English (Memoirs of Babur). Trans. by A.S. Bereridge, London: Luzac and Co., 1921, p. 127.
44. F.W. Mote, n. 2, p. 425.
45. Erik Hildinger, n. 24, p. 109.
46. P. Ratchnevsky, *Genghis Khan: His Life and Legacy*, Trans. by T.N. Haining, (Oxford, U.K.: Blackwel Publishers, 1991), p. 167. see also, Jonathan Tucker, *The Silk Road*, p. 220, Quoted from *Tabaqat-i-Nasiri*.

47. Jonathan, Tucker, n. 5, p. 220.
48. M. Hussain has translated relevant sections of the *Rehla* of Ibn Batutah (GOS, cxxii, 1953), p. 198.
49. Mahapandita Rahula Sankrityayana, n. 12, p. 256.
50. F.W. Mote, n. 2, p. 441.
51. Grousset, R., *The Empire of the Steppes: A History of Central Asia*. Trans. by Naomi Walford, (New Brunswick: Rutgers University Press, 1970), p. 183.
52. Jonathan, Tucker, n. 5, p. 224.
53. *Ibid.*, p. 224.
54. Wolfram, Eberhard, n. 3, p. 237.
55. Firdausi, *The Epic of the Kings: Shah-Nama*. Trans. by Reuben Levy, London: Routledge & Kegan Paul, 1967, p. 387.
56. Jonathan, Tucker, n. 5, p. 366.
57. *Cambridge Economic History of Europe, Trade and Industry in the Middle Ages*, Vol. II, (eds.) Postan, M., and E.E. Rich, Cambridge University Press, 1952, p. 287.
58. L. Boulnois, trans. by Dennis Chamberlin, *The Silk Road*, (Ruskin House-Museum Street, London: George Allen and Unwin Ltd., 196l), p. 218.
59. Jonathan Tucker, n. 5, p. 266.
60. *Ibid.*, p. 266.
61. *Ibid.*, p. 266.
62. *Ibid.*, p. 266.
63. L. Boulnois, n. 43, p. 615.
64. *Ibid.*, p. 615.
65. L. Boulnois, n. 43, p. 219.
66. Jonathan, Tucker, n. 5, p. 267.
67. F.W. Mote, n. 2, p. 615.
68. *Ibid.*, p. 722.
69. Boxer, C.R., *South China in the Sixteenth Century*, (London: Hakluyt Society, 1953), p. 97.
70. L. Boulnois, n. 43, p. 218.
71. L. Kinross, *The Ottoman Centuries*, (New York: Marrow Quill, 1977), p. 167.
72. *Ibid.*, p. 229.
73. James J. Reid, *Tribalism and Society in Islamic Iran*, (Malibu: Udena Publications, 1983), p. 115.
74. Zhou, Xuejun and Song, Weimin (ed.), *Archaeological Treasures of the Silk Road in Xinjaang Uygur Autonomous Region*. Exhibition catalogue, Shanghai Museum, Shanghai: Shanghai Translation Publishing House, 1998, p. 124.

3

Independence of Central Asian Republics and the Revival of Silk Route

Following the disintegration of the Soviet Union in December 1991, new independent states came into existence in Central Asia. Lying to the east of the Caspian Sea, these states, five in number, are Kazakhistan, Kyrgyzstan, Tajikistan, Turkmenistan and Uzbekistan. These states are regarded as constituting a natural region, characterized not only by contiguity and interdependence, but also by a dense web of shared socio-cultural characteristics. The Central Asians themselves have been enthusiastic proponents of this idea of a common regional identity.

Yet in recent years two contrasting trends have emerged that challenge this idea of Central Asia as a discrete region. On the one hand, these states have adopted markedly divergent political and economic systems. Increasingly, the dissimilarities seem to outweigh the similarities, calling into question the notion of a homogenous 'Central Asian' space. Various explanations can be advanced for such differences, but undoubtedly they owe something to the fact that traditionally, these societies were very diverse. Even today, the ancient divide between the nomad world of the north and the settled communities of the south is reflected in attitudes towards the ordering of society.

On the other hand, there has been a move to strengthening ties with neighbors to the south and east, as well as to the north and west. Again, this is not a new development but rather a revival – or rediscovery – of latent ethnic, cultural and economic linkages. In the context of these wider regional formations, the Central Asian states (in no small measure as a result of their common experience of Soviet rule) currently constitute a distinctive sub-region[1]. However, this situation is by no means immutable: there are already indications that this 'core' could fracture, with the possibility that the segments thrown off might be absorbed into different politico-economic configurations. Given this fluidity, it is pointless to impose rigid terminological definitions. Hence, 'region' will here be used in a loose sense to refer both to the five Central Asian states and to more extensive groupings of adjacent, or nearly adjacent, states.

During the Soviet era, the Central Asian republics were largely isolated from the external world. There were almost no direct communication or transport links with neighboring countries. Foreign relations were handled through Moscow. Consequently, with the exception of a handful of senior officials and eminent academics, very few Central Asians had any firsthand knowledge of life beyond the Soviet borders. At the same time, direct cooperation between the Central Asian republics was also limited, since the planning and organization of regional projects was directed from Moscow. Thus, when the Soviet Union collapsed – unexpectedly, with no transitional period – the governments of these new states were virtual novices in the field of foreign affairs at the international level, and also at the regional, intra-Central Asia level.

The first stage in the development of external relations was the very basic process of establishing an organizational infrastructure. Remarkably, this was accomplished within a very short period. Ministries of Foreign Affairs and Foreign Economic Relations were established in all the Central Asian states. They were soon able to open embassies in the USA and key European and Asian centers, also in the member states of the Commonwealth of Independent States (CIS). By the mid-1990s, each Central Asian state had established trade and diplomatic links with over one hundred foreign countries.[2] Foreign policy planners in these new states were confronted with several tasks simultaneously: finding their bearings in the international arena; defining their national interests; identifying friends and partners; and prioritising objectives.

One of the first priorities of the new states was to gain membership to the main international organizations. This was a crucial gauge of external recognition and acceptance. This in turn was a means of protecting and consolidating their independence. Moreover, participation in such organizations provided these small states with a voice in international affairs, and eventually, through the tactical use of voting rights, enabled them to extract benefits from larger, more powerful members. All five Central Asian states were formally accepted as members of the United Nations on 2 March 1992.[3] They subsequently joined the main organizations of UN funds, programs and special agencies (including UNDP, UNHCR, UNCTAD, UNESCO, International Civil Aviation Organization, International Labour Organization, the International Monetary Fund and the World Bank) as also the Economic and Social Commission for Asia and the Pacific. Kyrgyzstan is to date the only Central Asian state that has been accepted as a member of the World Trade Organization. In regional relations, the Central Asian states have followed a multitrack approach, joining a range of organizations. Most of these regional bodies have similar policy aims and objectives, though they differ in political orientation.

These regional organizations may be categorized in various ways, but an obvious difference is that one set comprises CIS members (though they are not necessarily pro-CIS), while the other set combines CIS and non-CIS members. All the Central Asian states joined the CIS in December 1991, on the eve of the formal disintegration of the Soviet Union. On 10 October 2000, this five-member group of CIS states signed a treaty on the formation of the Eurasian Economic Community (EEC), to take effect from 1 April 2001.[4] The new organization's highest policy-making body, the Inter-State Council, is to be located in Moscow. The Kazakh President Nazarbayev was elected chairman at the inaugural meeting held in Minsk on May 31. The primary aim of the EEC is to further economic cooperation (which the CIS signally failed to achieve).

The Central Asian Economic Forum (CAEF) developed parallel to the Eurasian Economic Union. Initially, it seemed as though moves to create a specifically Central Asian entity might lead to the defection of these states from the CIS, or at least to the formation of a strong sub-regional group within the CIS. In July 1998 the Central Asian Union was transformed into the Central Asian Economic Community. However, although economic issues were still ostensibly the main focus of the organization's activities, security concerns were becoming more prominent.

The acronym GUUAM designates an organization that comprises Georgia, Ukraine, Uzbekistan, Azerbaijan and Moldova. The founding members were Georgia, Ukraine, Moldova and Azerbaijan. The original intention of this alliance, first established in 1996, was to facilitate the development of a Eurasian Trans Caucasus transportation corridor (TRACECA) that would bypass Russia, thereby underpinning the independence of these former Soviet countries. GUUAM is firmly oriented towards the Black Sea and Central and Eastern Europe.

In the early 1990s, there was much speculation as to whether the newly independent Central Asian states would opt for an 'Iranian model' of governance (i.e. Islamic monocracy) or a 'Turkish model' (i.e. secular democracy), and by extension, whether they would adopt a pro-Western or an anti-Western stance. However, underlying this purported political-ideological rivalry, there was also cultural competition between the Turks, who belong to the same ethno-linguistic family as the Kazakhs, Kyrgyz, Turkmen and Uzbeks, and the Iranians, who share a similar bond with the Tajiks. Yet the Central Asians proved averse to the establishment of exclusive 'special relationships' with either Turkey or Iran. Nevertheless, both these countries have developed conduits through which to exert indirect influence. Thus, Iran has fostered the Economic Cooperation Organization, while Turkey has sponsored regular Turkic Summits.

The Economic Cooperation Organization (ECO) developed between Iran, Pakistan, and Turkey. In 1985 it was relaunched, on the initiative of Iran, under its present designation. An intergovernmental organization, it aims to promote economic, technical and cultural cooperation among member states. The principal policy and decision-making organs are based in Tehran. In November 1992, the five Central Asian states, as also Azerbaijan and Afghanistan, were admitted, bringing the total membership of the organization to ten. The institutional base was expanded and given new operational impetus. A sustained program of activities has been initiated, including projects to develop transport and communication networks; as also to encourage economic, commercial, cultural and scientific cooperation. Summit meetings are convened annually in the capitals of member states and regular working sessions are held between ministers and senior civil servants. The focus is firmly economic, not political. To date, ECO's greatest success has been in facilitating bilateral contacts between member states.

The Shanghai Cooperation Organization developed from efforts to resolve bilateral issues between China and adjacent CIS members. Its first priority was border demarcation. China shares long frontiers with Kazakhistan, Kyrgyzstan, Russia and Tajikistan. In the 1990s, several stretches of these borders were either not formally demarcated, or were regarded as disputed territory. China initiated moves to resolve these problems through bilateral as well as multilateral negotiations. On 26 April 1996, the five heads of state met in Shanghai to sign the 'Treaty on Deepening Military Trust in Border Regions'. This event marked the beginning of a series of annual meetings between the leaders of the so-called 'Shanghai Five' group. Regular working meetings were also convened at the ministerial level. The declared aims of the Shanghai Cooperation Organization (SCO) included the creation of 'a new international and political order featuring democracy, justness and rationality'.

The Central Asian states are still very young. They were created in haste, against a background of political upheaval and rapid social and economic change. Yet, all these countries have made significant progress in decentralizing their economies, expanding international links, diversifying and increasing production and trade.

Central Asian Economies

The extraction and export of their natural resources is the basic source of the economy of Central Asian countries. The countries in the region have developed little capability to utilize their own resources effectively. However, the worldwide economic recession has dashed Kazakhistan's hopes of developing its economy entirely on the basis of extraction and exports.

The Kazakhistan joint stock gold mining company, for instance, is on the verge of bankruptcy, although the volume of mined gold has gone up.[5] Inaccessible markets and lack of electricity has added to the problems. The company's debt to the workers is reaching an unpayable amount.[6]

Kazakhistan

Kazakhistan's oil reserves have been estimated to amount to as much as 2,100,000,000 tonnes,[7] along with huge amounts of natural gas reserves. The rivalry over various oil routes is generating inordinate amount of friction between the Central Asian states. The vast oilfields in Kazakhstan have remained unexplored. The Chevron oil company of the United States has the rights to these fields. Britain and France are also negotiating for rights over some oil and gas fields in Kazakhstan. Due to weaker demand from the main partners—Russia, South Korea and other East Asian countries—Is this word right? and nonferrous metals, which are another important source of development for Kazakhstan, dropped from 47.9 per cent of total exports in 1993 to less than 37.4 per cent in 1998.[8] Despite the price fall, because of increasing absolute volumes, the share of oil and oil products has grown from 25.3 per cent to 38.7 per cent of the total exports.[9] So together oil, oil products and basic metal comprised more than three-quarters of exports, and were hit by a sharp price decrease. The grain harvest was the lowest of the decade and exports fell by more than 42 per cent in value terms in 1998, compared to 1997.[10] The share of chemicals, machinery and equipment to total exports also dropped because of the development of the Russian ruble and diminished competitiveness in Russia, their traditional main market.[11]

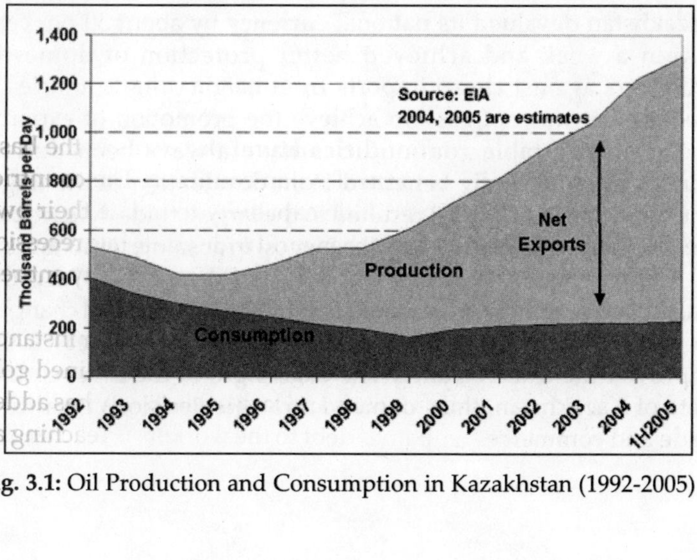

Fig. 3.1: Oil Production and Consumption in Kazakhstan (1992-2005)

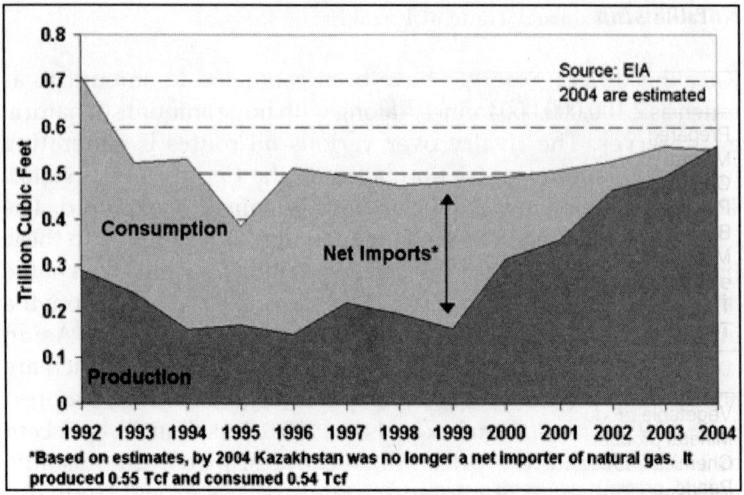

Fig. 3.2: Natural Gas Production and Consumption in Kazakhstan (1992-2004)

The cheap imports from Russia, Uzbekistan and Kyrgyzstan create difficulties for many Kazakh producers. Imposition of 20 per cent Value Added Tax (VAT) on all personal imports, mutual Quantitative restrictions in trade with Russia and 200 per cent tariffs on selected imports, mainly beverages and food stuffs, from Kyrgyzstan and Uzbekistan were not effective.[12] On April 5, 1999, Kazakhstan devalued its national currency by about 30 per cent within a week and achieved better protection of domestic producers against cheap imports from neighboring countries.[13] However, it was not easy to achieve the promotion of exports, because exportable commodities have always been dollar-dominated and hardly benefited from devaluation of the tinge. The developments in 1998 resulted in the largest trade deficit since the states independence; it was the biggest in absolute terms among all Central Asian states.[14] The efforts taken in 1999 by the Nazarbaev government have not yet brought about crucial changes. Nevertheless, rising price of oil and metals in the year 2000, improved the trade balance. The challenges of the independent state of Kazakhstan, thus, demand strategic decisions regarding trade and commerce.

Table 3.1: External Trade of Kazakhstan, Principal Commodities

(US$ Million)

Imports c.i.f.	*2001*	*2002*	*2003*
Prepared foodstuffs	331.0	320.9	426.0
Mineral products	904.4	822.9	1,007.2
Chemical products	667.1	715.7	909.6
Plastics and rubber	239.8	267.9	362.8
Base metals and articles thereof	889.5	737.9	993.2
Machinery, mechanical appliances and electrical equipment	1,852.2	1,881.7	2,152.5
Transportation equipment	625.0	803.2	1,222.8
Total (incl. Others)	6,446.0	6,584.0	8,408.7
Exports f.o.b.	*2001*	*2002*	*2003*
Vegetable products	392.7	408.2	659.5
Mineral products	5,028.8	5,917.5	8,316.3
Chemical products	405.9	418.6	440.0
Pearls, precious and semi-precious stones, and metals	264.6	269.5	249.9
Base metals and articles thereof	2,109.9	2,234.1	2,635.1
Total (incl. Others)	8,639.1	9,670.3	12,926.7

Table 3.2: Principal Trading Partners

(US$ Million)

Imports c.i.f.	*2001*	*2002*	*2003*
Belarus	46.3	54.8	94.9
China, People's Republic	172.0	313.0	523.7
Finland	71.4	73.4	97.2
France	141.6	110.2	196.2
Germany	490.2	586.2	734.2
Italy	268.9	219.1	250.2
Japan	142.0	164.6	212.0
Korea Republic	110.6	110.2	114.6
Netherlands	85.4	87.5	127.6
Poland	61.3	74.7	117.2
Russia	2,891.99	2,548.8	3,282.1
Switzerland	67.6	60.2	61.7
Turkey	137.0	173.7	209.0
Ukraine	155.0	217.1	209.0
United Kingdom	249.4	259.7	248.6
USA	349.1	461.4	470.4
Uzbekistan	81.1	86.5	89.7
Total (incl. Others)	6,446.0	6,584.0	8,408.7

(Contd.)

(*Contd.*)

Exports f.o.b.	*2001*	*2002*	*2003*
Belarus	1,221.2	2,011.3	2,192.6
China, People's Republic	659.6	1,023.0	1,653.1
Finland	56.1	48.5	108.9
Germany	501.8	220.3	146.4
Italy	956.3	904.2	1,013.1
Korea, Republic	43.4	48.9	55.5
Kyrgyzstan	87.0	108.6	156.4
Netherlands	144.2	123.6	1861
Poland	164.2	320.5	201.0
Russia	1,759.5	1,497.8	1,967.9
Switzerland	408.7	792.4	1,679.9
Tajkistan	61.2	45.7	75.7
Turkey	74.2	97.4	99.2
Ukraine	490.2	291.5	426.2
United Kingdom	294.3	131.8	143.2
USA	159.0	116.9	99.1
Uzbekistan	150.2	101.0	137.9
Total (incl.others)	8,639.1	9,670.3	12,926.7

Table 3.3: Transport

	2001	*2002*	*2003*
Railways (Estimated Traffic)			
Passenger-km (million)	10,384	10,449	10,686
Freight net ton-km (million)	135,653	133,088	147,672
Road Traffic (Motor vehicles in use at 31 December)			
Passenger cars	1,057.801	1,062,554	1,148,754
Buses and coaches	50,162	51,367	61,391
Lorries and vans	241,528	251,129	261,327
Motorcycles and mopeds	97,909	80,953	74,756
Shipping—Merchant Feet (registered at 31 December)			
Number of vessels	21	20	22
Total displacement (grt)	13,096	11,845	15,300
Source: Lloyd's Register-Fairplay, World Fleet Statistics.			
Civil Aviation (traffic on scheduled services)			
Passengers carried ('000)	884	1,036	1,275
Passenger-km (million)	1,901	2,179	2,654
Total ton-km (million)	44	53	94

Kilometers flown (million) 20 in 1996; 20 in 1997; 35 in 1998.
Source: *UN Statistical Yearbook.*

Kyrgyzstan

Kyrgyzstan has been relatively stable during the years but the country's economic downturn has continued. With few natural resources the country has little attraction for foreign investors, but the quasi-democratic system introduced by President Asker Akayev has bought his government considerable financial support from the World Bank, the IMF and Japan.[15] Nevertheless the future continues to be bleak for the country as acute shortage of fuel, food and other consumer goods has increased public dissatisfaction.

Kyrgyzstan has taken the most far reaching steps in privatizing its industrial, agricultural and banking economy. Of the 20 commercial banks functioning in Kyrgyzstan, 12 have gone down.[16] The noisy and scandalous collapse of financial institutions with foreign capital caused a major problem in Kyrgyzstan. A fall in export revenues of almost 15 per cent and an increase of import expenditures by about 17 per cent led to a trade deficit in 1998 comparable with the largest one since independence, recorded in 1996.[17] The 1998 official trade data for Kyrgyzstan indicated an unsustainably sharp increase of dollar dominated imports from the highly industrialized countries and a clear fall of exports of gold in value terms because of a drop in world prices.[18]

The share of trade with regional partners, especially on the export side has substantially decreased.[19] Attempts to improve trade with neighbors by increasing the re-export of imported consumer goods and beverages have forced in neighbor countries. Kyrgyzstan's difficult economic situation makes it imperative that the country try and increase sales of its surplus electric energy to its neighbors, but the lack of funds for new electric grids and major infrastructural projects make this difficult. Export of water to Uzbekistan and Kazakhstan is another opportunity but needs more funding for dams and canals which Kyrgyzstan does not have. Akaev remains especially vulnerable to a backlash against the economic revolution.

Uzbekistan

Uzbekistan is a major Central Asian state rich in natural resources. Despite the slowdown in the pace of reforms and privatization in

Table 3.4: External Trade of Kyrgystan

(US$ million)

Principal Commodities			
Imports c.i.f.	*2000*	*2001*	*2002*
Vegetable products	42.3	15.5	21.7
Prepared foodstuffs, beverages and tabacoo	31.0	35.8	47.4
Mineral products	133.3	129.5	163.4
Products of chemical or allied industries	59.3	67.3	78.4
Plastics, rubber and articles thereof	22.8	22.0	24.9
Textiles and fabrics	35.2	28.8	38.9
Metals and articles thereof	27.6	27.3	29.7
Machinery, electrical equipment and parts	98.2	56.5	89.6
Vehicles and transport equipment	41.8	31.8	32.1
Total (incl. Others)	554.1	467.2	586.8
Exports f.o.b.	*2000*	*2001*	*2002*
Vegetable products	14.4	13.3	19.9
Prepared foodstuffs, beverages and tobacoo	37.3	32.7	30.1
Mineral products	86.8	58.4	62.4
Products of chemical or allied industries	14.5	18.0	25.2
Raw hides and skins, leather, fur, travel articles and bags	7.6	10.3	24.2
Textiles and fabrics	42.8	29.5	59.8
Natural and cultured pearls, precious and semi-precious stones, precious metals and products, and coins.	196.9	226.7	164.8
Machinery, electrical equipment and parts	33.4	28.5	26.9
Vehicles and transport equipment	14.9	26.5	21.2
Total (incl. Others)	504.5	475.2	485.5

Uzbekistan, President Islam Karimov has notched up the country's first real economic gains since the country won independence. Uzbekistan, which is the second largest cotton fiber exporter and the eighth biggest gold producer in the world, has recently suffered much more than its neighbors from the simultaneous sharp fall of prices for its two major exports.[20]

Following the success of the Uzbek-US Zarafshan New Mount joint venture in gold production, several well known international companies are now holding stakes to set up gold mining in Uzbekistan.[21] Uzbekistan reportedly has reserves of around 100 different minerals, of which 60 are already being used in the national economy.[22] Uzbekistan has 100-plus protracted deposits, including 165 oil, gas and condensate deposits, 3 coal deposits, 46

Table 3.5: Principal Trading Partners

(US$ million)

Imports c.i.f.	*2001*	*2002*	*2003*
Belarus	6.0	5.1	5.9
Belgium	8.4	1.6	3.3
Canada	1.9	9.0	8.3
China, People's Republic	48.5	59.1	77.7
Germany	24.3	31.4	38.2
Iran	6.7	4.3	5.9
Japan	5.8	6.4	11.8
Kazakhstan	81.8	123.9	170.9
Korea, Republic	7.8	7.0	11.7
Netherlands	4.0	16.1	12.3
Poland	4.9	3.9	6.1
Russia	85.1	116.7	176.1
Sweden	0.9	7.4	2.0
Turkey	15.8	17.0	26.0
Turkmenistan	9.0	1.7	0.4
Ukraine	6.2	7.8	12.6
United Arab Emirates	6.8	7.3	7.8
United Kingdom	4.8	2.8	2.5
USA	26.8	47.4	47.9
Uzbekistan	66.7	60.1	39.2
Total (incl. Others)	467.2	586.8	717.0
Exports f.o.b.	2001	2002	2003
Afghanistan	1.6	4.4	6.1
Azerbaijan	2.1	5.6	2.0
China, People's Republic	19.4	41.1	23.3
France	1.8	5.6	0.2
Germany	94.4	1.8	3.0
India	1.4	6.1	0.7
Iran	8.2	4.7	2.1
Kazakhstan	39.0	36.8	57.1
Latvia	3.4	8.7	9.4
Russia	64.5	80.0	97.0
Switzerland	124.2	96.4	117.9
Tajikistan	6.7	10.2	18.9
Turkey	13.8	16.4	11.0
United Arab Emirates	0.5	68.8	144.3
United Kingdom	14.1	0.9	0.1
USA	7.1	36.1	6.5
Uzbekistan	48.0	27.8	16.3
Total (incl. Others)	476.2	485.5	581.7

deposits of precious meals, 17 of extracted raw materials and 21 of semi-precious materials, 495 deposits of building materials and

Table 3.6: Transport

Railways (Traffic)			
	2000	*2001*	*2002*
Passenger-km (million)	44	50	43
Freight ton-km (million)	338	332	395

Source: UN, Statistical Yearbook.

Road Traffic (vehicles in use at 31 December)			
	1997	*1998*	*1999*
Passenger cars	176,075	187,734	187,322
Motorcycles and mopeds	26,634	23,909	20,789

Source: International Road Federation, World Road Statistics.

Civil Aviation (traffic on scheduled services)			
	1999	*2000*	*2001*
Kilometres flown (million)	9	6	6
Passengers carried ('000)	312	241	192
Passenger-km (million)	532	423	363
Total ton-km (million)	56	44	39

Source: UN, Statistical Yearbook.

over 150 deposits of subterranean water sources.[23] There was a major downturn in Uzbekistan's critical agriculture based economy with cotton production down to 20 per cent below target in 1996-97 with a total production of 1.02 million tons.[24] The government abolished its monopoly over the export of raw cotton in order to increase foreign exchange earnings. Major sectors that recorded growth are metallurgy with 183 per cent growth, wool processing 118 per cent and chemical and petrochemical 115 per cent.[25] A joint Uzbek-South Korean car plant was expected to produce a total of 30,000 cars in 1997,[26] half of which were to be exported to other commonwealths of independent states. Other major economic gains came from the energy sector. Uzbekistan has nearly tripled its oil production since the Soviet era. Its current production of 160,000 barrels per day has made Uzbekistan self sufficient in oil and it hopes to export some 40,000 barrels per day.[27]

Tashkent's main foreign investment hope lies in its proposed $1.3 billion gas joint venture with US energy companies. The joint venture will develop 11 new gas fields.[28] Uzbekistan also began holding negotiations with energy companies including Mobile, Texaco, Unocal, and France's Agip about developing new oil and gas projects.[29] US firms are also helping Uzbekistan convert tractors and trucks previously run on diesel to compressed natural gas. At this time, Uzbekistan has the largest number of representative offices of foreign banks in the region. Deutsch Bank, Chase Manhattan Bank, Malay Bank and 20 more from various countries are represented in Uzbekistan.[30]

Because of recent financial difficulties, falling export revenues forced Uzbekistan to cushion the negative effects of external trade shocks, and make ends meet, by reducing its imports.[31] The government used both direct and indirect restrictions to cut consumer goods imports as much as possible, and promoted massive imports of modern machinery and technology to facilitate further industrialization.

Table 3.7: External Trade of Uzbekistan

(US$ million)

Principal Commodieis			
Imports f.o.b.	*1998*	*1999*	*2000*
Chemicals and plastics	407.2	33.0	399.5
Metals	303.6	245.4	253.5
Machinery and equipment	1,553.7	1,393.5	1,044.1
Food products	512.2	408.1	361.1
Energy products	16.3	66.6	112.7
Total (incl. Others)	3,288.7	3,110.7	2,696.4
Exports f.o.b.	*1998*	*1999*	*2000*
Cotton fibre	1,361.0	883.7	897.1
Chemicals and plastics	51.7	101.8	93.4
Metals	180.7	138.9	216.7
Machinery and equipment	146.6	103.2	111.8
Food products	111.9	206.7	176.4
Energy products	277.8	371.5	335.2
Total (incl. Others)	3,528.2	3,235.8	3,264.7

Source: Centre for Economic Research, Taskhent, *Uxbek Economic Trends.*

Table 3.8: Principal Trading Partners

(US$ million)

Imports	*2001*	*2002*	*2003*
China, People's Republic	55.9	114.6	161.5
France	118.8	38.7	486
Germany	227.2	224.5	253.1
Kazakhstan	165.3	111.1	126.7
Korea, Republic	380.3	207.3	236.5
Russia	400.2	498.7	536.6
Tajikistan	95.9	80.2	91.5
Turkey	98.7	102.1	127.5
Ukraine	120.2	74.9	85.5
USA	162.5	151.9	282.5
Total (incl. Others)	2,292.6	2,076.9	2,477.3
Exports	*2001*	*2002*	*2003*
Germany	56.4	43.2	37.1
Italy	155.2	133.8	54.3
Japan	48.0	66.7	72.3
Kazakhstan	73.7	78.7	89.7
Korea, Republic	124.3	88.0	100.4
Kyrgyzstan	60.7	54.7	62.4
Russia	527.2	310.6	408.2
Tajikistan	137.0	120.3	137.2
Turkey	32.8	68.4	93.4
Ukraine	175.5	25.3	28.8
Total (incl. Others)	2,087.1	1,562.2	1,911.2

Source: Asian Development Bank, *key Indicators of Developing Asian and Pacific Countries.*

Table 3.9: Transport

Railways (Traffic)	*1999*	*2000*	*2001*
Passenger-km (million)	2	2	2
Freight ton-km (million)	14	15	16

Source: UN, Statistical Yearbook.

Civil Aviation (Estimated traffic on scheduled services)	*1999*	*2000*	*2001*
Kilometres flown (million)	37	39	57
Passengers carried ('000)	1,658	1,745	2,256
Passenger-km (million)	3,328	3,732	5,268
Total ton-km (million)	370	417	580

Source: UN, *Statistical Yearbook.*

Tajikistan

Tajikistan has gone through a long civil war. The end of the war and peace efforts have contributed to a certain amount of economic growth and improvement of the foreign trade balance deficit that had increased more than four times, reaching about one tenth of its GDP.[32] This huge deficit was also connected, first of all, with a sharp worsening of the terms of trade. International prices for major exports fell by almost 15 per cent and 17.7 per cent in 1998.[33] A decline of cotton-fiber exports of up to 88,400 tons aggravated the shortage of hard currency earnings. Overall decrease in export revenues was 19 per cent in 2000.[34] On the import side, devaluation of the Russian rouble promoted a greater inflow of consumer goods to Tajikistan. The rise of total imports in value terms together with a two-fold decrease of exports in 1998 resulted in the second largest trade deficit in the region in relative terms.[35]

Table 3.10: External Trade of Tajikistan

(US$ million)

Principal Commodities			
Imports c.i.f.	*1999*	*2000*	*2001*
Alumina	81	198	184
Natural gas	36	35	27
Petroleum products	54	48	76
Electricity	179	119	98
Grain and flour	46	45	38
Total (incl. Others)	663	675	688
Exports f.o.b.	*1999*	*2000*	*2001*
Aluminium	309	433	397
Cotton fibre	82	84	62
Electricity	175	92	79
Total (incl. Others)	689	784	652

Turkmenistan

Turkmenistan has the third rank in the world in gas resources and petroleum regions. President S. Niyazov has so far been foiled at every attempt of his to open up pipeline routes. Turkmenistan was one of the most isolated and least developed of the Soviet republics.

Table 3.11: Principle Trading Partners

(US$ million)

Imports c.i.f.	*2001*	*2002*	*2003*
Azerbaijan	33.5	41.1	46.9
India	34.4	31.6	36.0
Iran	10.0	15.6	17.5
Italy	20.0	25.8	8.0
Kazakhstan	89.1	72.3	82.4
Russia	129.4	163.5	135.8
Turkmenistan	62.3	47.1	53.7
Ukraine	63.6	80.5	91.8
Uzbekistan	150.7	132.44	151.0
Total (incl. others)	680.1	710.3	837.8
Exports	*2001*	*2002*	*2003*
Belgium	6.0	9.5	10.1
Hungary	38.8	39.9	45.5
Italy	5.8	6.9	46.4
Latvia	11.7	30.9	35.2
Netherlands	194.4	216.9	2.4
Russia	104.7	87.5	68.4
Switzerland	52.2	68.7	81.3
Turkey	75.1	118.5	141.6
Turkmenistan	9.7	9.9	11.3
Uzbekistan	87.2	72.9	83.2
Total (incl. other)	651.6	737.0	657.4

Source: Asian Development Bank, *Key Indicators of Developing Asian and Pacific Countries.*

Table 3.12: Transport of Tajikistan

Railway (Traffic)			
	1999	*2000*	*2001*
Passenger-km (million)	61	73	32
Freight ton-km (million)	1,282	1,326	1,248
Civil Aviation (Estimated Traffic on Scheduled Services)			
	1997	*1998*	*1999*
Kilometres flown (million)	7	5	4
Passengers carried ('000)	594	217	156
Passenger-km (million)	1,825	322	229
Freight ton-km (million)	166	32	23

Source: UN, *Statistical Yearbook.*

After gaining independence Turkmenistan has become the most repressive of all post-Soviet regimes and is ranked as one of the most repressive in the world. Oil and gas have potential roles in Turkmenistan. But their production has been monopolized by Niyazov. This stifles private enterprise and ensure that the president stays as the initial beneficiary of any foreign investment. Moreover, the country's distance from bodies of water and trade routes make energy resources less easily exploitable. Turkmenistan is in the process of becoming a "gas republic" in which the power of some major international companies and that of its megalomaniac president sit comfortably side by side.[36]

Turkmenistan had its largest trade deficit in 1998 since its independence in 1997, equalling 26 per cent GDP.[37] It was faced with a sharp decrease of its major export commodity, gas, from 80.9 billion cubic meters in 1990 to 24.3 billion cubic meters in 1996, 6.5 billion cubic meters in 1997 to 1.8 billion cubic meters in 1998.[38] An increase of production in oil and oil products, and cotton fiber – two major exports both affected by low world market price

Table 3.13: External Trade of Turkmenistan

(US$ million)

Principal Commodities			
Imports c.i.f.	*2001*	*2002*	*2003**
Food and live animals	129.4	114.3	130.3
Beverages and tabacoo	56.8	70.1	67.4
Mineral fuels, lubricants, etc.	39.1	25.7	17.7
Chemicals	178.6	210.8	271.2
Basic manufactures	448.7	394.2	487.7
Machinery and transport equipment	1,204.7	857.6	1,125.6
Miscellaneous manufactured articles	128.1	112.7	165.2
Total (incl. Others)	2,348.8	2,119.4	2,450.0
Exports f.o.b	*2001*	*2002*	*2003*
Crude materials (inedible) except fuels	123.7	83.8	152.4
Mineral fuels, lubricants, etc.	2,217.2	2,447.1	2,920.3
Basic manufacturers	141.6	150.6	196.6
Machinery and transport equipment	14.5	17.1	16.9
Total (incl. Others)	2,620.2	2,855.6	3,320.0

* Estimates.

Source: Asian Development Bank, *Key Indicators of Developing Asian and Pacific Countries.*

Table 3.14: Principal Trading Partners

(US$ million)

Imports	*2001*	*2002*	*2003*
France	10.9	32.6	87.6
Germany	197.9	103.7	160.9
Iran	121.4	80.9	90.4
Japan	161.2	8.3	7.4
Russia	396.7	360.9	281.3
Turkey	163.6	233.5	205.7
Ukraine	264.9	213.3	243.3
United Arab Emirates	138.1	181.9	203.2
USA	208.2	137.3	37.7
Total (incl. others)	2,210.0	1,819.1	1,846.0
Exports	*2001*	*2002*	*2003*
Cyprus	26.4	90.7	103.4
Germany	5.1	4.0	5838
Iran	301.6	355.6	399.5
Italy	473.0	486.8	101.5
Russia	153.5	22.9	24.7
Switzerland	87.3	3.8	4.5
Tajikistan	50.4	33.6	38.3
Turkey	126.8	168.1	185.3
Ukraine	1,198.0	1,346.1	1,535.2
USA	31.7	49.0	74.1
Total (incl.others)	2,555.0	2,710.4	2,729.0

Source: Asian Development Bank, *Key Indicators of Developing Asian and Pacific Countries.*

Table 3.15: Transport

Railways (Traffic)	*1996*	*1997*	*1999**
Passenger journeys (million)	7.8	6.4	3.1
Passenger-km (million)	2,104	958	701
Freight transported (million metric tons)	15.9	18.5	17.2
Freight ton-km (million)	6,779	7,445	7,337

Source: Railways Directory of Turkmenistan.

– could not make up for the revenue losses. And in 1998, Turkmenistan's exports were the lowest.[39] The collapse of output and exports of gas that badly affected both economic growth and trade indicators in 1997 and 1998, was a direct result of external shocks connected with complete dependence on Russian pipelines.

Therefore, creating alternative transit transport routes has become an important precondition for the promotion of trade and development, strengthening economic independence and integration with world economy.

Revival of the Silk Route in Independent Central Asia

The ancient Silk Route passed through the territories of the Central Asian Republics of Kazakhstan, Kyrgyzstan, Uzbekistan, Tajikistan, and Turkmenistan and also through the southern Caucasian Republic of Azerbaijan, Georgia and Armenia. Being landlocked, the Central Asian Republics do not have direct access to the world transport network and to the world markets. These Republics, possessing rich natural resources, need economically viable, cheap and safe access to the world markets. Hence the revival of the historical Silk Route has become one of the key policy issues of the newly independent Central Asian Republics.

These sovereign Central Asian states offer opportunities for cooperation in cultural, economic and political spheres on a new footing. The Central Asian states are keen to secure access to outside markets and to create regional transport and communication infrastructure. "They are enthusiastic about the moves by Iran and China to have a Trans-Asian rail link from Xingjiang through Central Asia to Iran which is a project of immense commercial, political and strategic importance. In other words, a modified system of the ancient Silk Route is being revived."[40]

Though the British and Russian governments could have helped in reviving the Silk Route during the 19th century, the monopoly of the British over Indian trade and the destination of Indian handicrafts and manufacturing inhibited the development of trade between India, Central Asia and Russia. Besides, restrictions imposed by the Tsarist administration on Indian trade passing through Bukhara also affected the growth of economic ties. The project submitted by S.I. Baranovsky, a Russian engineer, for the construction of a railway line from Orenburg to Peshawar as well as its later variant of the Indo-Volga Railway Line was turned down by the Tsarist authorities fearing penetration of British goods into Central Asia.[41] A Similar proposal by F. Lesseps for financing the construction of a railway line joining Orenburg with Samarkand and Peshawar as an extension of a line from

Lisbon to Orenburg was also rejected by Tsar Alexander Ï.[42] It was felt that the West European countries would gain more than Russia by the operation of this railway line.[43] "The first railway was built from Uzun-Ada on the Caspian to Kizyl-Arvat in 1881, and from there it was extended to the Amu-Darya in 1885 and thence to Samarkand in 1888. The line reached Tashkent in 1898, but Tashkent itself was not connected with Orenburg and thus to Russia until 1906."[44] The line was extended to Andizhan in 1899 and a branch line was built from Merv to Kushka on the Afghan frontier in 1898.[45]

The collapse of the world communist system created very favorable conditions for the restoration of the Silk Route. However, the historical necessity for the restoration of the Silk Route started earlier. The Soviet Union, over the territory of which the main section of the Silk Route passed, created obstacles. External trade was under state control. It may be asked why the USSR did not promote restoration of the Silk Route, which could bring sufficient dividends to the state by the levy of taxes for international transport through its territory, and also by the use of this route for the export of its goods to the world market? This can be explained by the following reasons. Firstly, the USSR joining the world transport network would have meant tremendous Soviet state investments for the reconstruction of old roads and the construction of new roads corresponding to world standards.[46] These expenses could be met not only by the profits from international transport through the territory of the USSR, but primarily by the export and sale of Soviet goods in other states.[47] However, Soviet goods, because of their low quality could not compete in the world market. Secondly, the Soviet state was against opening the country to the outside world. The international transport and road, and the openness of the state borders could have led to the penetration of new ideas from abroad, which would change the mind of the Soviet people.[48] In other words, the restoration of the Silk Route could lead to the destruction of the Soviet political system.

Joining the Central Asian Republics with the world transport system is one of the conditions of their socio-economic, political and cultural development, as well as their independence. The Central Asian and the Southern Caucasian states do not have direct access to the world transport network and through them to the world market. After independence, authoritarian presidential rule has emerged in all the five Republics along with important geopolitical and economic differences. Kazakhstan is the largest state, spanning an area eleven times the size of the U.K. but with a population of under 15 million; its geopolitical condition shaped by the two neighboring great powers, China and Russia.[49] By contrast, its main regional competitor, Uzbekistan, has the highest population density in the region, and it has on its borders the unstable states of Afghanistan and Tajikistan.

Tajikistan has partly emerged from a civil war that went on between 1992 and 1997; like Kyrgyzstan it is mountainous and inaccessible. Turkmenistan is similarly isolated; in fact, it was the most isolated of all Soviet republics during the Soviet period. Its border with Iran is an important geopolitical influence. Tajikistan has emerged as the poorest of the post-Soviet economies. As the Caspian littoral states, Kazakhistan and Turkmenistan stand to profit substantially from oil revenues if there is sufficient transport and network of pipelines. Like Kazakhistan, Uzbekistan also has gas as well as substantial cotton crop. Both Kyrgyzstan and Tajikistan have hydroelectric power and mineral resources

Interests of the Central Asian Republics in the Revival of the Silk Route

The Central Asian Republics are in the transitional period of their social, political and economic developments. The restoration of the Silk Route opens opportunities not only for expanding trade, and regional economic cooperation but also for the interchange of ideas and contacts between Europe and Asia. The current steady and dynamic development of political, trade and economic relations pre-suppose the strengthening of fraternal and mutually advantageous relations of partnership between all states of the Silk Route region. The arms race, the local conflicts, extremism and terrorism, the unlawful manufacture, distribution and consumption of narcotics substances, natural disasters and those brought about by technology or by man, and the crying social needs are problems that lead to a recognition of the natural and objective need for the revival of the Silk Route on a qualitatively new basis.

The Central Asian states are keen to revive the Silk Route due to various interests and prospects contained in the revival. Some of these factors are as described below:

Economic Interest

For the newly independent Central Asian Republics, the revived Silk Route is synonymous with their hope for economic development. The weaknesses inherited from the old Soviet system, and more recently by the precipitous economic collapse following the breakup of the Soviet Union, have created enormous difficulties for Central Asian Republics. Yet it cannot be denied that the long period of Russian and then Soviet domination brought out significant development of infrastructure, agriculture, mining, industry, education, and so forth, even if there was no all-round development of regional economy.

The economic crisis in Central Asia includes many aspects such as the breakdown of agriculture due to lack of machinery and replacement parts, formerly supplied from other areas of the USSR; the breakdown of industrial production, for similar reasons; the lack of supplies of crucial materials; the loss of former markets. In these circumstances the newly independent Central Asian states have been trying to diversify their economics and seek new partners in economic cooperation.

The underdeveloped industrial base continues to be the key problem in Central Asia. Local agricultural products, mainly cotton, and mineral resources like gold, silver, chromium etc., will have to be shipped to Russia and to the other republics of the CIS the Commonwealth of Independent States for processing, till such industries develop in Central Asia.[50] Another problem is that the indigenous labor force is low skilled, whereas two-thirds of the skilled industrial workers have been Slavs. And the departure of the Russians and Ukrainians from Central Asia has affected the industrial sector in the Central Asian states.

The states have intensified the process of privatizing their economies and opening up to foreign investments to stabilize and transform their systems. Underdeveloped production structures, disruption of previous economic ties and shortage of hard currency has forced these states to look for alternative sources of supply, markets and remunerative prices for their raw materials.

The states are keen to link their internal rail and road network to Iran, Turkey and Pakistan, in the same way as it stands presently connected to Europe via Orenburg and Moscow. They are eagerly looking for port facilities in these countries. In February 1993,

Kazakhistan's parliament approved the economic programme for 1993-95 that calls for "focus on construction of a trans-Asian railway and highways passing through Iran, Pakistan, Russia and China, and development of a large port system on the Caspian Sea in cooperation with Iran.[51] Central Asian societies now ascribe all the ills of their economy to erstwhile Soviet policies, and are searching their future in the revival of the Silk Route.

To consolidate the Central Asian states into a powerful economic bloc, the restoration of Silk Route is thus an unavoidable step. The Tashkent summit held in early January 1993, decided to bring about a common market with common taxation, customs, pricing, investment and export policies thereby moving towards the cooperation and integration of the economies of the region.[52]

The stabilization of the Central Asian economies would be possible only through strict control over monetary supply and budgetary deficits, and through expansion of production or import of consumer goods.[53] The Central Asian states have extremely underdeveloped production structures for expanding consumer products. Their ability to import consumer goods is limited. The viability and success of structural changes in the Central Asian economies is dependent on the speed and extent to which they can get integrated into the world economy. The economy of Central Asia will not become viable unless these states become part of a common economic space in the CIS or of the world economy. Since, the CIS does not constitute itself into a common economic space at present, and the future of the CIS is full of uncertainties, the only alternative available to the Central Asian economies is to become part of world economy.

Each of the Central Asian countries is small in size, either in terms of geography or population. Their income level is not high. A characteristic feature of small countries in the world is that they depend on foreign trade to a larger extent than bigger countries like Russia or the Ukraine for income, production and consumption. So, the foreign capital requirements of the Central Asian economies are enormous. The Central Asian states can meet the situation created by inadequate flow of foreign capital and also make their economies viable through the expansion of foreign trade along proper transport routes.

The Central Asian Republics are making all efforts to establish closer economic relations with other countries. In August, 1992,

Kazakhistan's Foreign Minister, Tuleutai Suleymenov, met the Foreign Minister of China, Li Ping, and had extensive talks.[54] Both countries signed seven documents including counsellor treaty; agreement on encouragement and mutual protection of investments, agreement on cultural cooperation and education etc. Being two large neighboring countries, these agreements can go a long way in protecting trade and economic cooperation, in improving means of communication, water management, building railways. This is a step in the revival of the historical Silk Route.

Other countries are also interested in the revival of the Silk Route through Central Asian states. A pipeline to Turkey would ensure supply of energy. Turkey can levy transit fee on transport from Baku and Ashkabat. Iran is keen not to be left out in sharing the transit tariff on its territory. China and Japan are looking from two clear economic angles: first to ensure abundant supply to their territories, and second to play second fiddle to no other country of the region.[55] Since all countries of the region are experiencing economic difficulties, the time is appropriate for them, more than ever before, to play crucial roles in trying to keep the region under control for their economic interests.

Prospects are especially bright for the three hydrocarbon rich states near the Caspian Sea – Kazakhstan, Uzbekistan and Turkmenistan. In these three Republics the energy sector holds the key to future economic development. Several oil companies have pinned great hopes on Caspian oil and have invested billions

Table 3.16: Asian Oil Demand Outlook (Mn B/D)

Country	*Actual 1997*	*8/97 Est* 2002*	*4/98 Est** 2002*
China	3.9	5.1	5.0
India	1.9	2.0	2.5
Japan	5.6	5.8	5.6
Indonesia	1.0	1.1	1.0
Malaysia	0.5	0.7	0.6
Other Asia	6.6	8.6	7.6
Total Asia	**19.5**	**23.7**	**22.3**

Source: Mobil

* Mobil's estimate in August 1997

** Mobil's estimate in April 1998

of dollars into Kazakhstan and Azerbaijan. They think that this region has the potential to become a future Kuwait.[56]

The Silk Route has a unique role to play in the fulfillment of the economic interests of Central Asian Republics. The restoration of the Silk Route is beneficial not only for the Central Asian

Table 3.17: Oil and Gas Reserves of Central Asia

Country	*Proven oil Reserves Bn. bld.*	*Potential Oil Reserves Bn. bld.*	*Proven Gas Reserves tr. cu. m.*
Kazakhstan	5.3	20.0	1.8
Turkmenistan	1.4	4.3	2.9
Uzbekistan		3.2 mt.	82.8 bn
Azerbaijan	1.2	15.0	0.1

Source: OPEC Bulletin, November/ December, 1996: for Uzbekistan Adelphi paper, 228.

Table 3.18: Central Asian Republics Oil Production and Exports

(*Thousand bbl/d*)

Country	*Production (1990)*	*Production (1997)*	*Net Exports (1990)*	*Net Exports (1997)*	*Possible Exports (2010)*
Kazakhstan	602.1	573.3	109.2	310.9	2000
Turkmenistan	124.8	107.3	69.0	39.2	50
Uzbekistan	86.2	182.4	-168.1	23.8	50
Total	**813.1**	**863.0**	**10.1**	**373.9**	**2100**

Source: United States Energy Information Administration.

Table 3.19: Central Asian Republics Natural Gas Production and Exports

(*Billion cubic feet/year*)

Country	*Product on (1990)*	*Production (1997)*	*Net Exports (1990)*	*Net Exports (1997)*	*Possible Exports (2010)*
Kazakhstan	251.2	215.4	-257.0	16.2	0-100
Turkmenistan	3099.5	610.9	2539.0	229.6	2100-2500
Uzbekistan	1439.5	1808.1	102.5	88.2	50
Total	4820.2	22634.4	2384.5	334.0	2100-2650

Source: United States Energy Information Administration

Table 3.20: Production of Energy Resources in Kazakhstan (1990-1997)

	1990	*1991*	*1992*	*1993*	*1994*	*1995*	*1996*	*1997*
Gas (Million Cubic Meters)	8.20	7.37	7.56	6.25	4.50	4.80	4.24	8.20
Coal (Million Tones)	131.3	130.3	126.5	111.8	104.3	83.2	76.9	N.A.
Crude Oil (Million Tones)	25.82	19.10	21.79	19.28	19.27	20.64	22.95	N.A.
Electricity (Million Kwh)	87.37	86128	79.17	65.1	66.66	59.00	51.98	N.A.

Source: Petroleum Economist, Europa Annual, 1997.

Table 3.21: Production of Energy Resources in Uzbekistan (1990-1997)

	1990	*1991*	*1992*	*1993*	*1994*	*1995*	*1996*	*1997*
Gas (Million Cubic Meters)	38.06	39.09	39.93	41.98	47.20	48.00	48.20	48.90
Hard Coal (Metric Tones)	26,73,000 (1989)	4,807	3,800		N.A.	N.A.	N.A.	
Crude Petroleum	3,293	3,943	5,517	5,500	N.A.	N.A.		
Electricity (Billion Kwh)	55,900	N.A.	N.A.	N.A.	N.A.	N.A.	N.A.	N.A.

Source: Petroleum Economist, Europa Annual, 1997.

Table 3.22: Production of Energy Resources in Tajikistan (1990-1997)

	1990	*1991*	*1992*	*1993*	*1934*	*1995*	*1996*	*1997*
Gas (Million Cubic Meters)	1989 3,03,000	93	72	49	1	1	N.A.	N.A.
Crude Petroleum (Million Tones)	(1989) 1,90,000	108	61	42	4988	64	N.A.	N.A.
Electricity Coal (000 Tones)		17,600	17,000	16,800	N.A.	N.A.	N.A.	N.A.

Source: Petroleum Economist, Europa Annual, 1997.

Table 3.23: Production of Energy Resources in Turkmenistan (1990-1998)

	1990	*1991*	*1992*	*1993*	*1994*	*1995*	*1996*	*1997*	*1998*
Gas (Million Cubic Meters)	81.90	78.64	56.06	60.91	35.80	32.30	35.18	17.30	15.50
Crude Petroleum (million Tones)	5812 (1987)		4,663	3,916	3,866	4,400	4,700	N.A.	
Electricity (Billion Kwh)			13,136		10.5	N.A.	N.A.	N.A.	

Source: Petroleum Economist, Europa Annual, 1997.

Table 3.24: Production of Energy Resources in Turkmenistan (1990-1998)

	1990	*1991*	*1992*	*1993*	*1994*	*1995*	*1996*	*1997*
Gas (Million Meters)	1.05 58.90	N.A.	72	42	39	36	26	45.6
Crude Petroleum (Million Tons)	23,000 N.A.	113	88	88	89	83	N.A.	
Crude Oil (Million Tons)	39,	37,000	N.A.	2, 15	1, 72	848	413	432
Electricity	14,903	N.A.	N.A.	12.7	N.A.	N.A.	N.A.	N.A.

Source: Petroleum Economist, Europa Annual, 1997.

Republics' economies, but also for some developed economically states. The revival of the Silk Route is an urgent goal put forward by the new, independent states of Central Asia. It is a means for strengthening and developing their independence: a key to the solution of their economic problems.

Political Interest

The revival of the Silk Route holds significance for the political interests too, of the Central Asian republics. The Republics need speedy modernization through market reforms. Politically, the new Silk Route provides democratic reforms and international cooperation for them. The TRACECA (Transport Corridor Europe – Caucasus-Asia) programme was adopted with the initiative of the European Union. Francois Lamoureux, the head of the European Commission delegation at the Baku conference, in his speech stated, that the TRACECA programme would support the political independence of the involved states by widening their opportunities to have access to the European and world markets by developing alternative transport routes.[57]

The restoration of the Silk Route offers opportunities not only for trade and economic development between Europe and Central Asia, but also for the interchange of ideas and values. The revival will accelerate the process of modernization of the Central Asian republics. Presently these states are in the transitional period of their social development.

The conduct of the Silk Route policy by CAR is based on the following principles:

- Equitable partnership, friendship and cooperation with all Silk Route countries.
- Interdependence.
- Mutual advantage.
- Long term perspective.
- Multifaceted development of international cooperation.

Equitable partnership, friendship and cooperation with all Silk Route countries are the important components of the policy, which would help create a favorable environment along its national borders and in the contents of bilateral and multilateral diplomacy. This policy is in full conformity with the universally acknowledged principles and norms of international law as laid down in the Chapter of the United Nations, comprising mutual respect for sovereignty, territorial integrity and inviolability of borders, non-interference in internal affairs, non-use of force, settlement of conflicts by peaceful means and equal and mutually advantageous cooperation.

The development of mutually advantageous international cooperation within the Silk Route region will allow all countries to find answers to many questions and solve their problems. The countries of the region are striving to create new transportation systems and diversify the existing ones so as to ensure the shortest and best means of access to world communications. They are encouraging and developing international trade, both within and outside the region; and they are stepping up cultural and humanitarian, scientific and tourism contacts between the countries of the region.

Necessity

The restoration of the Silk route is seen as a necessity in the development of the Central Asian Republics. The process of forming a Central Asian Federation which would mean a common Central Asian market and a strong united political block is going on.[58] At the Tashkent summit held in early January 1993, the heads of the five Central Asian states took a series of steps aimed at consolidating the Central Asian states into a powerful economic and political bloc. In a significant move, they decided to specify "Central Asia" as the collective term for all the five Central Asian states.[59] The Tashkent summit decided to bring about a common market with common taxation, customs pricing, investment and export policies, thereby moving towards cooperation and interaction of the economies of the region.[60] It was also decided to create a regional information network and set up a joint commission for oil production, power generation, agriculture etc. All the Central Asian states were unanimous in their resolve to expedite the construction of a railroad to Iran for getting access to the Persian Gulf and to Turkey.[61]

Following the disintegration of the former central Soviet economic structure and disruption of previous inter-regional economic ties, the newly independent Central Asian states have been trying to diversify their economies and seek new partners in regional and economic cooperation. Having huge resources of gas, oil, coal, ferrous and non ferrous metals, rare minerals and metals, hydro-electric power and irrigation network, besides being the main producers of cotton, wool, silk, etc., a new realization of their immense economic potential has dawned in Central Asia.[62] This has created high expectations among the Central Asian states to reap the economic fruits of their independence from the ex-Soviet Union. The Central Asian states have intensified the process of privatization of thier economies, and are opening their markets to foreign investment because of the down trend of their economies. Underdeveloped production structure, disruption in previous economic ties and shortage of hard currency has forced these states to look for alternative sources of supply, markets and for remunerative prices for their raw materials.[63]

Revival of the Trans-Siberian Railway

The construction of roads around the Takla Makan desert has provided access, to the vast natural resources of the region. The area is rapidly being industrialized and Urumchi, the present capital of Xinjiang has become a Chinese industrial city.

The sluggish trade between the people of Xinjiang and the CIS countries is picking up rapidly with a flourishing trade in consumer items.

The railway connecting Lanzhou to Urumchi has been extended to the border with Kazakhstan, when on 12th September 1990 it was finally joined to the Soviet railway system, providing an important route to the new Central Asian republics and beyond.[64] This Eurasian Continental Bridge, built for the revival of the Trans-Siberian Railway, has been constructed from Lian Yan Gang city in Jiangsu province (on the East China Coast) to Rotterdam.[65] The first phase of this development has already been completed, and the official opening of the railway was held on 1st December 1992. It is believed to be at least 20 per cent cheaper than the route by sea, and 11,000 kilometers shorter. From China, the route passes through Kazakhstan, Russia, Byelorussia and Poland, before reaching Germany and the Netherlands.[66] The double-tracking of the railway from Lanzhou to the border of the C.I.S. has now been put on the priority list of Chinese development.

Extension of Karakorum Highway to Silk Route

Following the independence of Central Asian states Pakistan planned to extend the Karakorum Highway (KKH) to Central Asia. China, Kazakhstan, Kyrgyzstan and Pakistan signed an agreement of "traffic in transit" to further promote trade relations through roads from Almaty eastward by using the historic Silk Route.[67] China has not only opened Xinjiang to cross-border trade and traffic with Central Asian Republics but has been evincing keen interest in the project for the revival of the Silk Route by extending the Urumchi-Almaty rail upto Iran.[68] China has opened 10 border points in Xinjiang for trade and traffic with Central Asia. The Urumchi trade fair is a regular event now. The Urumchi airport has become a hub of activity. It operates direct flights to Sharjah (UAE), Istanbul, Almaty, Tashkent, Osh, Bishkek, Andijan and Islamabad. More than six million tons of goods are estimated to be traded annually between Xinjiang and the Central Asian Republics, particularly Kazakhstan and Kyrgyzstan.[69] There are important historical, economic and strategic dimensions of communication linkage between South and Central Asia. Historically for centuries trade convoys from China used to travel via the Silk Route to the Indian sub-continent, West Asia and Europe. As per the agreement signed by China, Pakistan, Kazakhstan and Kyrgyzstan, the trade route will be extended from Karakorum highway to Kashgar, Bishkek and Almaty. The total length of the trade and transit route from Karachi to Almaty will be 3,726 kilometers[70] and work on the project has begun.

It is suggested that an alternate route to Karakorum Highway should be constructed from the Chiporson Valley.[71] This route will connect Pakistan to Tajikistan via the Wakhan corridor.[72] Already there exists a jeep track connecting the Karaborum Highway with Chiporson valley but there is need to improve this track and transform it to a proper road. The stretch from the Chiporson Valley to the border of Tajikistan is hardly 50 kilometers, which could be constructed despite the difficult terrain. The road from the border of Tajikistan to the other parts of Central Asia already exists.

Silk Route versus Oil Route

Central Asia being the world's largest land-locked region and having rich energy resources offers considerable trade and investment opportunities. But the lack of effective transport routes and relative isolation has made this difficult. The main Eurasian land-bridge rail line from China enters Kazakhstan through the Altai Pass, that crosses the border between Aktogay and the Kazakhstan frontier town of Druzhba.[73] From here, the main corridor runs via Kazakhstan's capital Almaty, through the agro-industrial area of Frunze and Dzambul, to Tashkent. Near Tashkent the corridor divides into two parts. One runs north-west parallel to the Syrdarya river to Aralsk, and through western Kazakhstan into European Russia, continuing via Orenburg, Kuybyshev, Moscow and Minsk into Central Europe. The second goes via the legendary cities of Samarkand and Bukhara, to Merv and Tedzhen in Turkmenistan and from there via the newly opened Tadzhen-Mashhad line into Iran and Turkey. Reaching southern Europe via Istanbul, this second route constitutes the new Silk Road.[74]

Thus, creating alternative transit transport routes has become important for the promoting of trade and development, strengthening economic independence and integration with the world economy. Many oil companies have been interested in developing the gas and oil fields in the Central Asian States and the Caspian Sea region. In December 1997, Turkmenistan started exporting gas to Iran via a newly built pipeline.[75] Two major systems, the newly constructed Baku-Tbilisi-Ceyhan line and the Tengiz-Novorossisk line will supply the oil to world markets.[76] The former will carry 1 million barrels a day and the latter will carry at least 400,000 barrels per day.[77]

A new pipeline is proposed to be laid from the Kazakh oilfields via northern Iran or right down to the Gulf. Both Kazakhstan and Iran would like to use such a route and the proposed pipeline was the subject of talks held in Astana by the Iranian Deputy Foreign Minister.[78]

For Central Asia, a land-locked part of the huge Euro-Asian continent, situated almost midway between the Pacific and Atlantic oceans, the alternative route to the West has certain advantages. It is the shortest one, and was put into operation on the basis of routes existing within the former Soviet Union (FSU) transport regulations, technical standards and administrative practices.[79] Under the European Union sponsored projects, this route (via the Trans-Caspian ferry, through Azerbaijan and Georgia to its part of Poti, and by the Black Sea ferry to Europe) has proved to be useful. Through this route, the cost of freight from Tashkent to Black Sea has been reduced by 30 to 35 per cent compared to the traditional routes.[80] Increasing quantities of cotton from Uzbekistan and oil from Kazakhstan and Turkmenistan are being shipped to the world markets through the Transcaucasian route.

A project put into operation in October 1998 between Shanghai in China and Germany crosses all the Central Asian independent states' routes.[81] It creates additional chances for the rebirth of the famous Silk Road traditions in trade and the business of oil, as well as information and cultural exchange on a modern technological basis. When the land bridge between east and west, and north and south through Central Asia begins operations and becomes more efficient, it will help to restore the importance of the region's Silk Route tradition as the main transit point along this route.

Caspian Pipeline Construction Route

The Caspian Pipeline Consortium was formed between Russia, Kazakhstan and Oman in 1992 to build a pipeline to transport oil from the Caspian region to the Black Sea. The CPC's original plan was to take advantage of the existing infrastructure by finishing a 1,600 km pipeline that had been 60 percent completed during the Soviet period.[82] This would link the Caspian littoral states with expanded port facilities at a total cost of $1.2-1.5 bn. The northern arm of the pipeline would extend from Tengiz around the northern

Table 3.25: Projected Global Oil and Gas Consumption, 1999-2020

Region/ Country	*Oil, MMbbl/d*			*Gas, tcf*		
	1999	*2020*	*Annual average growth 1999-2020, in percent*	*1999*	*2020*	*Annual average growth 1999-2020, in percent*
North America	23.4	33.7	1.8	26.1	40.7	2.1
US	19.5	26.7	1.5	21.7	33.8	2.1
Western Europe	13.9	15.8	0.6	14.0	25.9	3.0
Industrialized Asia	6.9	8.3	0.9	3.6	5.3	1.9
Japan	5.6	6.4	0.7	2.6	3.8	1.7
Former Soviet Union and Eastern Europe	3.7	8.0	3.7	22.5	36.4	2.3
Developing Asia	13.3	28.8	3.7	6.0	20.9	6.1
China	4.3	10.5	4.3	0.9	6.4	10.1
India	1.9	4.9	4.6	0.8	2.6	6.1
Central and South America	4.7	8.8	3.1	3.2	14.6	7.4
Middle East	5.0	7.8	2.1	6.8	14.6	3.7
Africa	2.5	5.3	3.6	2.0	3.5	7.4
World Total	**74.9**	**118.6**	**2.2**	**84.2**	**161.8**	**3.2**

Source: based on EIA, International Energy Outlook 2002, on-line version.

curve of the Caspian and then continue straight across to Tickorepk and so on to Novorossiysk.[83] The southern arm would link up with a pipeline from Baku at the Russia- Azerbaijan border passing through Grozny to Tikhoretok.[84] This would reverse the line from Baku to Grozny.

Tengiz–Baku–Ceyhan Route

As a competitor with Russia, Turkey's role in the region in exploring alternate oil transport route and collaborating in pipeline building is significant. Three countries – Azerbaijan, Kazakhstan and Turkey – have joined together to connect Tengiz and Baku with the Turkish Mediterranean port of Ceyhan. Ankara has displayed particular interest in the transit of Azeri and Kazakh oil through its territory. Azerbaijan and Turkey have signed on an agreement for the construction of the Baku-Ceyhan pipeline.[85] This 1,920 kilometers long pipeline is designed to handle 50 million tons of

Table 3.26: Oil Export Routes in the Central Asia and Caspian Sea Region

Name/Location	*Route*	*Crude Capacity*	*Length*	*Investment*	*Status*
Atyrau-Samara	Atyrau (Kazakhstan)	Current 0.2 million bbl/d;	N/A-Existing route	Increase would	Expands
	Samara (Russia)	increase to 0.3 million bbl/d	expansion	cost $22 million	existing pipeline To Russia. Completion due 1999
AIOC-Main Export Pipeline	Multiple routes considered from Baku (Azerbaijan)	1 million bbl/d	1100 miles it to Ceyhan, Turkey	$2.3-$3.7 billion if to Ceyhan, Turkey	Final Route Selection
AIOC-Early Oil Western Route	Baku (Azerbaijan) Supsa (Georgia)	0.1 million bbl/d design capacity; possible upgrade to 0.3 or 0.6 million bbl/d	550 miles	$590 million with no upgrade	Exports began 1999
AIOC-Early Oil Northern Route	Baku-Novorossisk (Russia) via Chechnya	0.1 million bbl/d design capacity; possible upgrade to 0.3 or 0.18 million bbl/d	868 miles; 90 miles are in Chechnya	$600 million to upgrade to 0.3 million bbl/d	Exports began late 1997
Northern Route-Chechnya Bypass	Baku- Dagestan (Russia) Novorossisk	0.6 million bbl/d	868 miles	$1.2-$1.5 billion	proposed by Russia 10/98 rejected by SOCAR. (Earlier Proposal 9/97to just build 176 Chechen Bypass Baku-Terskoye (Russia)
Caspian Pipeline Consortium (CPC)	Tengiz (Kazakhstan)-Novorossisk (Russia)	1.34 million bbl/d peak	930 miles	$2.3 billion	Construction has begun. Flows mid-2001; peak early Next decade

(Contd.)

(*Contd.*)

Name/Location	*Route*	*Crude Capacity*	*Length*	*Investment*	*Status*
Trans-Caspian (Kazakhstan) Twin Pipeline	Kazakhstan coast- Baku could extend To Ceyhan (Turkey)	N/A	370 miles to Baku	$2-44 billion if to Ceyhan	Feasibility study agreement December 1998 Royal Dutch/ shell, Chevron, Mobil Kazakhstan
Kazakhstan-china	Aktyubinsk-Xinjing (China)	0.4-0.8 million bbl/d	1,800 miles	$3.5 billion	Agreement 1997; feasibility study due 1999
South Pipeline (Central Asia Oil pipeline	Kazakhstan- Turkmenistan Afghanistan- Gwadar (Pakistan)	1 million bbl/d	1,056 miles	$3 billion	Memorandum of Understanding
Iran- Azerbaijan	Baku-Tabriz (Iran)	N/A	N/A	N/A	Proposed
Kazakhstan-Turkmenistan	Tengiz –Turkmenistan-	0.5-1.0 million bbl/d	1060 miles Tengiz Tehran	Total (France) est. $2 billion for 0.5	Proposed
Iran (KTI)	Khrag Island on Persian Gulf (Iran)		1300 miles Kazakhstan-Persian Gulf	million bbl/d pipeline Co. (France) est. $1.6 billion for 0.9 million bbl/d Pipeline to Persian Gulf	

Table 3.27: Natural Gas Export in the Central Asian and Caspian Sea Region

Name/Location	*Route*	*Gas Capacity*	*Length*	*Investment*	*Status*
Central Asia-Russia Europe	Turkmenistan-Kazakhstan-Russia	N/A	Existing route	Existing route	Uses existing Russian system Export had been halted over dispute with Gazprom-Turkmenistan Export to Ukraine to resume in 1999
Turkmenistan-Iran	Ekarem (Turkmenistan)-Iranian border. Iran has also proposed a new line from Serakhs (Turkmenistan)-Tehran (Iran)	283 bcf./year 2005; 530 bcf./year 2020	90 miles	$190 million	Completed-Exports began 1997
Turkmenistan-Iran-Turkey	Ekarem (Terun-Tabriz)	1 Tcf/year	1,350 miles	$3.8-4.0 billion	Feasibility study done by Royal Dutch/Shell
Trans-Caspian (Turkmenistan)	Turkmenbashi (Turkmenistain)-Baku-Ezerum or Ceyhan (Turkey)	1 tcf/year	1000-1250 miles depending on final route	$2.4-$3.0 billion	Preliminary feasibility studies done by both Enron and Unocal; October 1998 preliminary agreement Turkey & Turkmenistan to Build Pipeline
Trans- Caspian (Kazakhstan Twin Pipelines)	Caspian coast –Baku-Azerbaijan-Ceyhan	N/A	N/A	N/A	Feasibility study agreement December 1998 Royal Dutch /shell Chevron, Mobil, Kazakhstan
China Pipeline	Turkmenistan-Xinjiang (China); may extend to Japan	1 tcf/year	5,000 miles; more if to Japan	$8.5; billion China; more if to Japan	Preliminary feasibility study done by Exxon, Mitsubishi & CNPC
Centgas (Central Asia Gas)	Dauletad or Yashlar Fields (Turkmenistan)-Sui (Pakistan), May extend to India	700 bcf./year	900 miles	$2-$2.5 billion	Memorandum Understanding Turkmenistan, Pakistan Afghanistan & Uzbekistan

Source: Different publications of the United States Energy Information Administration.

crude oil in a year.[86] Kazakhstan could export oil to the Turkish terminals at Ceyhan from where it could flow anywhere through the Mediterranean to the world market. In order to deliver Kazakh oil to the world market via Turkey or via Greece, Kazakh refineries have to be linked either with Azerbaijani or Russian oil transport systems. Earlier, it was the Soviet oil transport system.

Turkmenistan–Afghanistan–Pakistan Route

In October, 1997 the Turkmenian government, the Unocal Delta of Saudi Arabia and various companies from Japan, Pakistan and South Korea formed a consortium called Central Asia Gas Pipeline Limited, to construct a gas pipeline from Turkmenistan right up to Karachi. Led by Unocal, they have undertaken this ambitious project to build this 1,271 kilometers pipeline from Charjow in Turkmenistan via Afghanistan to Multan in Pakistan with plans to extend it to India too.[87]

Kazakhstan–Turkmenistan–Iran Route

Geographical proximity has brought these three countries together in a joint quest for building gas and oil pipelines. The Kazakh-Iran Protocol envisages Iranian finance of $ 49 million for the reconstruction of the part of Akhtau that would link it with the Tengiz oil field. Only 100 kilometers of oil pipelines need to be built in order to see Kazakh oil flow via the Iranian Caspian Sea port of Bander-e-Anzali to the Tehran, Tabriz, Arak and Esfahan refineries.[88]

A more realistic, southward oil export route is possible through Turkmenistan, but it would depend on the Russians for the upkeep of the gas fields and handling the entire "transportation of 40 billion cubic meters of gas supply, mainly to the former Soviet Republics".[89] Turkmenistan has also been looking forward to developing alternative, stable channels of export of its natural gas to the hard currency market. Collectively, Kazakhstan, Turkmenistan and Iran could balance out the Russian leverage to a large extent by devising an alternative transport system.

Uzbek–Kazakh–China–Japan Pipeline

The Turkmenian leaders have also planned another trans - Asian Gas pipeline which will pass through all these countries along a distance of 8,000 kilometers. The world's three oil giants-American Exxon, Japanese Mitsubishi and Chinese National Oil Corporation-signed an agreement in Beijing in August, 1995 for building this pipeline.[90] This is an ambitious project in the Asia-Pacific energy sector that is being worked out at the expert level for implementation. This line will integrate the gas reserves of both Kazakhstan and Turkmenistan and cater to the domestic and foreign needs of many countries of the Asia Pacific.

Tengiz–Kumkol–Pavlodar–Chimkent Pipeline

This pipeline will join the existing active refineries in western and southern Kazakhstan. The Kumkol deposits have an estimated 89.4 million tons of oil and 8.75 cubic meters of gas.[91] In June 1995 Munaygaz of Kazakhstan and International Pipeline Consortium signed a memorandum of mutual understanding in Almaty for starting a joint company, and the job has been undertaken.[92]

Eurasian Corridor

The concept of the Eurasian infrastructure corridor, which has been developed by Lydon Larouche and circulated worldwide in Executive Intelligence Review's 1997 Special Report on the Eurasian Land Bridge, has attracted serious attention. The presidents of Azerbaijan and Georgia with the support of the European Union hosted an international conference on the "Restoration of the Historic Silk Route" on 8th September, 1998 in Baku, Azerbaijan.[93] The presidents of Azerbaijan, Bulgaria, Georgia, Kyrgyzstan, Moldavia, Romania, Turkey, Uzbekistan and Ukraine, transport ministers and experts from 32 countries, and representatives[94] of international organizations attended this conference. The participants emphasized the importance of the revival of the Great Silk Route and highly appreciated the contribution of the TRACEA project to that end, implemented within the European Union's TRACIS (Transportation on Commonwealth Independent States) programme as a Eurasian

Land-Bridge.[95] At the end of the conference the "Final Communiqué of the Conference", was signed as the "Baku Declaration ", foreseeing further international cooperation for the development of TRACECA. In the Euro-Asian Transport Conference in St. Petersburg, Russia on Sept. 12-13, 2000, five main corridors were discussed:[96]

(a) The TRACECA (Transport Corridor Europe – Caucasus-Asia) corridor, from Eastern Europe via the Black and Caspian Seas to Central Asia.
(b) The Central corridor, from southern Europe, via Turkey, Iran and Central Asia to China.
(c) The Southern corridor, which runs from southern Europe to Iran as the Central corridor, but reaches China via Pakistan, India and Southeast Asia.
(d) The Northern corridor, from Europe via the trans-Siberian railroad to China, North and South Korea, and Japan.
(e) A new North-South sailship corridor, which goes from Northern Europe to Russia, crosses the Caspian Sea to Iran, and via Iran's southern ports across the Arabian Sea to India.

These corridors, with their numerous branches, form a unified network, providing a foundation for the development of a gigantic economic zone of about four billion human beings.

Problems and Prospects of the Restoration of Old Silk Route

The Silk Route is reappearing, with new opportunities, potential and promises for peace and shared prosperity among the nations with links to one another. The new Silk Route for the 21st century covers all modes of transportation including road, rail, and maritime infrastructure as well as oil and gas pipelines and communication infrastructure.

Problems

The new Central Asian states are on their way to integration with the world economy and have faced several problems in reviving their trade and transport routes. The main problems within the region, affecting development, are endemic political corruption; organized crime; political instability. The Nogorno – Karabakh war and the associated political maneuvering of all involved, has had a detrimental effect on oil development and export projects[97]. Terrorism on the part of Kurdish separatists could pose a problem for the security of any transport route and pipeline through Turkey. Technical problems include the lack of commercial, legal and financial expertise in most of these countries. The absence of a substantial western style legal structure to support and build confidence among investors is also causing problems

The rivalry between Turkey, Russia, Iran and other powers over the oil and gas resources of Central Asia is a complex one. Decisions on long term oil exports from the region imply major strategic, political and economic consequences. There is competition for control of the region's energy resources.The ongoing pipeline politics in the Caspian and Central Asian regions has remained surcharged with real fears of continuing hostility[98]. Ethnic tensions, political instability and persisting apprehensions about the region are some of the practical problems. As pointed out recently by Professor Xue Jiaji, a Chinese economist from the Provincial Academy of social sciences, "one nagging factor in the development of the Eurasian land bridge is that the transit tariffs are different between countries, the rates remain unstable and there are many taxes and incidental expenses".[99] Leaders of Central Asian republics and other countries interested in the rebuilding of Silk Route are making efforts to overcome these problems.

Prospects

The restoration of the Silk Route offers opportunities to the Central Asian Republics not only for trade and economic cooperation, but also for new values and ideas for development. The revival of the Great Silk Route will make it possible to create all the necessary conditions for the transformation of the region into an area of stability, security, friendship, cooperation and equitable partnership.

The economic crisis in Central Asia also includes many aspects typical of the situation that exists in other parts of the former Soviet Union. These are: the breakdown of agriculture due to lack of machinery and replacement parts, formerly supplied from other parts of USSR; breakdown of industrial production, for similar reasons; lack of supplies of crucial materials; loss of former markets. And the situation has been further complicated by the intervention of foreign interests to exert control over oil, gas and the other vast material sources that have remained untapped in the region. Today, only the rapid development of the European infrastructure corridors can effectively overcome the present crisis, and tap the vast economic potential of the region.

Improvements in rail lines, pipelines and other transport infrastructure provide means to expand the income of the Central Asian countries, by making it easier to deliver the new capital equipment urgently needed to modernize and expand extraction and processing facilities, and to transport the product for sale to the widest possible market. By linking transport infrastructure corridors, immediate access will be available to the investors for such improvement, and also to the rapidly growing market throughout Eurasia.[100]

"The Russian Federation, which claims to look after the interests of Russians living in the 'near abroad', can help revive ailing enterprises and industries in Central Asia, which can provide employment opportunities for spilled Russians. Russia can also render assistance to the Central Asian republics in establishing and rejuvenating Russian educational and cultural institutions across Central Asia".[101]

Interest in the revival of the Silk Route began at the end of the 19th century. Imperial Russia and Britain competed for trade opportunities in Kashgar and other cities of Central Asia. The discovery of ruins, ancient artifacts, buried cities and manuscripts attracted world wide attention. The Silk Route today is a series of paved roads and train tracks that connect east to west along the paths of the old caravan routes. The new Silk Route of the 21st century covers all modes of transportation including road, rail as well as oil and gas pipelines and communication infrastructure. The revival of the historic Silk Route will facilitate regional cooperation among the Central Asian republics. However, building up alternative infrastructures and new link routes will take time and investment, but will be justified if trade benefits for all Central Asian countries involved exceed the costs of construction and promote development opportunities of the region through further integration with the world economy. The Silk Route has become one of the key policy issues of the newly independent Central Asian

Republics and other countries of the Silk Route region. Being landlocked and having rich natural resources, these Republics need economically viable, cheap and safe access to the world markets. From this aspect the New Silk Route is seen as a strong, viable option by these Republics and other states.

The present day Great Silk Route creates favorable circumstances for the intensification of international cooperation in the joint solution of the global problems that are facing mankind on the threshold of the third millennium. The expansion of the geography of the Great Silk Route will make it possible to make full use of the existing opportunities and create rich potential for intensifying international trade and economic, cultural and humanitarian, scientific, technical and tourist contacts between all countries and peoples.

The new Central Asian Republics are rapidly picking up a flourishing trade in consumer items as well as heavy industry. And trade with China is, therefore, starting to fulfill this demand. The developing trade requires new modes of communication among these countries. In the process, the old networks of roads and railways are being revived to facilitate trade. To export natural gas and oil, pipelines are being opened among the Asian and European countries. The network of transport corridors in Central Asia and adjoining countries will provide a foundation for the development of gigantic economic zones.

The transport network connections of Asia with Europe pass through the territory of Eurasia. Russia has been having a monopoly over the transportation network with Central Asia that was built assiduously over the past hundred years or so. But after their independence, the Central Asian Republics are keen to develop other transport networks and routes, so that they are dependent on Russia to the least degree. Hence the proposal to revive the Silk Route connecting Asia with Europe by constructing the transport corridor through the Central Asian Republics and the Southern Caucasian states has been mooted.

NOTES

1. Shirin Akiner, *Cultural Change and Continuity in Central Asia* (London: Kegan Paul International, 1991), p. 89.
2. *Ibid*, p. 104.
3. *The Europa World Year Book*, 46th Edition, Vol. II, Pub. Rutledge Taylor & Francis Group London and New York, 2005, p. 2467.
4. International Studies in Sociology and Social Anthropology – *Central Eurasia in Global Politics – Conflict , Security, and Development*, (ed.) Mehdi Parvizi Amineh and Henk Houweling Pub – Brill, London, 2004, p. 97.
5. Ramtanu Maitra, 'Importance of Eurasian Land bridge for the Central Asian Development', in Shams-ud-din (ed.), *Geopolitics and Energy Resources in Central Asia and Caspian Sea Region*, (New Delhi: Lancer Books, 2000), p. 183.
6. *Ibid.*, p. 183.
7. Sally N. Cummings, n-11, p. 49.
8. Bakhtior A. Islamov, *The Central Asian States Ten years After: How to Overcome Traps of Development, Transformation and Globalization*, (Tokyo: Maruzen Co., Ltd., 2001), p. 181.
9. *Ibid.*, p. 181.
10. *Ibid.*, p. 181.
11. *Ibid.*, p. 181.
12. Michael Gentile, 'Former Closed Cities and Urbanization in the FSU: An Exploration in Kazakhstan', *Europe-Asia Studies*, Vol. 56, No-2, (London: Carfax Publishing, March,2004), p.-269.
13. 'Central Asia- Developments in 1997', *World Focus*, Volume 19, Number 3, (New Delhi, March 1998), p. 19.
14. Sally N. Cummings, n. 11, p. 65.
15. 'Central Asia-Developments in 1997', *World Focus*, Volume 19, Number 3, (New Delhi, March 1998), p. 19.
16. Shams-ud-Din, n. 16, p. 184.
17. Bakhtior A. Islamov, n. 18, p. 181.
18. *Ibid.*, p. 182.
19. K. Warikoo, n. 13, p. 152.
20. BBC *Summary of World Broadcast*, SU/4039 G/1 9 Jan. 2001.
21. Ramtanu Maitra, n. 16, p. 184.
22. *Ibid.*, p. 184.
23. 'Quarterly Country Reports and Annual Country Profiles: Kazakhstan, Turkmenistan, Uzbekistan, Kyrgyzstan and Tajikistan', *The Economist Intelligence Unit*, (London: 1998-2000).
24. Bakhtior A. Islamov, n. 19, p. 183.
25. *Ibid.*, p. 183.
26. *Ibid.*, p. 184.

27. Ramtanu Maitra, n-16, p. 185.
28. 'Central Asia-Development in 1997' *World Focus*, Vol. 19, number 3, (New Delhi March 1998), p. 21.
29. *Ibid.*, p. 21.
30. Bakhtior A. Islamov, n-19, p. 183.
31. *Ibid.*, p. 184.
32. BBC, *Summary of World Broadcast*, 28, March, 2000 (Via Nexis).
33. Bakhtior A. Islamov, n-19, p. 182.
34. Shally N. Cummings, n-11, p. 110.
35. Bakhtior A. Islamov, n-19, p. 183
36. Olivier Roy, *The New Central Asia: The Creation of Nations*, (London: I.B. Tauris, 2000), p. 194.
37. Bakhtior A. Islamov, n-19, p. 184.
38. *Ibid.*, p. 184.
39. *Ibid.*, p. 184.
40. K. Warikoo (Ed), *Central Asia: Emerging New Order*, Issued under the auspices of Himalayan and Cultural Foundation (India), (New Delhi: Har-Anand Pub., 1995), p. 8.
41. Allwarth Edward, *Central Asia, A Century of Russian Rule* (New York, London, 1967), p. 59.
42. G. Wheeler, *The Modern History of Soviet Central Asia*, (London, 1964), p. 71.
43. R. Pierce, *Russian Central Asia: 1867-1917: A Study of Colonial Rule*, (Berkeley and Los Angeles, 1960), p. 189.
44. G. Wheeler, n-4, p. 71.
45. *Ibid.*, p. 71.
46. Abid Sharifov, 'New Life of the Ancient Silk Road', *Silk Road*, (Baku, 1998), No. 3.
47. *Ibid.*, p. 19.
48. Etibar Najafov, 'Corelation between Culture and Civilization in the Social Development of Azerbaijan' *Proceedings of the International Education Society Conference*, (Urbana–Champaign, USA, Oct. 31-Nov. 2, 1997), see also (web on line) www.eduiuc.edu/EPS/MWSIES97/najafov.html
49. Sally N. Cummings, *Power and Change in Central Asia*, (London: Rutledge Pub., 2002), p. 1.
50. K. Warikoo, n-1, p. 25.
51. BBC, *SWB* SU/1618 20 Feb. 1993.
52. K. Warikoo, n-1, p. 31.
53. *Ibid.*, p. 129.
54. *Central Asia News File*, August, 1992, p. 5.
55. P.L. Dash, 'Oil Transport and Trade: Dilemmas and Options Facing Kazakhstan and Turkmenistan', in Sums-ud-Din, (Ed), n-16, p. 103.
56. 'US-Russian Cooperation and the Future of Central Asia', An

Interview with Andrew Kuchins, in *World Focus*, March , 2004, vol., 25, Number 3, New Delhi, p. 22.
57. Francois Lamoureux, 'Materials of the Baku Conference', see (web on line) www.muza.com.kg/silkroad
58. K. Warikoo, n-13, p. 31.
59. BBC, *SWB* SU/1579, 6 Jan. 1993. & BBC, *SWB* SU/1581, 8 Jan. 1993.
60. BBC, *SWB* SU/1579, 6 Jan. 1993.
61. BBC, *SWB* SU/1581, 8 Jan. 1993.
62. K. Warikoo, n-1, p. 24.
63. *Ibid.*, p. 25.
64. Brian Hook (ed), *The Cambridge Encyclopedia of China*, (Cambridge: University Press, 1991), 2nd ed, p. 367.
65. *Ibid.*, p. 367.
66. Oliver Wild, *The Silk Road*, 1992, see (web on line) www.ess.uci.edu/ /~oliver/silk.html. p. 8 of 9.
67. M.B. Naqvi, 'Regional Transport Scheme in Asia', *Dawn*, (Pakistan: December 12, 1998).
68. K. Warikoo, 'Central Asia and China: The Geopolitical Imperatives', in Shams-ud-Din (ed) *Geopolitical and Energy Resources in Central Asia and Caspian Sea Region*, (New Delhi: Lancer Book, 2000), p. 262.
69. *Ibid.*, p. 262.
70. Rafiq Abazov, 'Independence of Kyrgyzstan: 10 Difficult years on the Silk Road' *Eurasian Studies*, Special Issue, summer 2001, (Turkish Interview Cooperation Agency: Ankara), p. 190.
71. *Ibid.*, p. 196.
72. *Ibid.*, p. 196.
73. Jonathan Tennenbaum, *et al.*, 'The Eurasian Land-Bridge – The 'New Silk Road' –locomotive for worldwide economic development', *Executive Intelligence Review*, Special Report, (Washington D.C.: January, 1997), p. 154.
74. *Ibid.*, p. 154.
75. Bakhtior A. Islamov, n-19, p. 185.
76. Emmanuel Karagiannis, 'The US-Iranian Relationship After 11 September 2001 and the Transportation of Caspian Energy', *Central Asian Survey*', June-Sep., 22 (213), 151-162, (London: Carfax Publishing), p. 156.
77. *Ibid.*, p. 156.
78. R. Ebel and R. Menon (Eds.), *Energy and Conflict in Central Asian and the Caucasus*, (New York: Rowman &Littlefield, 2000). p. 157.
79. Bakhtior A. Islamov, n-19, p. 186.
80. *Ibid.*, p. 186.
81. Gulshan Sachdeva, 'Joint Ventures and Exports Routes in the Caspian Sea Region', in Shams-ud-Din, (Ed), n-16, p. 148.
82. Edwards Mathew, 'The New Great Game and the New Great Gamers:

Disciples of Kipling', *Central Asian Survey,* (March, 2003) 22(1), 18-102, (London: Carfax Publication), p. 85.
83. Shams-ud-Din, n-16, p. 23.
84. *Ibid.*, p. 83.
85. *Ibid.*, p. 97.
86. *Ibid.*, p. 97.
87. Rajan Menon, 'After Empire: Russia and the Southern Near Abroad', in Michael Mandelbaum, (Ed) *New Russian Foreign Policy,* (New York, A council of Foreign Relation Book, 1998), p. 106.
88. 'Daily Report', *FBIS,* (11 August, 1995), p. 71.
89. R.G. Gidadhubli, 'Russia: Oil Politics in Central Asia', *EPW,* (January 30-February 5, 1999), p. 262.
90. 'Daily Report', *FBIS,* (25 August, 1995), p. 67.
91. Bakhtior A. Islamov, n-19, p. 59.
92. P.L. Dash, 'Oil Transport and Trade: Dilemmas and Options Facing Kazakhstan and Turkmenistan', in, Shams-ud-Din, (Ed), n-16, p. 100.
93. Gulshan Sachdeva, n-74, in, Shamus-ud-Din, (Ed), n-16, p. 148.
94. *Ibid.*, p. 148.
95. Jonathan Tennenbaum, *et al., EIR* Report, n-66, p. 44.
96. Dr Etibar Najafov, *The Restoration of the Silk Road as a Factor of Modernization,* (Baku: Baku Slavik University, 2000), pp. 2-4.
97. Shams-ud-Din, (Ed), n-16, p. 10.
98. Rajan Menon, n-80, p. 108.
99. Ramtanu Maitra, n-16, p. 181.
100. Ramtanu Maitra, n-16, p. 188.
101. K. Warikoo, 'Russians in post Soviet Central Asia: Issues and concerns', in Touraj Atabaki and Sanjyat Mehendale (ed.) *Central Asia and the Caucasus: Transnationalism and Diaspora,* (New York and London: Routledge Pub. 2005), p. 80.

4

Role of External Powers in Silk Route Revival

The revival of the Silk Route is beneficial not only for the independent states of Central Asia, but also for some external powers. These external countries are interested in widening the scope of their economic activity and doing their business in the new markets of Central Asia. The geography of the Silk Route presents no hurdles in the increase of business and trade among Central Asian and other countries. Due to the geographical proximity of Central Asia to China, Russia, West Asia and South Asia the region has emerged as a distinct geo-political entity stimulating global attention and interest. Neighboring countries like Iran, Turkey, Russia, Pakistan, India and China are pursuing competing strategic, economic and cultural interests in Central Asia. China considers herself to be an important player in the new geopolitics of the region not only because it shares nearly 3,000 kms.[1]

The "International Symposium on Economic Development of Regions along the Euro-Asia Continental Bridge" took place in Beijing on May 7-9; 1996, with the participation of over 460 experts and diplomats from 36 countries.[2] This symposium was a part of an extraordinary foreign policy initiative of the Chinese government, to bring the nations of Europe and Asia together in a new sort of alliance for development. The immediate goal of that alliance is to build up an ultra-modern, integrated infrastructure for transport, energy and communication, stretching from the Atlantic to the Pacific, thereby providing the backbone for rapid economic development of the entire Eurasian landmass in the new millennium.

The transport corridor – known as the new Silk Route – will run from Central Asia through the Caucasuses and the Caspian across the Black Sea and then on to parts in Ukraine and the Mediterranean.[3] The European Union wants the Silk Road of the 21st century or the Super Highway, to complement existing transport routes to Europe, including the traditional and often heavily over loaded outlet via Moscow. The goal is to create a fully integrated transport network including upgraded highways, railroads, ports and ferries that will make it easier for the Central Asian and Caucasuses countries to trade not only with each other but also with the Europeans.

The new Silk Route project was launched at a conference in Brussels in May, 1993 which brought together trade and transport ministers from the three Caucasian states (Armenia, Azerbaijan, Georgia) and the five Central Asian countries of (Kazakhstan, Uzbekistan, Turkmenistan, Kyrgyzstan and Tajikistan).[4] The programme was named TRACECA (Transport Corridor Europe Caucasus Asia).[5] In December 1998, a high profile conference was held in Baku. The leaders and representatives of twelve international organizations and 34 countries, including Georgia, Azerbaijan, Moldavia, Romania, Bulgaria, Uzbekistan, Kyrgyzstan, Ukraine, Turkey, Armenia, China, Iran and Kazakhstan took part in this conference.[6] By 1998, The EU had already spent $ 75 million on TRACECA projects, and was soliciting another $ 300 million in loans. Additional funds were pledged by the European Bank for Reconstruction and Development (EBRD).[7]

To promote the Silk Route as a destination of cultural tourism, UNESCO and the World Tourism Organization (WTO) jointly launched a long term programme in 1994. Certain activities launched in the Silk Road project have been incorporated in the new UNESCO project "East-West Intercultural Dialogue in Central Asia".[8] A document edited by the UNESCO office in Tashkent, "Rebuilding the Silk Roads: Cultural Tourism and Revival of the Heritage of Uzbekistan", describes some thirty restoration initiatives costing around $ 40 million. The revival of the Silk Route includes various interests of external countries. These external powers have specific roles in its revival.

Role of China

China's present and near-future strategy considers the revival of the Silk Route as a primary regional strategic initiative. The land based transportation system – stretching along the traditional Silk Route – is of crucial significance to the consolidation of the Trans-Asian Axis and the key to Beijing's global power image and strategic security. China's self-acknowledged naval inferiority reduces the strategic use of the Indian Ocean, and thus increases the importance of the land based lines of communication for the consolidation and enhancement of the Trans-Asian Axis. As an emerging superpower with a rapidly expanding economy, China is seeking a way, to become a modern, industrialized nation state. Thousands of kilometers of new rail lines and highways are being built; vast energy and water projects have been launched. In 1999, Chinese officials and economists held a one day seminar in four cities to apprise their people of the second Eurasian Land bridge. The title of the seminar was: Asia-Europe Economic and Trade Relations in the 21st century and the second Eurasian land bridge.[9] The objective of these meetings was to provide a progress report on the work that started from 1986.

China which has the advantage of sharing its borders with Kazakhstan, Kyrgyzstan and Tajikistan has been following a policy of encouraging border trade between Xinjiang and its Central Asian neighbors. The direct rail link between Alma Ata and Urumchi, which was completed in mid-1991 has facilitated a two way traffic across the international borders. Through these developments "the Old Silk Route is actually in the process of revival."[10] The level of transportation has progressively increased on the Eurasian land bridge from Lianyungang Harbour to Europe. A project for the Eurasian land bridge has also begun in Northeast and Southeast China. China's railway ministry has also organized five regularly scheduled trains from Kunming to Chengdu and Xian to the Altai mountain pass.[11]

China and other countries have already invested billions of dollars in the development of "the New Silk Road" and the projects connected with it. With the completion of two crucial "missing links" in the Eurasian rail system, two new transport corridors between China and Europe have been created.[12] Modern communications – cables, new pipelines for crude oil and gas, as well as other rail and road projects – are being completed. In China itself, the regions along the main railway lines in the directions of Europe are being transformed into development corridors.

This positive development for the New Silk Route opens the perspective for Eurasian economic miracle based on large scale development of modern infrastructure. The construction of intercontinental infrastructure networks means the beginning of a new era of civilization. The conference in Beijing on "Economic Development of the Regions Along the Euro-Asia Continental Bridge" participated by the 460 experts and diplomats from 36 countries, made it clear, that the New Silk Road is no longer a mere vision for the future. A series of large scale infrastructure projects have begun to link China through Central Asia, Russia, Iran and beyond, all the way to Europe.

The railway line, which begins at the port city of Lianyungang on China's west coast, traverses in the northwestern direction, passing through Sinkiang into Kazakhstan. From there this rail runs via Moscow, Minsk, Warsaw and Berlin, all the way to the "Europort" at Rotterdam as the western terminus. This approximately 11,000 kilometers rail line was finally opened for traffic along its entire length.[13]

Xinjiang, one of the five autonomous regions of the People's Republic of China (PRC), has the highest strategic importance. There are positive interactions between Xinjiang's rapid techno-economic modernization and the revival of the Silk Route. In a highly volatile region Xinjiang appears, by sharp contrast, as a pole of stability and economic development. Xinjiang's recent history is marked by economic achievements. With a gross regional product per capita of 11,199 yuan (US$1,390) in 2004, Xinjiang ranks 13th among China's administrative entities.[14]

The Lanzhou (in Gansu province) and Xinjiang railway reached Urumqi in 1962. By 2001, 3,000 kms of railway lines were operating across the region. On the axis of the 10,900 km Eurasian land bridge from Lianyungang (north of Jiangsu province) to Rotterdam, Xinjiang is a centre of Eurasia. In 1949 Xinjiang had a road system of little more than 3,000 kms; by 2001 the region's highways were extended to 80,000 kms, including 428km of expressways. The highway running through the Taklamakan desert (known by the local people as the *shamo gonglu*, the Desert Highway) is the first in the world built on shifting sands. The autonomous region currently has 11 airports, with international routes connecting Urumqi with Almaty, Tashkent, Moscow and Islamabad.

Xinjiang is also the corridor though which energy supplies from Kazakhstan can transit to serve the needs of fast-growing coastal China. China's first cross-border crude-oil pipeline was opened recently and it is pumping oil from Kazakhstan. The Sino-Kazakh pipeline will carry 10 million tons of crude oil a year from Atasu to Xinjiang's Alashankou. Constructed under a 50-50 joint venture between China National Petroleum Corp (CNPC) and KazMunaiGaz, it is a strong symbol of Central Asia's integration by transnational projects – and China's Xinjiang is at the center of this new configuration. Three land ports- Karasu at the border with Tajikistan, Ushi at the border with Kyrgyzstan and Kanas in the Altay are opening in Xinjiang to stimulate the economy of neighboring countries and Xinjiang.

A new route will soon become one of the main axis of world trade. They have double-tracked 2,000 kilometers of the Chinese section of this route, electrified larger sections and built numerous parallel lines and branch lines.[15] This transport route was opened between Europe and East Asia which is considerably shorter than the northern route via the Trans-Siberian railroad, and connects directly to the core regions of China.

China has a significant role in the revival of the Silk Route, because it is a terminus country of the new Silk Route. A new "southern route" has been created between China and Europe, running from China to Kazakhstan and then southward through Uzbekistan, Turkmenistan and Iran, then reaching Europe via Turkey and the Balkan countries.[16]

The project of revival of the Silk Route and related infrastructure projects are seen by the leaders of China as a unique means, not only to develop positively oriented foreign policy, but also to solve some of the internal problems of the country. One big problem is the need of energy for their growing economy. Kazakhstan and China signed a declaration on closer cooperation in the 21st century and a border demarcation communiqué after a visit of Kazakh President Nursultan Nazarbaev to China, on 24th November, 1999.[17] The communiqué declared that the demarcation of the 1,700 km border between the both countries was over.

Both China and Kazakhstan have been drawing up an economic cooperation programme for the period until 2010, Nazarbaev announced at a news conference in Beijing after talks with his counterpart, Jiang Zemin.[18] China reaffirmed its commitments under a project to lay an oil pipeline from western Kazakhstan to western China. The pipeline will be 3,000 kms long, have a minimum annual capacity of 20 million tons and cost between 3bn and 3.5bn dollars to build.[19] The project is based on a deal which was signed by Nazarbaev and Jiang in 1997. The Chinese President Jiang Zemin confirmed that his country was interested in developing an Asian security mechanism (cooperation and confidence-building measures in Asia).[20]

At a press conference in Washington on December 22, 1998, Yushuning, Chinese Minister-Counsellor for press affairs, said that China had invited the U.S. business community in the Chinese market for building the second Eurasian land bridge. He stated that the Chinese side had provided the U.S. with three lists. The first two lists comprised 28 projects worth about $ 20 billion, he said.[21]

The third list comprised 25 sectors, areas for cooperation between the two sides in the period from 1998 through to 2005. The value of these projects is estimated at $ 600 billion.[22] And, finally, China's Minister Yushuning, told the U.S. side that during this period, from 1998 through 2005, China would import equipment, technologies and products worth U.S. $ 1.5 billion.[23] Within China, the New Silk Route is expected to serve several purposes:

- Enhancing exchanges between nations and regions located along the New Silk Route. This will involve closer contact with nations on various aspects of development along the route from China to Europe.
- Cooperation in resource development along the lines of the new Silk Route. This large area with rich resources has remained relatively backward, but provides vast scope for development.
- Launching major efforts within China to develop and equalize economic development along the new Silk Route. Foreign countries have been invited to participate in this effort.

The corridor will be characterized by the integration of East and West, common two-way development and mutual promotion.

China views Central Asia as a huge energy resource and a market which would extend her reach through Iran to Persian Gulf. China has been evincing keen interest in the project for the revival of the Silk Route by extending the Urumchi-Alimaty rail and other various transport systems up to Iran. Gradually, Xinjiang is rising as an important base and bridge tower of China, and an international transit base for commodities. The Urumchi airport has become a hub of activity. It operates direct flights to Sarjah (UAE), Istambul, Almaty, Tashkent, Osh, Bishkek, Andijan and Islamabad.[24] China's 'open door policy' for promoting foreign trade is designed to carve out a definite area of Chinese influence in the Central Asian Republics.

Russia's Role

Russia, the successor to the Soviet Union has a significant role in the building of the New Silk Route. Russia is destined by geography and history to play a unique role in the development of the Eurasian super continent. The construction of the famous Trans-Siberian Railroad created the first link between Europe and Asia. The northern Eurasian route, together with its rail connection southward to the areas of the Black Sea, Caspian Sea, Central Asia and China has been central to entire economic and political history of Russia over the last one hundred years.

The Russian energy company Gazprom is paying close attention to the vast natural gas and oil reserves of Central Asia. Gazprom represents Russian state interests and owns huge assets in Central Asia. Turkmenistan provides Russia with cheap natural gas, which is later sold to the rest of the world at international market prices. Turkmenistan, which possesses vast reserves of natural gas, claims it could continue to supply cheap gas to Russia under the terms of its agreement with Gazprom, and simultaneously take part in the Trans-Caspian project. This proposed pipeline would carry natural gas from Central Asia and Azerbaijan though Georgia to Ukraine and on to the rest of Europe. The viability of the project depends on how much interest and investment of European countries it can attract.

Russia has undergone periods of economic crises. The supply of agricultural machinery and fertilizers has been critically cut off in recent years. Over 50 per cent of the food consumption of 148 million Russians is imported from the outside.[25] A large part of the income from oil, gas and other primary materials has not even stayed within the country, but has instead flowed into the West.

At a seminar hosted in April 1996 by Leonid Abalkin, Russia's most famous economist and one of the fathers of economic reforms, La Rouche reiterated his call for cooperation between the United States, Russia and China, together with other nations, to force a reorganization of the international financial system and launch an economic recovery centered on the development of Eurasian infrastructure corridors.[26]

Russia's role as a bridge between East and West is an important factor in the revival of the Silk Route. In fact, Russia in the late nineteenth century was called "The Empire of Railroads". By the beginning of World War I, Russia's railroad network was over 72,000 kilometers long,[27] second only to the United States. Railroad development in Russia facilitated its industrial, mining and agricultural development, the settlement of its population, and economic growth. A large part of the Eurasian railroad network existing today dates back to the period of Russian rail-building.

Building up a dense infrastructure of development corridors along the Trans-Siberian Railroad (and certain parallel east-west routes, including Baikal-Amur Mainline) is today the key to the economic future of Siberia and Russia.[28] The Trans-Siberian Corridor is a crucial element in any economic recovery programme for Russia and at the same time a crucial element in the entire Eurasian system of development corridors. Russia completed the electrification of the Trans-Siberian Railway from Moscow to Vladivostok in 2002.[29] It will be fully electrified system for the first time in the history of railway transport.

The electrification of the Trans-Siberian Railway is a major project of the 21st century. An agreement has been reached on restoring the railway connection between the Democratic People's Republic of North Korea and the Republic of South Korea.[30] The Trans-Siberian railway will stretch to the port of Pusan, South Korea, and will become the most important transport bridge linking Europe and Asia.[31] The construction of tunnels and bridges to link the continent with Japan via Sakhalin will start soon. Railways Ministry of Russia believes that a railway connecting Tokyo with London will become reality in the second decade of the 21st Century.[32]

The Sakhalin project is of strategic importance for Russia as a bridge connecting East and West. The tunnel when built will enable the open passenger and freight railway traffic to Tokyo from Amsterdam. From Japan to Sakhalin, the tunnel, which is intended not only for railway transport, but for gas and oil pipeline as well, will be built by Japan.[33]

In preparation for the "Iron Silk Road" era, the Russian government will also push for the involvement of the Organization for Collaboration of Railways (OSJD), a railway cooperation body. The OSJD, founded in 1956 on the initiative of the former Soviet Union, has 27 member countries, including China, North Korea and Yugoslavia.[34] The Russian Railway Ministry intends to rebuild 930 kilometers of the Trans-Korean railway line in North Korea from Khasan station to the border with South Korea, and the Trans Korean railway will be connected to the Trans-Siberian line.[35] At present, the delivery of cargo from South Korea to Western Europe through the Suez Canal takes 40-45 days, but the new transport corridor will reduce the container delivery time to 10-12 days and the tariff for the owner of the container reduced by nearby 400 dollars.

The First Russian Deputy Minister for Railways, Aleksandra Misharin declared that Russia would have a railway outlet to South Asia via Iran.[36] He said that Iran was now building a railway spur to one of its Caspian ports. When it is ready, Russian trains will be ferried from Astrakhan to this Iranian port, whence they will proceed to Pakistan, India and other countries via Iran. This Transport Corridor, is not only in Russia's interests, but of the European countries too, which will be able then to carry their goods to South Asia and vice – versa much quicker and cheaper. Today, they have to ship them via the Suez Cannel, Misharin said.

Interests of Japan

The technical feasibility exists to massively upgrade the role of Russia in the New Silk Route through the Trans-Siberian Corridor and to stimulate the development of the entire eastern Siberian and Far Eastern region of Russia, by establishing direct land connections to Japan and the United States.

These revolutionary projects in trade and development in the entire Pacific region will be the centre of world economy in the

21st century. The first project involves extending the Baikal-Amur Mainline, via a short tunnel connection to the island of Sakhalin. The project was fully planned, and some digging even begun in the 1940s and 1950s. The connection to Japan would be provided by a north-south railroad on Sakhalin, together with a 50 kilometer undersea tunnel to Japan's Hokkaido Island. The rail connection from Hokkaido to Japan's biggest island, Honshu, is already provided by the 54 km Seikan Tunnel, the longest in the world.[37]

A second project is the land connection to the United States which would be achieved by an approximately 85-kilometer long tunnel across the Bering Strait to Alaska. This project requires the construction of major railways on both sides: A Bering Strait Connector from Yakutsk to the Bering Strait on the Russian side, and a much needed railroad from northern Alaska to British Columbia on the North American side.[38] This great project would be a crucial step toward linking the railroad, network of Europe, Africa, Asia, and North and South America, into an integrated global system – a world railroad network. In this respect, the revival of the historical Silk Road will give considerable impetus to the expansion of cooperation between countries in Europe, the Caucasuses and Asia.

Role of Iran

Because of its strategic and sensitive location, various trade caravans have been passing through Iran since time immemorial, making it an important part of the ancient Silk Route. This role has assumed more importance since the collapse of the Soviet Union, the independence of Central Asian countries and the revival of the famous Silk Route. This is because the land-locked countries in Central Asia and the Caucasuses can be connected to the Persian Gulf and open seas via Iran or to Europe via Turkey, making use of the reliable railway network of the country for export and import of goods.

With the breakup of the Soviet Union and the formation of the new republics, good opportunities became available for the Islamic Republic of Iran, which became the hub of global economy and the political relations of Central Asia and Caucasus. This role of a linking hub has its roots in Iran's geographical location, as well as its pragmatic foreign policy. All Central Asian Republics, except Georgia, are land-locked, and would pass through Iran for direct and indirect economic connections with the rest of the world. Most countries realize that to have economic ties with the republics of Central Asia and Caucasus there is no alternative but to use the land and air routes of Iran. Iran has its borders with the Central Asian republics, and its land and sea routes are linked to Central Asia, the Caucasus, and Russia.

The independence of the new Republics brought about a great cooperative relationship with the Islamic Republic of Iran. In addition to geographical contiguity with the Central Asian countries and the Caucasus, the two sides – Iran and the new Republics – have many things in common, including a shared faith, history and culture. Iran welcomed the independence of the Republics by embarking on an all-out and relentless effort to expand mutually beneficial tier and reinforcing political, commercial, economic, cultural (tourist, oil, and maritime) relations. Iran also welcomed the joining of these states to the Economic Cooperation Organization (ECO) as new members, and has proposed the establishment of the Caspian Sea Economic Cooperation Organization (CSECO), comprising Russia, Iran, Azerbaijan, Kazakhstan and Turkmenistan.[39]

One of the chief branches of the Silk Route traversed western China, then followed the oasis route (Khotan, Kashgar, Samarkand, Bukhara, Merv) across southern Central Asia into northern Iran, and thence westward on to the Black Sea or the Mediterranean Sea.[40] The advent of the railway has given new importance to these terrestrial links. The concept of recreating the Silk Road has acquired a potency far beyond its economic significance: it has become a symbol of rebirth for the entire region.[41]

Iran signed a series of bilateral agreements with Turkmenistan in 1994 in railway lines, freight transport, customs arrangements and border trade. Despite the United States' disapproval, Turkmenistan opted for the Iranian route to export its natural gas to Europe and both countries signed an agreement in 1995 to construct a gas pipeline between Korpeje (Turkmenistan) and Kurt Kuly (Iran).

The opening in May 1996 of the rail link between Iran's great north eastern city of Mashad and Turkmenistan's rail junction of Tejend, briefly attracted world attention, with romantic allusions to the revival of the historic Silk Route. Iran's president at the time, Ali Akbar Hashemi Rafsanjani, presided over the inauguration ceremony along with eleven heads of neighboring countries and dignitaries from over fifty countries. Ambitious plans were announced to set up a well-equipped free-trade zone in the Iranian border town of Sarakhs, across the "Bridge of Friendship" from Turkmenistan's twin town of Serakhs.

Iran's capacities are limited in the undertaking of large scale investment in mega projects. Its main problem is its isolation from the international community. Besides, Iran has expressed its appreciation for the cooperation of China in constructing segments of railway networks to make possible the first running of a train from Lianyungang harbor to Tashkent in November 1995.[42] The geopolitical advantage of Iran and its position as a regional and continental linking bridge make significant its role in the restoration of the Silk Route. The linkage of its railway system with the railway network of Russia and the Central Asian Republics has been realistic in approach. The construction of the 300 kilometers long Mashhad-Sarakhs-Tejend railway, which complements the 700 kilometers long Bafq-Bander Abbas railroad, has materialized. This railway network was inaugurated on 14 May, 1996, in the presence of the heads of states and dignitaries of more than 32 countries.[43] This grand project which was described by ESCAP (UN Economic and Social Commission for Asia and the Pacific) as the Iron Silk Route, was finished by the experts of Iran with the help of Turkmenistan.

Mr. Broujerdi, Deputy Minister of Foreign Affairs said that Iran had now constructed the missing link in the Euro-Asian railway network.[44] With the operation of Bafq-Bander Abbas railway, Lianyngang port on east China will be connected to Bander Abbas at the Persian Gulf via the cities of Urumchi, Almaty, Tashkent, Sarkhs, Mashhad, and Tehran. This project provides access to the open seas for the land locked Central Asian nations, on the one hand, and links the railroad to Rotterdam via Tehran, Istanbul and Europe, on the other.

A new project of a 2,750 kilometers rail link being implemented now, is outlined below:

"Bander Abbas–Tehran	1,500 kilometers
Tehran–Mashhad	950 kilometers
Mashhad–Sarkhs	170 kilometers
Sarakhs–Tajan (Turkmenistan)	130 kilometers."[45]

The implementation of this project is of international economic significance and can provide the best and safest transportation and transit routes to the CIS states, particularly in Central Asia and China. Starting in Xian, China, this route will revive the historic the Silk Route that has been called the East-West bridge. Linking the new Silk Route with land connections from Central Asia, to China and the Pacific Coast in north and the east, and the subsequent connections of sea routes from the Persian Gulf and Indian Ocean to ports in Canton, Shanghai, and Lianyungang via the Malacca Straits, will create a new cycle of exchange of raw materials, finished products, and technology between west and South Asia.

The revival of the Silk Road will enhance the advantageous position of Iran in the Euro-Asian trade. The road network from Central Asia to China and the shipping lanes from the Indian Ocean to the Pacific herald a prosperous future and greater friendly and fraternal relationship among the nations of the region. It will create new export opportunities for countries around the wider periphery, by providing the options of shorter, more direct linkages.

Role of Turkey

The unique geographical location of Turkey leads her to act not only as a springboard for regional markets but also to serve as a bridge between East and West in the heart of Eurasia. Turkey's location at the center of huge potential markets can be used as a base of operations to launch projects in the region stretching from the Adriatic Sea to the Great Wall of China.[46] Turkey attaches great importance to developing relations with her neighbors. Turkey supports both politically and economically the efforts of Central Asian countries to consolidate their sovereignty and independence and to facilitate their transition into market-oriented economies.

Turkey, in its endeavor to complement the efforts for the revival of the Silk Route, has contracted for the construction of the Eastern Black Sea Road, which will upgrade the link between the TRACECA (Transport Corridor Europe Caucasus Asia) corridor and the Pan-European transport network.[47] Furthermore, the implementation of projects for the Bosphorous railway tunnel and the Kars-Tbilisi railway are under way. The coordination of these two projects will help in creating an unbroken link between Asia and Europe via Turkey. Central Asia and the Transcaucasus are important for Turkey's interests in terms of oil and gas and trade prospects in general. On the strategic level, the area provides an opportunity to Turkey to strengthen its influence and prestige at the expense of Russia and to a lesser extent, Iran.

Role of Pakistan

The emergence of six independent Muslim states, five in Central Asia and one in the Caucasus has attracted the attention of the Muslim state of Pakistan to a large extent. Pakistan has been active in fomenting anti-communist waves among the Central Asian Republics bordering Afghanistan. Pakistan wants to be the linchpin in the strategic chain which includes Afghanistan, Central Asia, the Middle East and China. As a geographically contiguous country, Pakistan provides access to India and the Arabian Sea. Pakistan is a potential importer of Caspian oil and gas, considering its large population and lack of energy resources.

Pakistan hoped to compensate for its strategic weakness vis-à-vis India by establishing control over Afghanistan and forging alliances with the Muslim states of the Caucasus and Central Asia. In pursuit of this strategic vision, there was heightened Pakistani activity in the region during the Gorbachev era and soon after the Soviet demise.[48]

The absence of direct communications and transport links was a major obstacle in the development of Central Asian relations with Pakistan. The necessity to overcome such obstacles, coupled with potential benefits of becoming the main access point between Central Asia and the outside world, prompted Pakistan to push for the construction of a transport infrastructure across Afghanistan. Pakistani planners have recognized that the shortest distance between Central Asia and the Indian Ocean lie through their territory. They could become not merely the pipeline outlet but the major port (Gwadar) for Central Asian goods.[49] Instability in Afghanistan has caused the failure of the Trans-Afghan pipeline project, although the Turkmenian President Niyazov and the Pakistani leader General Musharraf both sought to revive it during their May 2000 meeting in Ashghabad.[50] The two leaders also committed themselves to improving the transport infrastructure across Afghanistan. For the past few years there have been proposals regarding a gas pipeline from Turkmenistan through Afghanistan to Pakistan. The US company Unocol and some American and Turkmenian officials felt that the pipeline could be extended to India. The biggest obstacle to the project has been the political volatility in Afghanistan.[51]

Karakorum Highway as a Branch of New Silk Route

The fragile Karakoram Highway is an important overland gateway from Pakistan to China. Twisting through northern Pakistan along a narrow corridor and precarious mountain passes, the Highway enters western China where it feeds into Kashi (Kashgar) and the traditional roads encircling the Takla Makan desert. Work on the Karakoram Highway started in 1967. A passable road was completed only in 1978, and fully opened for traffic in 1986. The Karakoram Highway is a strategic breakthrough for Beijing and Islamabad. It broke the isolation of both countries, ensuring a corridor that can withstand blockade even during intense warfare.

The idea of communication linkages between Central and South Asia came in late 1998 when Pakistan, China, Kazakhstan and Kyrgyzstan signed an agreement of 'traffic in transit' to further promote the existing trade relations through roads from Almaty to Karachi, by using the historical Silk Route.[52] According to the agreement, the competent authority and the executive bodies responsible for the permit will be the Ministry of Communications of the People' Republic of China and its authorized Department of Communication of the Xinjiang Ugur Autonomous Region, the Ministry of Transport and Communication of the Republic of Kazakhstan, the executive department of which would be the Transport Inspection wing of the Kazakhstan Ministry of Communication, and the Ministry of Transport and Communication of the Islamic Republic of Pakistan. The agreement states that exchanges on the international road transiting territory shall be through consultation on the basis of reciprocity and mutual benefits.[53] The agreement says that the vehicles in transit will have permits, one permit for each vehicle and valid for a single to and from journey.

When the Karakorum Highway was inaugurated in 1978 for all-weather traffic, the idea of using the road for promoting trade relations between Pakistan and China was presented. It was only after the Soviet disintegration and the subsequent emergence of the Central Asian states that serious thought was given to broaden the scope of the Karakorum Highway to Central Asia. Khurshid Ahmed Kasuri, the Secretary General of Pakistan Democratic Alliance, in an interview with *The News*, said that there was lot of scope for the rapid expansion of economic and cultural ties between the states of the region.[54] The Karakorum Highway has been cut though the high mountain ranges of the Himalayas and the Karakorum mountains to connect Pakistan with China. It opens a passage through isolated hilly regions that had remained the cultural backwaters of humanity for millennia. The building of the highway should be regarded as the eighth wonder of the world.[55] Thousands of Pakistani and Chinese engineers and workers participated in the construction of the Highway. From Thakot to Khunjrab, the length of the road is around 760 kilometers.[56] When this trade route is extended from Karakorum Highway to Kashgar, Bishkek and Almaty, the total length of the trade and transit route from Karachi to Almaty will be 3,726 kilometers.[57]

Paradoxically, the efforts of Pakistan for promoting trade and commercial relations with China and Central Asian states via Karakorum Highway is a significant initiative in the revival of the Silk Road. Political instability in Pakistan and its hostile relations with India have been the traditional obstacles in its revival.

The importance of traffic on the strategic Karakorum Highway between China and Pakistan has become the subject of a broad cooperation. China is financing the modernization of the Karakorum Highway to make it usable throughout the entire year without interruption and the building of new approach roads. Kazakhstan, Kyrgyzstan, China and Pakistan have agreed on a common plan for the operation of the road.

In 1998 an accord was signed in which Pakistan, China and two Central Asian States, Kazakhstan and Kyrgyzstan agreed to provide trade and transit facilities via the Karakorum Highway to the port of Karachi.[58] It is the most important agreement as far as traffic in trade is concerned and this would further boost the existing trade relations and bring the people of these countries closer to each other.

Welcoming the Asian Development Bank's initiative for a

regional connectivity project to create road and railway links between South Asia and Central Asia, *Dawn* (17thMarch, 2002) says editorially "The land-locked but relatively rich Central Asian Republics would then find an outlet to the world – (Also) with the passage of time a linkage between SAARC and the Economic Cooperation Organization could also materialize for the mutual benefit of both the regional economic groupings".[59] The establishment of road and railway links between Central and South Asia has the potential to yield tremendous socio-economic benefits for the people of these two neighboring regions.

The western region of China acts as a bridge promoting Chinese trade with Pakistan and other neighboring countries. It has registered a record $ 3 billion in foreign trade in 2003, up by 45.8 percent in 2004.[60]

Work on the project began on May 1, 1999. In the winter of 2000, a test convoy of trucks ran over the Karakorum from Pakistan to Almaty.[61] It is estimated that 50-60 tankers/trucks carrying goods arrive from China every month into Pakistan.[62] Items like cloth and crockery are brought from China and sold in the markets of Sust (a border checkpost) and Gilgit. Some positive implications of the Karakorum Highway on the lives of the local people are-

The travel distance has been drastically reduced between far-flung areas after the construction of KKH. It used to take three days to travel on foot from Gulmit to Gilgit. Now it takes only two hours to cover the distance. Similarly, from Gilgit to Rawalpindi it used to take around a month but now it takes only 14 hours. From Gulmit to the Chinese city of Kashgar it now takes only 10 hours, while earlier, it used to take 15 days to cover that area.[63]

KKH has changed the lifestyle of the local people. Earlier, utilities like electricity and telephone were rarely available in this area but now there is massive electrification and better communication facilities. New markets and schools/colleges have also been established in the last few years.

New trade and business opportunities have emerged in the area along the KKH.

There has taken place a rapid rise in tourism because of the KKH. Both local and foreign tourists visit this area and enjoy the scenic beauty and terrain. Tourist inflow has created job opportunities along the KKH.

Some negative implications of Karakorum Highway are:

The cultural heritage of the Northern Areas is facing a serious threat because of more construction and contacts with the outsiders.

The growth crime and the use of drugs can also be seen as negative implications of Karakorum Highway.

Because of the strategic significance of KKH, the area seems to have attracted the attention of foreign powers. Sectarian tensions also tend to generate insecurity among the local people.

Pakistan considers the Karakoram Highway to be a symbol and manifestation of the unique Sino-Pakistani relationship and its strategic unity of purpose. Recently, Islamabad expanded this theme to include the emerging Silk Route. For example, Pakistani officials stressed in late December 1993 that "the role of China in the construction of the Silk Route has made the (our) bilateral relations as strong as the Karakoram Highway."

Nowadays most traffic on the Karakoram Highway consists of tourists and Hajjis – Muslims making a pilgrimage to Mecca – but small-scale trade has also revived. Pakistani businessmen come to Kashgar to buy thermos, enamel wash-basins, and other items sold cheaply in Chinese shops. They are also attracted by Kashgar's reputation as a place of pleasure. Apart from the Hajjis, a few Chinese find their way west. The Karakorum Highway, a branch of the New Silk Route or Eurasian land-bridge thus has great importance in present times.

Construction of Gwadar Port

Located at the entrance of the Persian Gulf and about 460 kms from Karachi, Gwadar has immense geostrategic significance. The endemic instability – in the Persian Gulf environment in particular – following the Iran/Iraq war, the Gulf war and the emergence of the new Central Asian States has added to its importance. Considering the geo-economic imperative of the regional changes, the Asian Development Bank's Ports Master Plan studies considered an alternate to the Persian Gulf ports to capture the transit trade of the Central Asian Republics (CAR) as well as the trans-shipment trade of the region. The ADB studies, however considered Gwadar as having the most advantageous location for such an alternative port in the region, which could handle ships and large oil tankers. Keeping that aspect in view as well as the inherent strategic and economic benefits that Gwadar Port offered, the transport programme of the 8th Five Year Plan (1993-94) of Pakistan included the development of Gwadar Port as an essential element of its aims and objectives. Technical and financial feasibilities, therefore, were undertaken resulting in decisions for the development of Gwadar Port by the Govt. of Pakistan. Pakistan is in the process of developing the Gwadar port complex, which can serve as a gateway to land-locked Central Asia and Afghanistan. This port will provide facilities for trans-shipment, transit, warehousing and industrial needs for international export import trade, especially for the Central Asian states and Afghanistan.[64]

Gwadar seaport has an important role in the development of the Eurasian land-bridge; it was inaugurated on the Arabian Sea coast in southern Baluchistan on April 2002. This port is strategically located at the opposite end of the Gulf of Oman and the Straits of Hormuz at the mouth of the Persian Gulf.[65] It will be beneficial to nearly 20 countries of the Middle East, Central Asia and South Asia. The project would also help Baluchistan, the least developed province of Pakistan. The complex would boost tourism and ancillary industries like fishing, ship building and other marine based enterprises. For land locked countries, the complex will help boost international trade and economic relations by providing an export outlet.

The Prime Minister of Pakistan Mr. Shaukat Aziz said "the Gawadar deep sea port could serve as a transit for Tajikistan's trade with the Gulf and other countries".[66] Gwadar port is important for the Turkmenistan-Afghanistan-Pakistan gas pipeline project. Turkmenian gas can be exported from this port to Japan and the Far-East.[67] A well-known Pakistani economist, Javed Burki, talks of the possibility of an economic and trading bloc involving seven "stans" – the five "stans" of Central Asia, Afghanistan and Pakistan. He says that this would create a zone of 223 million population with a gross domestic production of $114 billion and per capita income of $512. Since the Central Asian Republics need to export their enormous untapped oil and mineral wealth, the role of Pakistan and Afghanistan could become important,[68] and the Gwadar seaport project would be a new approach to the New

Silk Route. Gen. Pervez Musharraf, the President of Pakistan said that Pakistan was bound by geography to work with its land-locked neighbors, traditionally dependent on trade through Pakistani ports. "We have to interact with each other in a harmonious manner".[69]

The Gwadar deep-sea port project was supported by Mr. Pervez Musharraf for the prosperity of Pakistan.[70] It could transform Pakistan into a vibrant hub of commercial activity among the energy rich Gulf and Central Asian states, Afghanistan and China. Gwadar port will also provide the strategic depth to the Pakistani navy as a naval base along its coastline. The port has significance for China, as it will enable that country to diversify its crude oil import routes and extend its presence in the Indian Ocean. Thus China is contributing with technical assistance, 450 workers and 80 percent of the funds for the construction of the port.[71] The Pakistan Foreign Ministry spokesman, Masood Khan said "the *Gwadar port* is a symbol of Pak-China cooperation and is a part of our joint efforts to build a modern infrastructure project in Pakistan".[72]

Gwadar seaport is an issue of concern for neighboring India and Iran at Sino-Pakistan maritime activities. It has sparked a tacit competition over whether Pakistan's Gwadar port or Iran's Chabahar port, built with Indian assistance, will serve as Central Asia's conduit to oil and gas. The port is 450 kilometers farther away from the Indian border than Karachi.

Construction work of the Gwadar port began in March 2002 after the "Chinese agreed to provide $198 million of the $248 million required for Phase-I of the project. Phase-I involves the construction of three multipurpose ship berths and is slated to be completed early 2006. As the sign of the near completion of Phase-I, a Chinese cargo vessel carrying port related equipment successfully berthed at Gwadar. Phase-II, estimated at $600 million, will include the building of nine additional berths, one bulk cargo terminal, one grain terminal and two oil terminals".[73] China's interests in the Gwadar port lie in the continued consolidation of its relationship with Pakistan through large-scale collaborative development projects. This will diversify and secure its crude oil import routes and extend Chinese presence in the Indian Ocean. It ensures the security of its energy related shipments along the existing routes.

Gwadar port will provide a stable and proximate point of access to the Gulf ports. Just 250 miles from the Straits of Hormuz, through which nearly 40 percent of the world's oil supplies flow, the port is strategically located to serve as a key shipping point in South Asia. It will provide access to the land-locked Central Asian Republics, Afghanistan and the Chinese Xinjiang region to the Arabian Sea. A road from Gwadar to Saindak, which is currently under construction and runs parallel to the Iran-Pakistan border, will be the shortest route between Central Asia and the Arabian Sea.[74] Gwadar port will also enable the transfer of Central Asia's vast energy resources to world markets. The benefits of the development of Gwadar port are:

(a) Capitalizing on opportunities for trade between the landlocked Central Asian states and Afghanistan.
(b) Promoting trade and transport with Gulf states.
(c) Trans-shipment, essentially, of containerized cargo.
(d) Unlocking the development of the hinterland.
(e) The socio-economic upliftment of the province of Baluchistan.
(f) Establishment of shipping related industries in Pakistan.
(g) The creation of export processing and industrial zones.
(h) Reducing congestion and dependence on other existing ports.
(i) Will become a regional hub for major trade and commercial activities.

China's interests in the Gwadar port are to consolidate its relationship with Pakistan, diversify and secure its crude oil import routes, and extend its presence in the Indian Ocean. China has also pledged to develop its western regions including Xinjiang as part of its "Go West" policy. Xinjiang has already demonstrated its economic potential by registering $4.8 billion in foreign trade and $22.7 billion in GDP in 2003, up by 10.8 percent from the previous year. Seeking to capitalize on Xinjiang's rising fortunes and strengthening Sino-Pakistani economic ties, Prime Minister Shaukat Aziz during the visit of the Governor of Xinjiang to Pakistan in October 2004 called for expanding trade links with Xinjiang and offered Gwadar port's services for facilitating trade.

India and Iran have been warily watching the construction of Gwadar port in their backyard. The port could endanger the Indian naval security. Iran's response to the Gwadar port has been to construct its own Chabahar port and tacitly compete with Pakistan in capturing access routes and energy-related trade from Afghanistan, Kazakhstan, Kyrgyzstan and Tajikistan.

EU's Policy and Action for New Silk Route

With the support of the European Union, the presidents of Azerbaijan and Georgia hosted an international conference on the "Restoration of the Historic Silk Route" on 8th September, 1998 in Baku, capital of Azerbaijan.[75] The Presidents of Azerbaijan, Bulgaria, Georgia, Kyrgyzstan, Moldavia Romania, Turkey, Uzbekistan, and Ukraine, transport ministers and experts from 32 countries and representatives of international organizations attended this conference. The participants emphasized the importance of the revival of the Great Silk Route and highly appreciated the contribution to that end of the TRACECA project, implemented within the European Union's TRACIS (Transportation in Commonwealth Independent States) programme as a Eurasian Land-Bridge.

One important conference, "Euro-Asian Transport in St. Petersburg, Russia" was held on Sep. 15-13, 2000. At this conference, five routes from Europe to Asia were discussed.[76] These are: (i) The TRACECA (Transport Corridor Europe–Caucasus–Asia) corridor, from eastern Europe via the Black and Caspian Seas to Central Asia, (ii) The Central corridor, from southern Europe, via Turkey, Iran and Central Asia to China, (iii) The southern corridor, which runs from southern Europe to Iran, as central corridor, but reaches China via Pakistan, India and the south east Asia, (iv) The northern corridor, from Europe via the trans-Siberian rail road to China, North and South Korea, and Japan (v) A new north-south sail ship corridor, which goes from Northern Europe to Russia, crosses the Caspian Sea to Iran, and via Iran's southern ports across the Arabian sea to India. These corridors, with their numerous branches, form a unified network, providing a foundation for the development of a gigantic economic zone.

Europe and China thus represent the natural "development poles" of Eurasia. The European Union policy towards the New

Silk Road is mainly articulated around the following complementary poles or pillars:

- EU's TACIS programs (Technical Assistance Programs), which constitute the world's largest donor grant finance to the newly New Independent States (NIS), covering the whole spectrum of the necessary economic and political modernization of these countries.
- EU partnership and cooperation agreement with each of the NIS: These are comprehensive frameworks covering economic issues, political dialogueing, and democratic institution building.
- The European Energy Charter and its Treaty, which is legally binding and which came into force in November 1998.
- INOGATE (Interstate Oil and Gas Transport to Europe), a specific technical assistance programme.[77] Energy Charter and INOGATE are designed to create opportunities for Central Asian and Caucasus countries to exploit and export energy resources as a concrete basis for their economic development.

Europe – especially Germany, its neighbors, and Italy – represent the greatest single concentration of productive capacity, developed infrastructure, and qualified labor force in the world. In particular, Europe possesses the greatest potential in the world for the production and export of high technology investment goods. It is in this context, that it lays stress on the endeavour of the "New Silk Road". By 1998, the EU had already spent $75 million on the TRACECA project, and was soliciting another $300 million in loans. Additional funds were pledged by the European Bank for Reconstruction and Development (EBRD).[78]

In July 1999, the European Union convened a conference in Kiev attended by 50 delegations from the countries of the former Soviet Union, Central and Eastern Europe and the Black Sea Region, and from international financial institutions, to initiate the INOGATE Umbrella Agreement.[79] This accord envisages a single legal and administrative framework to facilitate cooperation among the INOGATE member countries, under a secretariat to be established in Kiev. In December 1999, the European Union approved a new seven year TACIS programme with a price-tag of € 3, 138.39 million.[80]

The TRACECA and INOGATE projects represent the quest for routes circumventing Russia, and even an attempt to drive a wedge between Russia and other CIS members. Indeed, the EU's strong backing for the revitalization of Romania's Black Sea port of Constanza, its partial funding of the Baku-Supsa pipe line and financial assistance for a new ferry service between Georgia's Black Sea port of Poti and Ilyichevsh in the Ukraine, could be perceived as attempts to by pass Russia.[81] The East-West road link from Baku through Alyat to the Georgian border is one of the main access routes for goods to and from Azerbaijan, and is supported by the European Union's TRACECA as a main link in the proposed revival of the Silk Route.

Role of the USA in the Revival of Silk Route

The USA has particular economic, strategic and political interests along the Silk Road countries. Sam Brownback, a senator of USA in his report dated March 19, 1997 "Pursuing a Silk Road strategy"[82] underlined the five US priorities in Central Asia and the Southern Caucasus, as under:

1. Central Asian and the Southern Caucasus states are the major factors in containing the spread northward of anti-extremist fundamentalism from Iran and other nations.
2. The Caspian Sea basin contains oil and gas reserves which, potentially, could rank third in the world after the Middle East and Russia, and exceed four trillion dollars in value. Investment in this region could ultimately reduce US dependence on oil imports from the volatile Persian Gulf.
3. Strong market economics near Russia and China can only help to positively influence these two countries on their rocky path towards freedom.
4. These countries, some of them nuclear capable ones, are also at the forefront of stemming the flow southwards of proliferation of weapons of mass destination.
5. This region offers to USA historic opportunities to spread the ideals of freedom and democracy.

The United States today, in economic and military terms, is the most powerful country, which, after the disintegration of the Soviet Union has become the only superpower of the world. The special role of the United States in the revival of the Silk Road is crucial. The United States supports the Eurasian development strategy of the New Silk Road, and, together with other nations, takes the necessary steps to reorganize the financial system. At the podium, the wife of the American economist Lyndon La Rouche, Helga Zepp was well positioned to voice an enthusiastic and credible "Yes !" on behalf of the West, to the "New Silk Road" policy.[83]

Some countries are considering establishing the Euro-Asia-America Continental Bridge, as the means of a bridge or tunnel across the Bering Strait. The narrowest stretch of the Bering Strait between Chukchi, Russia and the North America-Alaska Peninsula, is just 85 km. wide. Already in 1905, the Cross Alaska-Siberia Railway Company was set up by Russia and America. In 1986, a tentative plan for establishing a Bering Strait undersea tunnel was put forward.[84] Since then, in 1992, 1993 and 1994 three successive international meetings have been held especially to discuss this issue. As soon as the Bering Strait Tunnel is finished, the USA, Russia, China and other Asian countries will be connected together. So, Qinhuangdo Port, Jingtang Port, and Huanghua Port of Hebei province will be among the nearest ports of China from the western exit of the tunnel, and it will also become one of the bridgeheads connected with the Asian and North American Continental Bridge.[85]

Oil is the key determinant of United States foreign policy towards the Caspian region and Central Asia, and the revival of the Silk Route. The American foreign policy establishment thinks that control over the Caspian region by any power other than itself will be against American national interests. Therefore it opposes all those who show interest in the region, Iran or China, Russia or Europe.[86] The Ceyhen-Baku pipeline project is a case illustrating this. This pipeline is considered a main export outlet by Turkey and USA in their scheme of an East-West Energy Corridor.

The United States seeks to assume the leadership of Eurasia and fill the power vacuum caused by the eclipse of Soviet power. Beside, US interests are to counter Russian influence, reduce Russian monopoly on oil exports from Central Asia and the

Caspian Sea region, counter the influence of fundamentalist Islam in the region by installing pro-American regimes and bringing them into the fold of the market economy-oriented western world.[87] America's major interest lies in not allowing the rise of any other power with aspirations and capabilities to compete with the U.S. for the leadership of and control over the Eurasian region and its resources.

World Bank and UNESCO Support

The World Bank is joining an international effort to revive the old Silk Route connecting China and Central Asia with Europe. With a US$ 40 million credit on May 9th, 2002, The Bank supported the project of reviving the Silk Route.[88] "The Azerbaijan–Highway Project aims to help promote economic growth and private sector development by improving access and lowering transport costs for goods and passenger traffic",[89] said Akbar Noman, the World Bank's Azerbaijan Manager. "It will also lead to better transport services for the low income rural population living in the vicinity of the road as well as all road users by improving the organization, efficiency and maintenance practices of the Azeravtoyol road agency", he added.

In pursuit of its mandate "to increase the means of communication between peoples and for the purposes of mutual understanding", UNESCO has given significant support to initiatives that have greatly enhanced Central Asia's cultural heritage. The ten year UNESCO project of Silk Roads through a broad programme of studies, seminars, publications and expeditions sheds new light on the heritage of the Silk Road. The Steppe Route Expedition undertaken in 1991 through Turkmenistan, Tajikistan, Uzbekistan, Kyrgyzstan and Kazakhstan, widely reported in world media, has made for a revival of interest in Central Asia and the Silk Route. With a view to promoting the Silk Roads as a destination of cultural tourism, UNESCO and the World Tourism Organization (WTO) jointly launched, in 1994, a long term programme in Central Asia.[90]

Certain activities launched during the Silk Roads project have been incorporated into the new UNESCO project "East-West Inter-Cultural Dialogue in Central Asia". The main aim of this project is to bring to light elements which illustrate the concept that emerged during the Silk Road project, of a common heritage and plural identity". Within the framework of this project an international forum "Culture and Religion in Central Asia" was held in Bishkek in September 1999.

The second international meeting on the Silk Road was held in Tehran in April 1997, also supported by UNESCO. The primary aims of the meeting were to increase international understanding and expand cultural exchanges, both within the Silk Road region, and between individual countries. The meeting suggested a number of measures for the Silk Road countries with a view to achieving a high degree of sustainable tourism development.

The third international meeting on the Silk Road was held in Tbilisi from November 2-5 1998 with the aim of continuing with the planning and marketing process which the project started four years ago and take stock of the current situation to decide how to proceed. Through the project, the United Nations' Development Programme (UNDP) and the World Trade Organization will identify eight to ten cities along the route for awarding the title "UN Silk Road City" to encourage their commitment to and long-term planning for the protection of cultural assets. The Samarkand Declaration on Silk Road Tourism adopted in 1999 by 19 participating countries under the inspiration of the President of Uzbekistan and the then Secretary General of World Tourism Organization was a landmark.[91] A special logo of WTO Silk Road Tourism Project was subsequently adopted to unite all the countries' organization and their private sectors under a common visual banner.

In September 1994, at the 49th session of the UN Assembly the UN Secretary General presented a report on "Transit Transport System in the Newly Independent and Developing Landlocked States in Central Asia and their Transit Developing Neighbors: Current Situation and Proposals for Future Action".[92] Khalid Malik, UN resident co-ordinator and UNDP resident representative in China stated that the Silk Road Regional Programme (SRRP), a joint initiative between United Nations Development Programme (UNDP) and the governments of China, Kazakhstan, Kyrgyzstan, Tajikistan and Uzbekistan, will be carried out in three areas – trade, investment and tourism with the aim of reviving traditional economic co-operation.

In June 1995, the second meeting of governmental experts from landlocked and transit developing countries, representatives of donor countries, financial and development institutions, was held by UNCTAD in New York with proposals for the development of a global framework for transit transport cooperation.[93] UNCTAD conducted a "Central Asia External Trade and Transit Transport Initiative" technical meeting in Ankara where the issue of the Euro-Asia corridor was again discussed.[94]

Many international organizations put forward some related projects, such as UNESCAP's (UN Economic and Social Council for Asia and the Pacific) with the project of a New Iron Silk Route, ADB (Asian Development Bank) with the project of an Asian Expressway, and the GIF (Global Infrastructure Fund) of Japan's Mitsubishi Research Institute with the EATTS project.[95] All these development activities and initiatives clearly indicate the great potential for economic development and cooperation within the New Iron Silk Route region.

NOTES

1. Prof. K. Warikoo, Central Asia and China: The Geopolitical Imperatives, in Shams-Ud-Din (ed.), "Geopolitics and Energy Resources in Central Asia and Caspian Sea Region", (New Delhi, Lancer Books, 2000), p. 253.
2. Jonathan Tennenbaum, *et. al.*, 'The Eurasian Land-Bridge – The 'New Silk Road' – locomotive for worldwide economic development', *Executive Intelligence Review,* Special Report, (Washington D.C.: January, 1997), p. 28.
3. Gordon Feller, 'Central Asian States Find neither Privatization nor Political Reforms Correlate Exactly Economic Growth', (online web), www.washington.report.org, page 3 of 5.
4. R. Hrair Dekmejian and Hovann H. Simonian, *Troubled waters the Geopolitics of the Caspian Region,* (London, New York: I.B. Tauris Publishers, 2001), p. 141
5. *Ibid.,* p. 141.
6. Jeremy Brantsen, 'Conference Paves Way for Transport Corridor, Azerbaijan: Silk Road' (online web), www.washington.report.org.
7. Jeremy Bransten, 'Central Asia/Caucasus: Silk Road Conference Agrees on Eurasian Corridor', (web on line), www.washington.report.org.
8. (online web) www.unesco.in.ca. html page 1 of 2

9. Ramtanu Maitra, 'Importance of Eurasian Landbridge for the Central Asian Development', in Shams-ud-din (Ed), *Geopolitics and Energy Resources in Central Asia and Caspian Sea Region,* (New Delhi: Lancer Books, 2000), p. 179.
10. K. Warikoo (Ed), *Central Asia: Emerging New Order,* issued under the auspices of Himalayan and Cultural Foundation (India), (New Delhi: Har-Anand Publications, 1995), p. 29.
11. Ramtanu Maitra, n-8, p. 180.
12. Jonathan Tennenbaum, n-1, p. 6.
13. Dieter Dettke (Ed), *A Great Game No More: Oil, Gas, and Stability,* (Washington: Friedrich–Ebert–Stiftung, 1999), p. 65.
14. *China Statistical Yearbook,* 2005.
15. Jonathan Tennenbaum, n-1, p. 30.
16. Dr. Etibar Najafov, *The Restoration of the Silk Road As a Factor of Modernization,* (Baku: Slavik University Press, 1998), p. 3.
17. BBC, *SWB,* SU/3702 G/1, 26 November, 1999.
18. BBC, *SWB,* SU/3703 G/1, 27 November, 1999.
19. BBC, *SWB,* SU/3702 G/1, 26 November, 1999.
20. BBC, *SWB,* SU/3703 G/1, 27 November, 1999.
21. Ramtanu Maitra, n-8, p. 181.
22. *Ibid.,* p. 181.
23. *Ibid.,* p. 181.
24. *Ibid.,* p. 262.
25. Jonathan Tennenbaum, n-1,p. 163.
26. R. Hrair Dekmejian and Hovann J. Simonian, n-3, p. 44.
27. D. Kaushik, *Central Asia in Modern Times,* (Moscow: Progress Pub., 1970), p. 72.
28. Jonathan Tennenbaum, n-1, p. 168.
29. BBC *SWB* SUW/0673 WA/15, 12 Jan, 2001.
30. BBC *SWB* SUW/0673 WA/15, 12 Jan, 2001.
31. *Ibid.*
32. *Ibid.*
33. *Ibid.*
34. BBC *SWB* SUW/0677 WA/16, 9 Feb, 2001.
35. BBC *SWB* SUW/0683 WA/17, 23 March, 2001.
36. BBC *SWB* SUW/0683 WA/18, 23 March, 2001.
37. Friedrich–Ebert–Stiftung, *A Great Game No More: Oil, Gas and Stability in the Caspian Sea Region,* (Washington: D.C., 1999), p. 46.
38. Jonathan Tennenbaum, n-1, p. 172.
39. Ajaya Patnaik, 'Central Asia in Global Setting', in *World Focus,* Vol. 23, No. 6, (New Delhi, June-2002), p. 6.
40. K. Warikoo, n-9, p. 251.
41. *The UNESCO Programme* 'Integral Study of the Silk Road' launched in 1988, acted as a catalyst not only by reviving and publishing the

concept of the "Silk Road", but also by giving it practical support in the form of the expeditions and conferences that were organized throughout the region. (online web) www.unesco.worldpaper.com
42. Ramtanu Maitra, n-8, p. 183.
43. Dilip Hiro, 'Turkmenistan and Iran: US Advice Ignored', *Middle East International,* no. 551, May 30, 1997, pp. 19-20.
44. The speech presented by Mr. Broujerdi, Deputy Minister of Foreign Affaires of Iran, On May 7, 1997, (online web) www.muza.com.kg/silkroad
45. Jonathan Tennenbaum, n-1, p. 48.
46. Gareth M. Winrow, *Turkey in Post-Soviet central Asia,* (London: Royal Institute of International Affairs, 1995), Bolukhasi, pp. 80-94.
47. R. Hrair Dekmejian & Havann H. Simonian, n-3, p. 108.
48. Anthony Hyman, 'Central Asia's Relations with Afghanistan and South Asia', in Peter Ferdinand (ed) *The New Central Asia and its Neighbors,* (London: Pinter Pub., 1994), pp. 86-93.
49. Michael Collins Dunn, 'Great Games and Small: Afghanistan, Tajikistan, and the New Geopolitics of South West Asia', *Middle East Policy* – 5, no. 2, May 1997, pp. 146-7.
50. R. Hrair Dekmejain & Hovann H. Simonian, n-3, p. 119.
51. C. Raja Mohan, 'Central Asia's Pipeline Dreams', *The Hindu,* New Delhi, 12 October 1996; see also, 'India can join as pipeline', *The Times of India,* New Delhi, 20 April 1995.
52. Moonis Ahmar, 'Connecting two Asia's', *The News International,* Karachi, December 12, 1998.
53. 'Road transit pact to enhance trade with Cars' *The News International,* Islamabad, December 30, 1998.
54. K. Warikoo, n-9, p. 311.
55. *The New Encyclopedia Brittannica* (Chicago, Encyclopedia Brittanica, Inc., 1995), S. 9.
56. Prof. Ahmad Hasan Dani, *Human Records on Karakorum Highway,* (Lahore: Sang-E-Meel Pub., 1995) p. 11.
57. Moonis Ahmar, 'Communication Linkage Between Central And South Asia: A Case Study of Karakorum Highway (KKH)', *Eurasian Studies* 20, Special Issue, Summer 2001, p. 190.
58. *Ibid.,* p. 189.
59. *Public Opinion Trends* (POT) Analysis and News Service, (New Delhi August 31, 2004), p. 4094.
60. *Ibid,* November 5, 2004, p. 5177.
61. 'The New Eurasian Land Bridge: Building Our Way Out of the Depression', *Executive Intelligence Report,* 2002. p. 4.
62. Moonis Ahmar, 'Comminication Linkage between Central and South

Asia: A Case Study of Karakoram Highway' article in *Eurasian Studies*, 20, Special Issue, summer 2001, p. 193.

63. *Ibid.*, p. 94.
64. Ajay Patnaik, 'Strategic Games and South Asia-Central Asia Relations' in Mahavir Singh & Victor K., (ed) *Eurasian Vision*, (New Delhi 2003), p. 274.
65. *Ibid.*
66. *Public Opinion Trends* (POT), News Service, Pakistan September 15, 2004, p. 4336.
67. Ajay Patnaik, 'Strategic Games and South Asia-Central Asia Relations' in Mahavir Singh & Victor K., (ed.) *Eurasian Vision*, (New Delhi 2003), p. 274.
68. Shahid Javed Burki, 'Bringing Together the Stans', *Dawn*, Pakistan, 5 March, 2002.
69. *Public Opinion Trends* (POT), News Service, Pakistan, December 29, 2001, p. 5702.
70. Ziad Haider, 'Baluchis, Beijing, and Pakistan's Gwadar Port', *Georgetown Journal of International Affairs*, Winter/Spring 2005, pp. 95-96. (online web) http://www.unescap.org/tcd/countrypapers.htm
71. *Ibid.*, p. 96.
72. 'Beijing Lauds Best Medical care to Injured Chinese', *The News* (Pakistan), 6 May 2004.
73. 'Gwadar: Government of Pakistan Board of Investment Report', (online web) http://www.pakbai.gov.pk/html/gwadar.html (date accessed: 12 July, 2004).
74. Ziad Haider, 'Baluchis, Beijing, and Pakistan's Gwadar Port', *Georgetown Journal of International Affairs*, Winter/Spring 2005, pp. 95-96. (online web) http://www.unescap.org/tcd/countrypapers.htm
75. R. Hrair Dekmejian & Hovann H. Simonian, n-3, p. 140.
76. Dr. Etibar Najafov, n-14, pp. 2–4.
77. Friedrich–Ebert–Stiftung, n-35, p. 65.
78. Jermy Bransten, 'Central Asia/Caucasus: Silk Road Conference Agrees on Eurasian Corridor', *RFE/RL Weekday Magazine*, 9 September, 1993.
79. R. Hrair Dekmejian & Hovann H. Simonian, n-3, p. 141.
80. 'EU/Ex-USSR: New TACIS Programme Approved', *European Report*, 7 January, 1999.
81. BBC *SWB*, EE/W0557/WB, 1 October 1998.
82. Friedrich–Ebert–Stiftung, n-35, pp. 74–78.
83. *Ibid.*
84. By the people's Government of Hebei Province, "The 'Flying Bird' of the Bohai Bay River," in EIR Special Report, 1997, Washington, D.C. (online web) www.washington.edu.com
85. *Ibid.*

86. Girijesh Pant, America's Caspian Oil Policy' in Shams-ud-Din (ed.), *Geopolitics and Energy Resources in Central Asia and Caspian Sea Region*, (New Delhi: Lancer Pub., 2000), p. 174.
87. D. Kaushik, (ed.), *Contemporary Central Asia,* Vol. VI , Number 1-2 April-August, 2002. (New Delhi and Maulana Abul Kalam Institute of Asian Studies, Kolkata, India: Published jointly by the Central Asian Studies Foundation), p. 23.
88. BBC *SWB* SUW/0678 WA/17, 9 May, 2002.
89. Report of World Bank on Silk Route Revival, (New York: World Bank Pub. 1996). (online web) www.worldpaper.com/archivewp
90. Report of the UNESCO Programme and the WTO (World Tourism Organization) focusing on Central Asia, (New York: WTO Pub. 1994).
91. WTO, Annual Report, 'International Trade Statistics', (New York: UN Pub. 1999).
92. Jonathan Tennenbaum, n-1, p. 44.
93. *Ibid.*
94. UN, Management and Financing for Road Maintenance Report/ *ESCAP*/World Bank Seminar, 17–20 Sep., 1996, (online web), www.worldpaper.com
95. UN, Road Safety in Asia and the Pacific: Report/*ESCAP*/Asian Development Bank Seminar-cum-Workshop, 2–6 Sep., (Bangkok-New York: United Nations, 1997).

5

Eurasian Land Bridge and Its Implications

A main feature of economic development in the last decade of the 20th century has been the globalization of markets which brought with it increased demand for the unhindered movement of people, goods and services. In this new environment, transport has become both an economic resource and a means of economic activity. However, the increased demand for mobility can only be satisfied if two important conditions are met. One is the provision of safe and reliable international transport routes and networks. The other is the efficient management of the infrastructure including the 'software aspects' of transport relating to the necessary harmonization of the documents required and their speedy and unhindered transmission between the parties involved.

The New Silk Route whether in terms of the ancient trade routes between east and west or the Eurasian Land Bridge of the 21st century, covers all modes of transportation including road, rail, as well as oil and gas pipelines and communication infrastructure. This Eurasian Land Bridge will give considerable impetus to the expansion of cooperation between Europe, the Caucasus and Asia. It will create new opportunities, potential and promises for peace and shared prosperity among the nations with links to one another.

The revival of the Silk Route is believed to be beneficial not only for the independent states of the Central Asia, but also for the economically developed countries like Germany, France and Britain. These countries are interested in widening the scope of their economic activity and doing their business in the new markets of Central Asia. The concept of the Eurasian infrastructure corridor as the Eurasian Land Bridge has attracted the serious attention of various developed countries. A number of seminars have been held by these countries emphasizing the importance of the revival of the Silk Route.

With the end of the cold war era, a number of nations gained their independence, and democratic norms and globalization became the dominant factor in world politics. The idea of reviving the Silk Route as a corridor linking Europe and Asia was launched in 1993, under the umbrella of TRACECA (Transport Corridor Europe Caucasus Asia). The project envisages a Eurasian Land Bridge consisting of highways, railroads, fiber optic cables, oil and gas pipelines and expansion of seaports.[1]

Europe and China represent the natural "development poles" of Eurasia.[2] China's rapid development process has a powerful stimulating effect on the other countries of Asia, an effect which will be further strengthened by the policy of the "New Silk Road" and the "Eurasian Land Bridge". Economic development is originating largely from these two aspects, spreading mainly along the development corridors of the Eurasian Land Bridge, which runs through Siberia on the north, through Iran and Turkey in the middle, and through the Indian sub-continent and Southeast Asia, in the south. Other Asian countries have positive economic impulses connected either directly or indirectly with the rise of the Eurasian Land Bridge economy.

India: India possesses a large, well-rounded industrial and scientific-technical base, and an agricultural sector which has shown an impressive capacity for development. But despite its enormous potential, India is not yet able to function as a prime locomotive for Eurasian development in the way China does presently. India has displayed its keen interest in the future course of strategic alignments around the Caspian and the Eurasian Land Bridge.

Recently there have been signs of growing interest in India about the Eurasian Land Bridge development as a potential means for addressing both the external and internal problems of the country. Positive developments in multilateral relations between India, Russia, China, Iran and other countries of the region reflect a growing orientation toward mutually beneficial economic cooperation, in which the Land Bridge is a central element.[3] The rapidly expanding economy of India, combined with its near total dependence on energy imports makes India a potential consumer of Central Asian Caspian oil and gas. And India is interested in developing export markets in Central Asia for both its inexpensive consumer goods and its high-tech products.[4] India's integration into the Eurasian Land Bridge system would mean an enormous gain for the economy of Eurasia as a whole.

Japan: Japan has already shown its interest in the new Eurasian Land Bridge, and in numerous related projects in China, the Tumen and Mekong regions and Central Asia. As the leading industrial nation in Asia, Japan obviously has a decisive role to play in future Eurasian development.

Japan has extended major credits to Uzbekistan and Georgia. A package of loans in 1995-96 to Uzbekistan, worth $600 million, targeted modernizing the Ferghana oil refinery, upgrading communications, investing in the energy sector, developing foreign trade and expanding three airports.[5] The Eurasian Land Bridge strategy is key to defining Japan's future economic role as a leading supplier of modern machinery and other high-technology capital goods to rapidly-growing markets on the Eurasian land mass. Building a land connection between Japan and the Korean peninsula (Fukuoka-Pusan), would have great potential benefits.[6] The Eurasian Land Bridge would help to highlight the real strength and mettle of Japan.

Rusia: As the main successor state to the Soviet Union, the Russian Federation is the repository of most of the latter's geopolitical status, military might and economic resources. Russia has been in the centre of the development of a trans-Eurasian infrastructure, and it was the main vehicle for the spread of modern science and technology. The Eurasian development corridors represent a unique opportunity to revive this tradition in Russia, and to mobilize, for positive purpose, the scientific and technological potential represented by the military- industrial-scientific complex of the former Soviet Union.[7]

The oil and gas sector is a major component of Russia's industrial base. In proven oil reserves Russia ranks eight, with an estimated 50 barrels; it also contains the world's largest natural gas reserves.[8] Oil and gas exports are Russia's largest Currencyearning commodities, but the deterioration of transport infrastructure is the important factor to decline the Russian exports. Within these circumstances the Eurasian Land Bridge will provide fast momentum in the development of economic activities.

The New Silk Route being built as the Eurasian Land Bridge will serve as fundamental link between the East and the West, shaping cultures, political ideas, technologies, beliefs and peoples. The idea of the Eurasian Land Bridge signifies a road of peace and shared prosperity.

A Factor of Promotion in Relationship

The Eurasian Land Bridge will foster international cooperation and level up the transit tariffs which are different between countries, as the rates remain unstable, there being many taxes and incidental expenses.[9] In order to overcome this hurdle, the leaders of China visited Central Asia and Russia a number of times.

China has made it known that it is important to strengthen the communication of international economy and technology, impel the economy to recover and foster prosperity. Moreover, China has noticed the European community's promotion of an "Eastern strategy" to develop partnership relationships with Asia. The development of the main axes of traffic, through large projects for infrastructure in transport, energy, water and communication will be the groundwork for the industrial development of the Eurasian land mass. And by this process the relations among the Eurasian countries will be improved.

Destroying the Drug Route

International efforts to revive the old Silk Route connecting China and Central Asia with Europe can also be used as a means of drug trafficking. The International Narcotics Control Board is concerned about the rapid spread of illicit crop cultivation and the trafficking and abuse of drugs, especially heroin, in the countries of Central Asia (Kazakhstan, Kyrgyzstan, Tajikistan, Turkmenistan and Uzbekistan) and the Caucasus (Armenia, Azerbaijan and Georgia).[10] In view of the overall rise in criminal activities in Central Asia and Caucasus, there is need for adequate resources to deal with the problem of drug abuse and illicit drug trafficking.

The opiates originating in Afghanistan are smuggled through Central Asia. The largest share of these drugs is transported through Iran and Turkey or from Pakistan to Iran and to other countries in the Persian Gulf area before being sent to its final destination. Turkey continues to be the major transit point for heroin destined for Europe.[11] The Caspian Sea is increasingly being used to trans-ship larger amounts of both opiates and cannabis from Afghanistan through Turkmenistan to the Russian Federation and other countries in Europe.[12]

"Drug traffickers have taken advantage of the absence of control on the borders between CIS member states and transportation links established in West Asia, especially in Central Asia. It has been reported that heroin with a high purity level, smuggled via Central Asian countries and the Russian Federation, has been introduced on the illicit market in a number of European countries".[13] The scenario described in those lines characterises the drug trail of which the famous New Silk Route is very much an important part. The Taliban, who had warm relations with Turkmenistan used this opportunity to transport the contraband stuff to the Caspian region and beyond. President Rakhmanov disclosed at a conference on drugs in 1998 that at any moment 2,000 tons of narcotics were ready to be transported across Central Asia for European and other markets.[14] The state of the borders in Central Asia is instable, allowing the transit of drugs, arms and other contraband items to various parts of Asia and Europe.

Grand Design for Peace and Development

The integrated infrastructure programs of the Eurasian Land Bridge connects the industrial centers of Europe and Asia. The development of the main axes of traffic is the precondition for the grand infrastructure project in transport, energy, water and communications. The groundwork of this project will be the main factor in the industrial development of the Eurasian land mass. The economic cooperation, in the interests of all participating nations, can mean the basis for peace building tasks in the 21st Century.

The Eurasian Land Bridge network of high-speed trains for transport of persons and goods connects most of the sixty big cities with each other.[15] This infrastructural integration will mean an enormous increase in the economic efficiency of the connected economic area along the Eurasian Land Bridge. The construction of new ports within the project of reviving the Silk Route will lay the foundation for a dramatic expansion of maritime trade.

The idea of building a tunnel between Japan and Russia to the Sakhalin Island, the integration of the South-North Korean railway with the Siberian railway to have the Siberian railway open up the northern regions of Russia which are a tremendous wealth of raw materials, could lead to the development of the entire continent.[16] The Chinese government is now moving very fast in the direction of connecting the Old Silk Route with the European and Middle Eastern regions.

Promoting India–China–Russia: Tripartite Cooperation

The opening of the new Eurasian Land Bridge and the old Silk Road trade routes can provide new opportunities for cooperation between India, China, and Russia. In the grim situation facing the world today when the United States has turned into a new imperial power by unleashing a war on Iraq to gain control of its oil wealth, the Eurasian vision of cooperation is the only hope for the world to overcome the crisis into which it has been plunged by the international speculative financial capital of a unipolar world order.[17]

The triangle is based on peaceful cooperation among the three great powers – India and China the two powers of Asia, together with the Eurasian power, Russia. These powerful states are constituting the keystone of the future multipolar world. This triangle is not conceived by its advocates in Moscow, Beijing and New Delhi as a military alliance or a power bloc, but an alliance for peaceful cooperation among the three great powers.

In 1998, during his visit to India, the Russian Prime Minister, Yevgeni Primakov, casually made a suggestion for a Russia-China-India strategic triangle. The idea of such a triangle had surfaced much earlier, in 1938, August 21, when Jawaharlal Nehru, in an article, "Why India should support China", called for united action by the national freedom movements in the two countries, and cited the example of the Soviet Union which had "definitely discarded imperialism".[18]

India has the best of relations with Russia and is working to improve relations with China. India and China appear to have taken a strategic decision to transform their troubled relations. This is evident from two agreements signed by the leaders of the two sides. The memorandum on border trade signed by the Chinese Commerce Minister Lu Fuyuan and India's External Affairs Minister Yeshwant Sinha shows that China has decided to recognize the accession of Sikkim to India.[19] China also agreed to reopen the Old Silk Route, the route through Sikkim's Nathu La pass having the shortest distance between India and China.[20]

Prime Minister A.B. Vajpayee did pick up the threads again during his visit to China in 2003, and opened the doors for a more purposeful negotiation on the boundary dispute and an approach to future economic cooperation.[21] Before his departure, Vajpayee told the press that in view of the dramatic changes in the world in recent years "two of the world's largest and most populous developing countries, India and China, should remain in close touch on global issues of concern to developing countries".[22] A decision was taken to open border trade through the Nathu La pass in Sikkim, which amounts, to a kind of revival of the ancient Silk Route.

The mega project of the Silk Route revival, such as constructing a land-bridge across Eurasia alone is the axis or the hub of the creation of the Russia-China-India strategic triangle. There are two important areas of increased economic cooperation between the three countries: first, the management of economic governance; second, the management of energy security.[23]

New Silk Route as a Factor in Energy Security for India and China

India and China are energy deficient countries. Both have started tapping the Russian, Iranian and Central Asian energy sources. Energy experts in India have pointed out that the easiest and cheapest alignments of pipelines are by or along the existing railway lines, roads and river beds in the region. Some possible routes include[24]:

(a) West Siberia — Tyumen — Omsk — Semay — Druzhba —Urumchi—Kuqua—Aksu—Kashgar—Yarkand—Shahidullah—India.

(b) West Siberia — Tyumen — Petropavlovsk — Astan — Karganda — Bishkek — Issykkul — Naryn — Kashagar — India.
(c) North Siberia — Tomsk — Novosibirsk — Barnaul — Semeny on to Kashgar and India.
(d) Iran — Baluchistan — Sindh — India.

Several other routes have been suggested linking Central Asia and Iranian gas to Russia, China and onward to India. Various routes have been suggested such as Shahidulla in Xinjiang, to India; routes via the Karakoram pass and Khardung-la to Leh; via Aksai Chin and the Xinjiang-Tibet road up to Tashigang and then down to the Indus Valley from Demchok to Leh; from western Tibet to India along the river Satlaj.[25] Rail or road links to connect India with the CARs by the most viable route of Jammu and Kashmir is very important for the revival of the Silk Route. It is possible for China to transport oil from West Asian sources piped straight from Indian ports into China along these very routes. That is, gas coming from Central Asian and Caspian regions through China into India, and oil coming from West Asia through India to China. This kind of cooperation in the energy sector can provide the necessary security in the field of energy for both nations.

The revived Silk Route can also help create popular and economic foundations for closer relations between India and China. Economic cooperation is necessary to create a popular base. As the experience of the European Union shows, popular support for regional cooperation can be built on the foundations of tangible economic and cultural projects. Energy security can be one such area of bilateral cooperation.

Factor in Modernization of Central Asia

The twenty-first century version of the traditional Silk Route – a road on which for centuries our forefathers traveled with goods and ideas – is a factor in the modernization of Central Asia. The restoration of the Silk Route offers opportunities not only for trade and economic cooperation with Central Asia, but also for the interchange of modern ideas and values. Presently the Central Asian states are in the transitional period of their social and political development.[26] At the same time, these states are accepting the western European model of modernization based on western values such as democracy, market economy and the principle of the supremacy of law.

The new Silk Route will integrate the Central Asian states – Kazakhstan, Kyrgyzstan, Tajikistan and Turkmenistan – with the world transport system. This is necessary for their socio-economic, political and cultural development as well as their independence.[27] The Central Asian States do not have direct and stable accesses to world transport networks and through them to world markets. The states need economically effective and safe exits for their natural resources to world markets. Presently they are not able to produce exportable goods and the essential source for their foreign currency revenues continues to be the sale of their natural resources (oil, gas, cotton etc.) and taxes for transportation through their territory.

The restoration of the Silk Route will thus be beneficial for the development of regional cooperation among the Central Asian states. The lack of effective transport routes and relative isolation has made it difficult for all the five republics to access international markets in the heels of their independence in 1991. The rebirth of the Silk Route and its traditions in trade and business, as well as information and exchange of ideas will increase regional cooperation among Central Asian states, leading to the modernization of the peoples of Central Asia.

Land Bridge for Global Trade

After the disintegration of the Soviet Union the international situation has witnessed some new characteristics. Globalization is erasing boundaries and building networks between nations and peoples, economics and cultures. In international relations, while the role of ideology and the military have been on the decrease, the significance of the economic factor is on the increase. Economic globalization and regional economic cooperation have gathered further momentum. President Jiang Zemin of China said that[28] "We need an 'all-win' economic globalization in which all countries, North or South big or small, are all beneficiaries; we need an economic globalization in which all countries can participate as equal members".

The Eurasian Continental Bridge starting from Lianyungang and Rizhoo port in China, terminating in Rotterdam, the Netherlands, has a total length of 10,900 kilometers across Europe and Asia.[29] This is a giant international corridor. To the east, it links up Northeast Asia and Southeast Asia, through the numerous seaports in China and can further connect with the western coastal cities; to the west after track-transfer at the Alataw pass, in Xinjiang, it joins the Central Asian railway network at the border station in Kazakhstan, extends farther westward to Aktogay, and from there, via three routes, namely, the northern, the middle and the southern, can join the European railway networks and reach Europe:[30]

The Northern Route: connecting Aktogay in Kazakhstan, or Bishkek in Uzbekistan, northward by the Siberian railway and onward to West Europe and North Europe.[31]

The Middle Route: starting from Kazakhstan via Russia, Belarus, Ukraine, Slovakia, Hungary, Austria, Switzerland, can trans-ship from Germany and France to the ports of the English Channel. Or it can go south from Aktogay, Kazakhstan, along the border of Kyrgyzstan, through Tashkent, Uzbekistan and Ashkhabad, Turkmenistan, west to Krasnovodsk, via the Caspian Sea to Baku, Azerbaijan, then to Tbilisi, Georgia, the Black Sea, Verna in Bulgaria, Romania, Hungary, thus reaching the Central European countries.[32]

The Southern Route: starting from Ashkhabad, Turkmenistan, south down into Iran, then from Mashhad go west via Tehran, Tabriz, to Turkey, through the Straits of the Bosphorus, and via Bulgaria and Yugoslavia, reach Central Europe, West Europe, and South Europe.[33]

An important characteristic of the region of the new Eurasian Land Bridge is that it links east and west, the Pacific and Atlantic economic centers, which belong to the developed region, but lack space capacity and natural resources. Thus the Eurasian Land Bridge has a very strong feature of inter-dependence and mutual advantage.

The Land Bridge is important for the promotion of global trade.[34] The building up the infrastructure of the Bridge will take time and investment, but will be justified as the trade benefits all the countries on a global level. The new world economic order, based upon the Bridge has immense scope for trade expansion. It has not any national boundary and other barriers for global trade. It lays the bases for an international trading system.

Implications of the Eurasian Land Bridge

Some progress on the Eurasian Land Bridge as a means of connecting Central Asian markets with world markets has been made at practical levels. Over the past ten years, the United States, the European Union and China have emphasized the important role of the countries of the Caucasuses and Central Asia in the development of East-West energy and transport routes, linking Central and South Asia with Europe. The World Bank is joining the international effort to revive the old Silk Route connecting China and Central Asia with Europe.

The Eurasian Land Bridge has favorable long-term consequences for all countries located in the Great Silk Road region[35]. The implication of the New Silk Road as a Eurasian Land Bridge is making it possible to create all the necessary conditions for the transformation of the region into an area of stability, security, friendship, cooperation and equitable partnership.

Present Situation: Prospects from the Trans-Siberian Railway

Building up a dense infrastructure development corridor along the Trans-Siberian Railroad and certain parallel east-west routes, including the Baikal-Amur Mainline are also among the keys to the economic future of Eurasia. The implication of the Trans-Siberian Corridor is as follows:

(a) The Russians constructed 3,377 km of railway line and 14 railway repair workshops and depots in their time.[36] Now the Trans-Siberian Railroad constitutes the Asian section of the Eurasian Land Bridge, the 11,200 kms long Northern route connecting the Atlantic Coast of Europe with the Pacific Coast of Asia.[37] For many years, the Trans-Siberian Railroad has been a major shipment route for goods between Japan and the Northern Pacific region (including Korea), and Europe. Improvements in technical quality and logistical organization of the Trans-Siberian line, already planned, can greatly increase the competitive advantages of this vis-à-vis the much longer sea route between Japan and Europe, especially for higher-value goods. Even after the completion of the Southern Route from China to Europe, the Trans-Siberian Corridor remains a key transit route from Japan, Northern China, and the Korean Peninsula, via the Vladivostok, Chit-Harbin, and Ulan-Ude-Ulaanbaator-Beijing connections.[38]

b) The Baikal-Amur-Mainline and other lines connected to Trans-Siberian Railroad open up access to gigantic reserves of every raw material required by modern societies – oil, gas, coal and other metals and minerals.

The transformation of the Trans-Siberian Railroad will lead to the development of the Eurasian Land Bridge Corridor. The projects drawn up during the Soviet period have been reviewed and modernized by the American engineer Hal Copper, together with two colleagues from the far Eastern city of Yakustsk.[39] They link the rail projects with the tapping of the rich petroleum reserves in the Far East, including Sakhalin Island.[40] This is a network of gas and oil pipelines with the rail lines, which has extended to North Korea and South Korea, China, and on to Japan.

On 1st January 2001 the first electric train ran along the newly electrified section of the Trans-Siberian railway.[41] The length of the electrified section of Russia's main railway was extended by 83km, up to the Guberovo station in Maritime Territory. The remaining 270 kms long section in Guberovo to Sibertsevo is yet to be electrified.[42] The head of the Far Eastern railway has stated "we will complete the electrification of the Trans-Siberian railway from Moscow to Vladivostok and it will be fully electrified for the first time in the history of railway transport".[43]

The electrification of the Trans-Siberian railway is a major project of the 21st century. An agreement has been reached on restoring the railway connection between the Democratic People's Republic of Korea and the Republic of Korea. The Tran-Siberian railway will stretch to the port of Pusan, South Korea, and will become the most important transport bridge linking Europe and Asia.

Sakhalin Rail Tunnel

One other center of gravity of international energy cooperation is the ongoing project for tapping the offshore gas and oil fields of Russia's Sakhalin island, in the Sea of Okhotsk, whose proximity to Japan and other markets in the Pacific makes such a project especially attractive. There are seven projects for the exploitation of natural gas and oil around Sakhalin.[44] On investment of $ 25-45billion on the transport and production infrastructure of the island is planned for the coming years. The connection to Japan would be provided by a north-south railroad on Sakhalin together with a 50-kilometer under-sea tunnel to Japan's Hokkaido Island.[45] The rail connection from Hokkaido to Japan's biggest island, Honshu, is already provided by the 54 kms long Seikan Tunnel, the longest on the world.

In 1999, the first crude oil flowed from the Sakhalin-2' project.[46] Cargo in containers is carried mostly between Asia-Pacific countries and European countries. The construction of tunnels and bridges to link the continent with Japan via Sakhalin started from 2001. The Railway Ministry's experts of Japan believe that a railway connecting Tokyo with London will become a reality in the 21st century.[47]

The Russian Railway Minister Nikolay Aksenko told ITAR-TASS in Berlin that the construction project of Sakhalin Bridge Tunnel had been approved by the Russian president.[48] The project is of strategic importance for Russia as a bridge connecting East and West, the Minister added. The tunnel will enable the opening of passenger and freight railway traffic to Tokyo from Amsterdam. It would mean a revolution in trade and development in the entire Pacific region, which is to be the centre of the coming times.

Development of the Tumen Region

This area, of approximately 10,000 square kilometers, is situated at the mouth of the Tumen River in the border region of Russia, China and North Korea.[49] It is the most interesting development area pertaining to the Northern Eurasian Land Bridge. The general area is delimited by the Russia port city Vladivostok, which is the terminal of the Trans-Siberian railway, together with the Chinese city of Yanji and the North Korean coastal city of Chongjin.[50]

One of the key projects here is the construction of an improved railway line linking the port cities of Najin in North Korean and Posyet in Russia, via the Chinese network through Manchuria and the Hingan mountain range.[51] This would shorten the rail distance from Vladivostok harbor to Europe over the Northern Route by 1,700 kilometers.[52]

The Tumen River Economic Zone is destined to become a crucial hub for rail and oil and gas pipeline connections between North and South Korea, northern China and Russia. It forms, in a sense, the junction between the northern and southern sectors of the Eurasian Land Bridge. Already, the futures trade between the regions surrounding the Sea of Japan is sufficient to make this one of the busiest port areas of the world.

Transport Corridor Europe–Caucasus–Asia (TRACECA) Project

The President of Azerbaijan and Georgia with the support of the European Union hosted an international conference, "Restoration of the Historic Silk Route" on 8th September, 1998 in Baku, Azerbaijan.[53] The participants emphasized the importance of the revival of the Silk Route and appreciated the contribution to that end by the TRACECA project, implemented within the European Union's TRACIS (Transportation in Commonwealth Independent States) programme as the Eurasian Land Bridge. At the end of the conference the communiqué of the conference, was titled the "Baku Declaration", which foresaw further international cooperation for the development of TRACECA.[54]

The Interstate Oil and Gas Transport to Europe (INOGATE) programme was designed to create opportunities to exploit and export energy which would promote economy development and political independence. Under this programme, € 50 million were allocated for 1996-1999 to implement the following projects:

- The rehabilitation, expansion and modernization of regional gas transmission systems and of supply for oil and oil products.
- The assessment of the prospects for enhancing the transport of hydrocarbons from the Caspian Basin and Central Asia to European markets.
- The transfer of the know-how needed to ensure conformity with international standards.
- The feasibility of alternative routes, notably, new routes across the Caspian Sea.[55]

These initiatives represent a policy of creating a regional balance of power that would prevent the establishment of hegemonic control by any outside or local state.

By 1998, the EU had already spent $ 75 million on TRACECA projects, and was soliciting another $ 300 million in loans. Additional funds were pledged by the European Bank for Reconstruction and Development (EBRD).[56] In a further step to extend the TRACECA project, the European Union approved a new seven year program with a price tag of € 3,138.39 million in December 1999.[57] The TRACECA project was of strategic importance for the Central Asian countries and Caucasus region, said the Deputy Minister of Kazakhstan.[58]

The TRACECA project's objective is to create conditions facilitating shipments of oil, petrol products and cotton to Europe by introducing standardized documents, customs procedures, machinery types, etc.

New Silk Road Initiative between Xinjiang and Eurasia

The Chinese government is expanding, constructing, exploiting and utilizing the new Euro-Asian Bridge for developing cooperation between Asia and Europe. In 1999, the Chinese government announced big plans to develop the economically less developed western region. Beijing plans to spend 100 billion yuan over the next few years on infra-structure, energy development and pipelines.[59]

In May 1999, in the western Chinese province of Xinjiang, a new 1,451 km long railroad was completed from Turpan on the mainline of the Eurasian land bridge, along the northern edge of the Takla Makan desert to the legendary "Silk Road" outpost of Kashi (Kashgar), the westernmost major city of china.[60]

The western development project relates to China's opening of border trade and investments between Xinjiang and Eurasia. Kyrgyzstan approved on November 13, 2002 the Bishkek-Naryan-Torugart railway route to link with Kashgar between Central Asia and China.[61] The new rail line will link the Ferghana valley to Xinjiang, and make possible direct rail links between Uzbekistan, Kyrgyzstan and China. President Askar Akayev signed a law on priority treatment to the project of building the Balykchi-Dzhalal-Abad-Torugart railway line, which would give access to China.[62]

The document was the final plan for the construction of the Kyrgyz section of the Europe-Asia transport corridor, the Kyrgyz Transport Minister said. The Minister presented the project to officials of the organizations involved – TACTS, the World Bank, the European Bank for Reconstruction and Development and the Asian Development Bank.[63] The opening up of the Trans-Eurasian railroad through Central Asia in 1990 and the linking of Almaty and Urumchi by railroad in 1992 ensured a long term role for China in Central Asia.[64] A joint Central Asian-Chinese initiative of reviving the Silk Road has also brought a dramatic change in the Sino-Central Asian frontiers. The most ambitious plan of cooperation between China and Central Asia is the proposed construction of a pipeline that would carry Central Asian oil to China. "If the Chinese build a pipeline, Central Asia's importance to China will shift immeasurably in the 21st century, as will Chinese military attitudes towards safeguarding their strategic oil reserves".[65] In 1994, sixtenn Silk Route countries signed the Samarkand declaration on Silk Road tourism.[66] The signatories agreed to help stimulate travel and business by updating and improving accommodation, transportation and other travel services along the route. All these development activities and initiatives clearly indicate the great potential for economic development and co-operation between Xinjiang and Eurasia.

The new initiative of the Chinese government, called the policy of the "New Silk Route" in reference to the ancient trade routes between east and west or "the Eurasian Land Bridge" has opened various dimensions for the restoration of the Silk Route. The Eurasian Land Bridge has been constructed from Lian-Yan-Gang to Rotterdam. The revival of Trans-Siberian Railways, the extension of the Karakorum highway, the opening of the North-South corridor from Finland to the Islamic Republic of Iran as Euro-Asian Transport, the construction of Gwadar port, the opening of the Sakhalin Rail-Tunnel between the Japan and Russia, the development of the Tuman-Region and the Transport Corridor Europe-Caucasuses-Asia (TRACECA) project are the main constituents of the Eurasian Land Bridge as the New Silk Route.

North-South Corridor for International Transport

The North-South sail ship corridor was discussed in the Euro-Asian Transport Conference at St. Petersburg, Russia on September 12-

13, 2000. This corridor which goes from Northern Europe to Russia, crosses the Caspian Sea to Iran, and via Iran's southern ports across the Arabian Sea to India.[67] At this conference, the transport ministers of Russia, Iran and India signed a historic agreement for the development of a highway-efficient north-south transport corridor, which would raise the level of economic cooperation between these three nations to a new height.[68] The agreement establishes a combined land-sea corridor.

First of all, freight will be transported from the western ports of India by ship to the Iranian port of Bander-e-Abbas, and there after via rail road lines to Bander-e-Anzali on the Caspian Sea. From Bander-e-Anzali the ship route goes to the Great Russian port of Astrakhan, and then by railroad or truck to destination points in Russia, further on to Europe.[69] The North-South Corridor is useful for transport between northern Europe and India, as an alternative to the usual sea route. Thus the long detour through the Suez Canal is eliminated, shortening transportation times considerably. Transport costs could be reduced by 20-25 percent or more.[70]

The international agreement on the transport along the North-South corridor, between Russia, India and Iran has been signed by Belarus, Kazakhstan, Oman, Tajikistan, Syria, Armenia, Azerbaijan and Bulgaria.[71] In 2002, a total of 7 million tons of freight was transported through the Russian ports via the North-South corridor, while in 2003 the figure increased up to 8 million tons.[72] Russia also hopes that the connecting of four Pan-Eurasian transport corridors with the North-South corridor would ensure the further development of the corridor.

A Trans-Asian Railway network in the North-South corridor of routes between Europe and the Persian Gulf with onward connections to South and South-East Asia was identified by the participating railway organizations on the basis of the three core routes. These three routes have been defined as follows:[73]

- Route I, the Caucasus route,
- Route II, the Central Asian route, and
- Route III, the Caspian Sea route.

The Caucasus Route

The Caucasus Route connects Finland with the Islamic Republic of Iran through the territories of Armenia, Azerbaijan and the Russian Federation. In Finland, the route originates in the port of Helsinki and goes to Vainikkala (283 km), the border station between the Finnish Rail Administration and the Russian Railways at Buslovskaya. From there it goes 3,221 kms to Samur at the border between the Russian Federation and Azerbaijan. After Samur the route joins Azerbaijan's rail system at Yalama and continues to Baku and Osmanly Novaya. It runs about 50 kilometers in Armenia and at Djulfa the route connects with the Iranian Railways. From Djulfa, the Caucasus route covers a distance of 882 km to Teheran through Tabriz, Maraghah, Zanjan and Qazvin. From Teheran it goes south to the port of Bandar Abbas over another 1,443 km passing through Qum, Meybod and Bafq.

The Central Asian Route

The Central Asian Route connects Finland with Iran through the territories of Kazakhstan, the Russian Federation, Turkmenistan and Uzbekistan. From Finland the route connects with the railways of the Russian Federation at Buslovskaya. From there it covers the distance of 2,513 km to Akrarayskaya through Saint Petersburg, Bologoye, Moscow, Kochetkovka, Rtishevo, Saratov and Volgograd. At Aksarayskaya the route junctions off eastward and covers around 85 km. to connect with the railways of Kazakhstan at Ganushkino. From Ganushkino the route goes through Makat and Beyneu and travels further south to the Kazak-Uzbek border.

Exiting the territory of Kazakhstan, the Central Asian route connects with the Uzbekistan Railway at Karakalpakia, from where the route continues south to Pitnyak over a distance of 593 kilometers. Exiting the territory of Uzbekistan, the route connects with the Turkmenistan railway at Taxiatash from where it continues south to Chardjou, Merv and Sarakhs at the border with Iran over a distance of 1,002 kilometers.

After Sarakhs the route leaves Turkmenistan and connects with the Iranian Railways through the Sarakh-Mashad section. From Mashad the route continues over 926 kilometers to Tehran through Azadvar, Sharood and Garmsar, and from Tehran, it goes south to Bandar Abbas through Qom, Meybod and Bafq over a distance of 1,443 kilometers. The total length of the route works out to 7,549 kilometers.

The Caspian Sea Route

The Caspian Sea Route connects with the railways of the Russian Federation at Buslovskaya from Helsinki. From Buslovskaya it covers a distance of 2,513 km to Aksaraykaya through Saint Petersburg, Bologoya, Moscow, Kochetkovka, Rtishevo, Saratov and Volgogard, and from Aksarakaya, it continues over 49 kilometers to the port of Astrakhan, Russia's main port on the Caspian Sea.

There is no rail connection to the main lines of the Iranian Railways. Only Bandar-e-Anzali stands a chance of being a rail connection some time in the future as it is located on the Astara-Qazvin section that the Iranian Railways has marked for construction on its general development plan. Road movement is necessary between the port and the nearest railheads, i.e. Qazvin for the port of Bandar-e-Anzali (around 210 km) and Tehran for the port of Noshahr (around 250 km).

All the three routes have two common sections. In the north a common section of 2,800 kilometers connects Helsinki (Finland) with Aksarayskaya station (Russian Federation). At Aksarayskaya, the routes branch off in different directions to go to Iran through (a) Armenia and Azerbaijan, (b) Central Asian Republics, or (c) the ports of the Caspian Sea.[74] In the south, a common section of around 1,450 kilometers located on the Iranian Islamic Republic Railways connects Tehran with the port of Bandar Abbas.[75]

Ultimately, the corridors can also facilitate the transportation of cargo destined for countries in South Asia, particularly India and Pakistan. Connections to countries in South Asia could be by rail or shipping. There are two alternatives to the corridors' continuation to India. The first and existing alternative is to use shipping services between Bandar Abbas and Mumbai port, which handles over 60 per cent of India's container traffic.[76] The other alternative is to depend on the completion of the Kerman–Zahedan line, to direct cargo to Mirjaveh and then on through Pakistan Railways to connect with India's rail system at Attari at the border between Pakistan and India.[77] These options can work effectively only after all railway systems in any given corridor implement track access agreements and charges.

Before such a development plan can be finalized, it is necessary to:

(i) Formalize a designated network for the Trans-Asian Railway in the North-South corridor between Northern Europe and the Persian Gulf;

(ii) Define the fundamental and operational priorities for the TAR in this corridor;

(iii) Agree on a follow-up plan of action for the resolution of information gaps, more detailed evaluation of the new lines construction programme, the formulation of suitable operational and commercial strategies and plans for the existing components of the corridor.

Given its geographical location, the corridor has the potential to serve a number of regions of which the most obvious are the Scandinavian countries, the countries of Central and Eastern Europe as well as the Central Asian countries. It may also attract traffic from regions east of the Ural mountains in the Russian Federation by providing import and export routes for goods between these regions and South and South-East Asia. In terms of market to the corridor could actually either compete with shipping, or provide shipping lines with the possibility to carry their containers from major ports in Europe (Bremerhaven, Hamburg, Helsinki, and Saint Petersburg) to hinterland places in the Russian Federation, the Caucasus region or Central Asia. It is important that the fundamental role and operational priorities for the TAR network in the North-South corridor be defined in terms of its advantages in satisfying international as well as sub-regional transport demands.

Reopening the Traditional Silk Route through the Nathula Pass

India and China have decided to launch a bold political initiative to break the impasse over the boundary dispute and have shown their readiness to seek a mutually acceptable solution. Bilateral relations improved further during Prime Minister Atal Behari Vajpayee's visit of China in June 2003.[78] A memorandum on border trade signed by the Chinese Commerce Minister Lu Fuyuan and External Affairs Minister Yashwant Sinha. The memorandum's preamble clearly notes that the two countries agree on the "opening of Nathula Pass in the Sikkim State on the India-China border"[79] for trade.

This trade route through Sikkim's Nathula Pass is the shortest distance between India and China. It is an all-weather pass situated at a height of 14,500 ft. It was closed after the Sino-Indian conflict in 1962. The reopening of this pass implies the revival of the ancient Silk Route over which the famed Chinese fabric was traditionally brought to India, to be traded for goods from the subcontinent.

From Nathula, Lhasa, Tibet's capital, is 416 km, the Tibetan trading station of Yatung is 21 km and the Chumbitang settlement only 9 km down the road into the Chumbi Vally, bound by the great peaks of Paunhuri and Chomolhar. In addition, Delhi is 1,785 km and Srinagar 2,595 km from the Pass.[80] This trans-frontier economic cooperation will restore historic trading routes, access roads and pilgrimage rights, and will create a new framework.

New Horizons About the Revival of the Silk Route

The volume of transportation on the Eurasian Land Bridge has progressively increased. Many projects have already begun. China has also set up an institution to coordinate work with other countries along the Bridge.[81] The institution's objective is to develop cooperation on joint transportation. Mongolia and Russia have already begun to coordinate their ventures with this institution.

To secure the required high-level coordination, it is important to set up a dedicated working group for the corridor consisting of senior professionals taken from within the railways as well as from outside. The tasks of the working groups will be to plan, organize and monitor activities as regards the technical, institutional and commercial aspects relating to the land bridge development. However, it is important to lay down the framework under which the progress of implementation has to be reported and milestone decisions approved. A coordinating council in charge of the corridor's development might provide such a framework.

India, China and Russia are the major powers of the Eurasian continent, and the main players in the sharing of the oil and natural resources of Central Asia via the various transportation routes. These three powerful states constitute the keystone of the future multipolar world. The opening of the new Eurasian Land Bridge can provide new opportunities for cooperation between India, China and Russia. The mega project of New Silk Route is the hub of the creation of the India-China-Russia strategic triangle for the cooperation and management of energy security.

Energy is an important source of revenue, particularly of hard currency for the Central Asian Republics. Energy resources have now assumed political significance for the Central Asian Republics because of their peculiar geographical location and uneven distribution over the Caspian region. During the last 15 years differences have surfaced among the energy rich countries of this region on issues such as the legal status of the Caspian, conflicting claims about the ownership of oil fields located on border regions, the building of the pipeline network for exporting oil and gas to world markets, the construction of railways and so on. Efforts have been made to resolve some of these issues and there seems to be some success on a few issues.

There is conflict among the Central Asian and Caucasian countries about their share and control over the oil and gas fields. These countries are trying to maximize their own share and increase economic benefits. Russia, being self-sufficient in energy, seems to be mainly interested in increasing its political influence over the region and has often used the energy resources of the Central Asian and Caucasian states as a means to enhance and regain its big power status. Russia wants to stop the growing American influence in the region and has made common cause in this regard with China.

Within the Central Asian and Caspian countries, the interests of the advanced industrial democracies such as the United States, Japan and Western Europe are both complementary and competitive. These countries share an interest in the political stability of the region because of its strategic importance and hydrocarbon wealth. From the perspective of these industrialized countries, the Caspian and Central Asian states are perceived as energy exporters, as importers of western products and as targets of investment.

The USA has its own geo-political and economic objectives in the Central Asian region in fighting international terrorism and also containing Russian influence. 9/11 has made some impact on the Central Asian region as it led to the US presence in several Central Asian and Caucasian countries here. On the issue of the possible routes for the transportation of oil and gas, the USA and other western European countries prefer pipelines that bypass the territory of Russia and Iran via Azerbaijan, Georgia and Turkey.

Consideration is given to supplying Turkmenian gas by the same route or via Afghanistan.

American interest in Central Asia and Trans-Caucasia has been best expressed by Zbigniew Brzezinski in his book *The Grand Chessboard: American Primacy and its Geostrategic Imperatives (1997)*. America's major interest lies in not allowing the rise of any other power with aspirations and capabilities to compete with the U.S. In the opinion of the US strategists, there are not many effective contestants for power and influence in Eurasia. Britain, China, Japan, Turkey, Iran, South Korea, Pakistan, Afghanistan, India do have interest in carving out their spheres of influence in Central Asia through the revival of the Silk Route, but with the exception of China none is a serious competitor of the United Sates.

The World Bank is joining an international effort to revive the old Silk Route connecting China and Central Asia with Europe. The East-West road link from Baku through Alyat to the Georgian border is one of the main access routes for goods to and from Azerbaijan, and this is supported by the European Union's TRACECA as a main link in the proposed revival of the Silk Route. A strong institution responsible for road planning and management, and adequate budgetary resources for road maintenance are key requirements at this juncture for the revival of the Silk Route project.

An agreement for the development of a highly efficient North-South transport corridor was signed by the transport ministers of Russia, Iran and India on September 12, 2000 at St. Petersburg,[82] seeking to raise economic cooperation between these three nations to a new level. The agreement establishes a combined land-sea corridor, by which freight from India to Russia will be transported from the western port of India by ship to the Iranian port of Bander-e-Abbas, and thereafter via the railroad lines to Bander-e-Anzali on the Caspian sea. From Bander-e-Anzali, the ship route goes to the great Russian port of Astrakhan, and then by railroad or truck to destination points in Russia, or further on to Europe. This North-South transport corridor in itself is not new, but coincides with the traditional "Sea Route" from India. The implication of the North-South corridor is a big step in the old Silk Route's revival in the century of globalization.

The construction of Gwadar deep sea port and Karakorum Highway are two important constituents of the revival of the Silk

Route in South Asia. The Gwadar port will provide a stable and proximate point of access to the Gulf ports. India and Iran have warily watched the construction of this port in their backyard. The port would endanger Indian naval security. At the same time it can be fruitful for the economic uplift of Pakistan. The simultaneous extension of Karakorum Highway provides good communication linkage between Central and South Asia. It is, therefore, imperative that a proper environment of cooperation is established in South Asia.

Paradoxically, the initiatives taken by Pakistan for promoting trade and commercial relations with China and the Central Asian states via the Karakorum Highway are facing difficulties for two reasons. Firstly, there has been no proper follow up after the understanding reached or the agreement signed to develop communication linkage with these countries. For instance the trade and transit agreement between Pakistan, China, Kazakhstan and Kyrgyzstan is yet to be implemented. Secondly, political instability in Pakistan acts as a stumbling block to give practical shape to the idea of building communication linkages with these countries.

The first of these involves the intensification of the process of inter-dependence and globalization, the introduction of the latest technologies, their phenomenal, rapidly developing communication systems and computer network and the acceleration of information and capital flows that erode national boundaries. The second trend reflects the high level of integration at sub-regional levels. The current steady and dynamic development of political, trade and economic relations would be unthinkable without the strengthening of fraternal trust and mutually advantageous relations of partnership between all states of the Silk Route region.

However, there are some obstacles in the way of the restoration of the Silk Route. Russia and Iran insist upon the other states acceptance of the itinerary offered by them. Another problem is that some states, such as the participants of the TRACECA programme are in armed conflict with each other. The solution of these problems as well as the restoration of the Silk Route require the participant countries to carry out their obligations towards the development of the Europe-Caucasus-Asia transport corridor.

The restoration of the Silk Route is a mean for strengthening the independence of Central Asian Republics. It is a key to the solution of their socio-economic, political and cultural problems.

It would promote the development of regional cooperation within Central Asia and Europe as well. It could be the mean for strengthen the economic, political and cultural relations of India with China and other neighbour countries if the old route from Jammu & Kashmir to China and Central Asia will reopen with modern technology. On the eve of the third millennium, the idea of the revival of the Silk Route has met with broad international support and an extremely warm response, largely as a result of the existence of the inter-dependent trends that characterize the development of the modern world.

NOTES

1. Michael C. Evans, 'Europe's Strategic Role in the Caucasus and the Black Sea', *Strategic Review*, 27, no. 2, spring 1999, pp. 4 – 10.
2. Jonathan Tennenbaum, 'The Eurasian Land-Bridge. The 'New Silk Road' – Locomotive for Worldwide Economic Development', *Executive Intelligence Review – Special Report*, (Washington D.C., January, 1997), p. 116.
3. R. Hrair Dekmejian and Hovann H. Simonian, *Troubled Waters the Geopolitics of the Caspian Region*, (London, New York: I.B. Tauris Publishers, 2001), p. 121.
4. Vijay Kapur, 'A Afghanistan And Central Asia: Differentiated Challenges and Priorities in the Twenty First Century' in K. Warikoo (ed), *Himalyan and Central Asian Studies*, vol. 8 Nos. 2-3, April-Sept. 2004, (New Delhi), p. 12.
5. 'Japanese Lending Targets Infrastructure Programmes', *Jamestown Foundation Monitor*, 31 October, 1996. (online web) www.silkroadproject.org
6. Jonathan Tennenbaum, n-2, p. 118.
7. *Ibid*, p. 119.
8. James P. Dorian, *Oil and Gas in Russia and the Former Soviet Union*, (London: Financial Times Energy Publishing, 1997), p. 21.
9. Ramtanu Maitra, 'Importance of the Eurasian Land-Bridge for the Central Asian Development', in Shams-ud-Din (ed). *Geopolitics and Energy Resources in Central Asia and Caspian Sea Region*, (New Delhi, Lancer Books, 2000), p. 181.
10. Mahendra Ved, 'Silk Route Turns Destructive Drug Route', *World Focus*, Vol-21, Number 8, August, 2000, New Delhi, p. 10.
11. 'The World Bank Group's Report' Washington, June 12, 2001. (online web) www.washington-report.org
12. BBC, *Summery of World Broadcast*, SUW/0672 WE/4, 5 Jan 2001.

13. Mahendra Ved, n-11, p. 10.
14. BBC *SWB*, SU/3703 G/1, 27 Nov., 99.
15. Jonathan Tennenbaum, n-2, p. 51.
16. Lyndon H. La Rouche, Jr., 'World in Crisis Needs a new Monetary System', *Executive Intelligence Review*, (Washington D.C., December 21, 2001).
17. D. Kaushik, 'The Triangle for Peace and Prosperity', *Contemporary Central Asia*, Vol. 24, Number 10-11-12 Oct.-Nov.-Dec., 2003, New Delhi, p. 48.
18. *Ibid*. p. 44.
19. Manoj Joshi, 'Reality Check on Sikkim, Tibet', *Times of India*, New Delhi, June 25, 2003.
20. *Ibid*.
21. C. Raja Mohan, 'India and China: A Shifting Paradigm', *Hindu*, New Delhi, July 29, 2004.
22. Ramatanu Maitra, 'Vajpayee's Historic Trip Strengthens India-China Ties', *EIR*, vol. 30, no. 26, (Washington D.C., July 4, 2003), p. 42.
23. Sanjaya Baru, 'Economic Cooperation and Globalization – China, India, and Russia Trilateral Cooperation: Some Issues' in *China Report*, 39:3 2003, (New Delhi, Sage Publications, Thousand Oaks/London), p. 367.
24. *Ibid*., p. 368.
25. Moonis Ahmad, 'Communication Linkage between Central and South Asia: A Case Study of Karakoram Highway': *Eurasian Studies*, 20, Special Issue, summer 2001, pp. 194—197.
26. K. Warikoo, n-4, p. 20.
27. Dr. Etibar Najafov, *The Restoration of the Silk Road as a Factor of Modernization*, (Baku Slavic university: Fulbright alumnus, 1998), pp. 1-2.
28. Jiang Zemin, 'Jiang Calls for Fair, Equitable New int'l Economic Order', *China Daily* Sep. 8. 2000.
29. Jonathan Tennenbaum, n-2, p. 40.
30. *Ibid*.
31. *Ibid*.
32. *Ibid*.
33. *Ibid*.
34. Mahavir Singh & Victor Krassilchtchikov (ed.), *Eurasian Vision*, (New Delhi, 2003), p. 105.
35. Askar Akaev, [President of the Kyrgyz Republic], 'Diplomacy of The Silk Road' (online web) www.http://cdf.gov.kg/c-krg-mfp-silkroad.htm
36. R. Pierce, "Russian Central Asia, 1867-1917; A Study of Colonial Rule" (Breaking and Los Angeles, 1960), p. 168.
37. Jonathan Tennenbaum, n-2, p. 168

38. Ramtanu Maitra, n-10, p. 188.
39. Jonathan Tennenbaum, n-2, p. 171.
40. *Ibid*, p. 172.
41. BBC. SUW/0673 WA. 15, 12 Jan 01.
42. *Ibid*.
43. *Ibid*.
44. 'The New Eurasian Land Bridge: Building Our Way Out of the Depression, *Executive Intelligence Report*, (Washington D.C., 2000).
45. Jonathan Tennenbaum, n-2, p. 172.
46. BBC *SWB*, suw/0673 WA/15, 12 Jan, 2001.
47. *Ibid*.
48. BBC *SWB*, SUW/0676WA/14, 2 Feb, 2001.
49. Mahavir Singh & K. Victor (ed.), n-35, pp. 120-121.
50. Jonathan Tennenbaum, n-2, p. 172.
51. The New Eurasian Land-Bridge: Building Our Way out of the Depression *Executive Intelligence Report*, (Washington D.C., 2002).
52. *Ibid*.
53. Jermy Brantsen, 'Azerbaijan: Silk Road, Conference Paves Way for Transport Corridor', *RFE/RL Weekday Magazine*, 4 September, 1998.
54. BBC, *SWB*, SU/D3668/F, 18 October 1999.
55. Rene Leray, 'European Union Policy and Action Toward Central Asia and Caspian Sea Countries', in Dieter Dettke (ed.) *A Great Game No More: Oil Gas and Stability in the Caspian Sea Region*, (Washington, DC: Friedrich-Ebert-Stiftung, 1999), p. 60.
56. Jermy Brantsen, 'Central Asia/Caucasus: Silk Road Conference Agrees on Eurasian Corridor', *RFE/RL, Weekday Magazine*, 9 September, 1998.
57. 'EU/NIS: INOGAATE Summit Opens Energy Umbrella Agreement Over NIS', *European Report*, 24 July 1999.
58. BBC, *SWB*, SU/3701 G/2, 25 Nov. 1999.
59. Sujit Dutta, 'China's Emerging Ties With Central Asia', in Nirmala Joshi (ed), *Central Asia: The Great Game Replayed: An Indian Perspective*, (New Delhi: New Century Pub., 2003), p. 160.
60. 'The New Eurasian Land-Bridge: Building our way out of the Depression', *Executive Intelligence Report*, 2002.
61. Sujit Dutta, n-60, p. 161
62. BBC *SWB*, SUW/0682 WE/3, 16Mar 2001.
63. *Ibid*.
64. Pashkun Dmitry, 'China's Image of Central Asia and It's Policy in the Region' (online web) http://www.depts.washington.edu/reecAS/events, p. 5.
65. Dianne L. Smith, 'Central Asia: A New Great Game?' Part V (online web) http://www.milnet.com

66. K. Warikoo (ed), 'Central Asia: Emerging New Order', (New Delhi: Har-Anand Pub., 1995), p. 130.
67. Dr. Etibar Najafov, *The Restorations of the Silk Road as Factor of Modernization*, (Baku: Baku Slavik University, 2000), pp. 2-4
68. Alexander M. Kadakin, 'Indo-Russian Relation: Problems and Prospects', Mahavir Singh & V. Krassilchtchikov (ed), *Eurasian Vision*, (New Delhi: Lancer Pub. 2003), p. 111.
69. 'The New Eurasian Land bridge: Building Our Way Out of the Depression', *Executive Intelligence Report*, 2002.
70. *Ibid*.
71. News and Analysis On Line Publication, *Pravda, RU: Russia*, 28/10/2005. (online web) http://news.pravda.ru/softhard
72. *Ibid*.
73. United Nations – ST/ESCAP/2182, Economic and Social Commission for Asia and Pacific studies, 'Development of The Trans-Asian Railway: Trans-Asian Railway in the North-South Corridor – Northern Europe to The Persian Gulf', (New York, 2001), pp. 7-34. (Online web) http://www.unescap.org/tctd/country papers.htm.
74. *Ibid*. p. 25.
75. *Ibid*. p. 24.
76. Source: Jane's World Railways – 2000-2001. (Online web) www.asiasources.org
77. United Nations ST/ESCAP /2182, n-74, p. 29.
78. Manoj Joshi, 'Reality Check on Sikkim, Tibet', *The Times of India*, New Delhi, 25 June, 2003.
79. Ravni Thakur, 'The Delhi-Beijing Route', *The Hindu*, New Delhi, 25, June, 2003.
80. Sudhir Sahi, 'Commerce at the Cost of Ecology? But it's Business', *The Times of India*, June 25, 2003.
81. Ramtanu Maitra, 'Importance of Eurasian Land bridge for the Central Asian Development', in Shams-ud-din (ed.), *Geopolitics and Energy Resources in Central Asia and Caspian Sea Region*, (New Delhi: Lancer Books, 2000), p. 180.
82. *Executive Intelligence Report*, Washington D.C., 2000.

ANNEXURE I

Silk Road Chronology

5000-500 BC

- 3200 Horse domesticated on south Russian steppe.
- 3000 Minoan civilization starts, the earliest in Europe.
- 3000 Silk first produced in China.
- 3000 Sumerians develop first writing system.
- 2500 Domestication of the Bactrian and Arabian camel, vital for desert travel.
- 1700 Horse-drawn chariot introduced in Near East.
- 1500 Iron technology developed in Asia Minor.
- 1500 Seminomadic stockbreeding tribes inhaabit steppes.
- 900 Spread of mounted nomadism.
- 753 Rome founded.
- 707 Cimmerians, earliest-known mounted nomads, defeat kingdom of Urartu in Near East.
- 900-700 Scythians and Sarmatians appear in the northern steppes – two of the first races learn to ride horses and wear trousers. stirrup.
- 600s Zoroaster born in Persia.
- 560s Buddha born in Nepal.
- 550 Achaemenid Empire established in Persia.
- 500s Chinese adopt nomadic style, wear trousers and ride horses.
- 450 Herodotus visits Greek trading colony of Olbia to gather information on Scythians.
- 551-479 Confucius born in China.

400 BC

- Empire of Alexander the Great expands into Asia. Greek culture into Central Asia.

300 BC

- Roman expansion begins.
- Greco-Bactrian kingdom develops in Central Asia.
- Parthians establish their empire in Iran.
- Qin dynasty unites the entire China for the first time.
- Chinese complete Great Wall as defense against the northern nomads' invasion.
- Han dynasty overthrows Qin and develops its vast empire.
- Buddhism begins to spread north. Gandhara art type emerges and starts a new art style – Serindian.
- Paper first made in China.
- Achaemenid Empire of Persia.

200 BC

- Stirrup appears in Indian and Central Asia
- Greek city-states come under Roman rule.
- The Xiongnu, later called Huns rise to power in Central Asia and invade Chinese western border regions.
- Han Emperor, Wu-ti's interests in Central Asia cause him to command the Chang Ch'ien expeditions to the West, (Fergana and the Yueh-chih). Celestial Horses introduced to China.
- Han power reaches Tarim region. The Silk road under China's control and the route to the West now open.

100 BC

- Mithridates, Parthian king, sends ambassadors to both Sulla and Wu-ti to provide an important link between Rome and China.
- Parthians defeat Romans at Carrhae. One of the most disastrous in Roman history.
- Roman conquers Gaul.

- Egypt under Roman rule. Gives Rome access to Red Sea and Spice Route trade.
- Rome officially becomes an empire.

1 AD

- Silk first seen in Rome.
- Buddhism begins to spread from India into Central Asia.
- Roman Syria develops the technique of blowing glass. The industry expands.
- Kushan Empire of Central Asia. Sogdians trading on Silk Route.
- Xiongnu raids upset Chinese power in Tarim region.
- Death of Jesus Christ. Spread of Christianity begins.
- Chinese General Pan Ch'ao defeats Xiongnu and keeps the peace in the Tarim Basin. The stability of the Silk road popularizes the caravan trades into two routes – north and south.
- China sends the first ambassador to Rome from Pan Ch'ao's command, but he fails to reach Rome.
- Graeco-Egyptian geographer, Claudius Ptolemy, writes his Geography, attempts to map the Silk road.

100 AD

- Rome sends the first Roman envoy over sea to China.
- Roman Empire at its largest. A major market for Eastern goods.
- Buddhism reaches China.
- For the next few centuries, Buddhism flourishes, becoming the most popular religion in Central Asia, replacing Zoroastrianism.
- The four great empires of the day – the Roman, Parthian, Kushan, and Chinese – bring stability to the Silk road.

200 AD

- Silk is woven into cloth across Asia, but using Chinese thread.
- Han dynasty ends. China splits into fragments.

- Sassanians rise to power from Parthians. Strong cultural influence along the trade routes.
- Barbarian attacks on the Roman Empire.
- Death of Mani in Persia. Manichaeism spreads throughout Asia, not to die out until the 14th century.

300 AD

- Stirrup introduced to China by the northern nomads
- Secret of sericulture begins to spread west along the Silk road.
- Xiongnu invade China again. China further dissolved into fragments.
- Constantinople becomes Rome's capital.
- Christianity becomes the official Roman religion.
- Dun Huang caves starts to appear and becomes the world's largest Buddha caves.
- Huns attack Europe.
- Roman Empire splits into two.
- Fa-hsien, one of the first known Chinese Silk road travellers by foot and a Buddhist monk, sets out for India.

400 AD

- A Chinese princess smuggles some silkworm eggs out of China. Silkworm farms appear in Central Asia.
- New techniques in glass production introduced to China by the Sogdians.
- Visigoths invade Italy and Spain.
- Angles and Saxons rise in Britain.
- Western Roman Empire collapses.
- Frankish kingdom formed.

500 AD

- Silkworm farms appear in Europe.
- Nestorian Christians reach China.
- Kingdom of Hephthalites (White Huns) in northern Asia, conquering Sogdian territory.
- Buddhism reaches Japan.

- Split of the Turkish Kaganate into Eastern and Western Kaganates. Western Turks move to Central Asia from Mongolian plateau. At the Chinese end of Central Asia, the Eastern Turks or Uighurs is in control.
- Sui dynasty reunites China.
- Sassanian Empire at its greatest extent in Central Asia.

600 AD

- Roman Empire becomes Byzantine Empire.
- Tang dynasty rules in China. For the first two centuries, the Silk Road reaches its golden age. China very open to foreign cultural influences. Buddhism flourishes.
- The Islamic religion founded.
- Death of Muhammad. Muslim Arab expansion begins.
- Xuan Zang's pilgrimage to India.
- The Avars from the steppes introduces stirrups to Europe.
- Sassanian Persia falls to the Arabs.
- Muslims control Mesopotamia and Iran, along with the Silk and Spice routes.

700 AD

- Arabs conquer Spain in Europe, which introduces much Eastern technology and science to Europe.
- Arabs defeat Chinese at Talas and capture Chinese papermakers, who introduces paper making into Central Asia and Europe.
- Block printing developed in China
- Tang dynasty begins to decline, and with it, the Silk road.
- Glassmaking skill introduced to China by Sogdians.

800 AD

- First porcelain made in China.
- Gunpowder invented in China and spread to the West by the 13th century.
- All foreign religions banned in China.
- Compass begins to be used by Chinese.

- Diamond Sutra dated 11 May 868, the world's oldest known printed book made in Dunhuang.
- Venice established as a city-state.

900 AD

- Kirghiz Turks in control of Eastern Central Asia, establish kingdoms at Dunhuang and Turfan.
- Tang Dynasty ends. China fragmented.
- England unified for the first time.
- Playing cards invented in China and spread to Europe toward the end of 14th century.
- The Islamic Empire divides into small kingdoms.
- Sung Dynasty reunites China.
- Porcelain developed in China and exported to western Asia.

1000 AD

- First Crusade. Exchange of technology between Europe and Middle East.

1100 AD

- China divided into Northern Sung and Southern Sung.
- Muslim oust the Franks from the Levant.
- Genghiz Khan unites Mongols. Expansion of Mongol Empire begins.
- Silk production and weaving established in Italy.
- Paper money first developed in China.

1200 AD

- Death of Genghis Khan.
- Mongols invade Russia, Poland, and Hungary.
- The Europe's first envoy to the East, Friar Giovanni Carpini leaves Rome for Mongol capital at Karakorum.
- Friar William Rubruck sent to Karakorum by the King of France.
- Seventh, and last, Crusade.

- Mongol control central and western Asia.
- Silk road trade prospers again under the "Pax Mongolica."
- Kublai Khan defeats China and establishes the Yuan dynasty.
- Paper money introduced to Central Asia and Iran by Mongols.
- Marco Polo leaves for the East.

1300 AD

- Turkish Ottoman Empire in power.
- Tamerlane, with capital in Samarkand, rises and conquers Persia, parts of Southern Russia, and northern India.
- Third Silkroad route appears in the north.
- Ibn Battuta, the first known Arab travels on a 750,000 mile journey to China via the Silkroad.
- The Black Death spreads throughout Europe.
- Paper made across Europe.
- Spinning wheel in Europe.
- Battle of Crecy between French and English, where cannons used first in Europe.
- Mongol Yuan Dynasty collapes. Chinese Ming Dynasty begins.

1400 AD

- Tamerlane defeats the Ottoman Turks, and causes the deaths of seventeen million people.
- Renaissance period in Europe.
- Chinese explore the Spice Routes as far as Africa
- Death of Tamerlane leads to the decline of Mongol power. Ottoman rises again in the Central Asia.
- Ottomans conquer Constantinople.
- Gutenberg printing press in use.
- China closes the door to foreigners.
- Fearing the power of Uighurs, Ming China reduces the trade and traffic dramatically in the Silkroad. The Silkroad comes to an end for purposes of silk.
- Lyon becomes the new center of the silk trade.
- Columbus reaches America.

- Vasco da Gama discovers the sea route from Europe to the East via the cape of Good Hope to Calicut in India.

1500 AD

- Islam becomes the religion of the entire Taklamakan region.

1600 AD

- Uzbek Turks appear from the north, settle in today's Uzbekistan.
- Prince Babur, descendant of Genghis Khan and Tamerlane, extends his empire from the Ferghana valley to India. Founder of Mogul dynasty.
- Manchuria rises and invades China. Qing Dynasty established.

1700 AD

- Numbers of severe earthquakes in Central Asia damage some of the great monuments.
- Porcelain produced in Europe.
- The Manchus, a Tungusic people from Manchuria, absorb the Gobi and Altai districts.

1800 AD

- German scholar, Baron Ferdinand von Richthofen uses the term "Silkroad" (Seidenstrasse) for the first time.
- Manchus take over the Tarim Basin.
- Xinjiang Province created under Qing Dynasty.
- Elias crosses the Pamirs and identifies Muztagh Ata. Recommends the Wakhan corridor be established.
- Younghusband crosses the Gobi Desert, pioneering a new route from Peking to Kashgar via the Muztagh Pass.
- Hedin explores the Kun Lun and Takla Makan desert, unearthing buried cities along the old Silkroad.
- Conway in the Karakoram Mountains.

- Stein's archaeological investigations of the Takla Makan and central Asia.
- The Great Game – Tsarist Russia and British India expand in Central Asia.

1900 AD

- Sven Hedin expeditions –1883-1935.
- Chinese revolution; end of Chinese dynasties – 1949.
- Tibet under China's control – 1950.
- Karakoram highway from Islamabad to Kashgar built by China and Pakistan – 1978.
- Beginning of Trans-Siberian Railways – 1916.
- Reopening of the Nathu La Pass – 2006.

Bibliography

Primary Sources-I

A.S. Altekar, *Corpus of Indian Coins*, Vol. IV, *The Coinage of the Gupta Empire*, Banaras, 1957.

Abhyankar, P.C., ed., trans. into Marathi by V.S. Abhyankar, *Vyakaranamahabhasya* of Patanjali, IV, Poona, 1966.

Afrasiab History Museum. Wall *paintings of Afrasiab (Reconstruction)*. Samarkand, 1997.

Alberuni's *Tahqiq-i-Hind* which is also available in English translation by E.C. Sachau, *Alberuni's India* (London, 1914).

Allan, B.C., *Monograph on the Silk Cloths of Assam*, Shillong, 1899.

Babur, Zahiru'din Muhammad. *The Babur-nama* in English (Memoirs of Babur). Trans. by A.S. Bereridge, London: Luzac and Co., 1921.

British Museum. Frozen tombs, *The Culture and Art of the Ancient Tribes of Siberia*. London, 1978.

Burrow, T.A., *Translation of the Kharosthi Documents from Chines Turkestan*. London: Royal Asiatic Society, 1940.

Central Asian Research Centre, *Cities of Central Asia*. London, 1961.

Chen, Yu, *Tales from Dunhuang*. Trans. By Li Guishan, Beijing: New Work Press, 1989.

Chinese Cultural Relics Promotion Center. *Treasures: 300 Best Excavated Antiques from China*. Beijing: New World Press, 1992.

Daily Life of Aristocrats in Tang China. Exhibition catalogue, Hong Kong: Regional Council, 1993.

Dhammapada, transl. Max Muller (Oxford, 1898).

Digha Nikaya (Hindi), Tr. Rahula Sankrtyayana and Jagadisa Kasyapa, Banaras, 1936.

Eggline, J., Tr., *The Satapatha-Brahamana*, III, Delhi. Varanasi, Patna reprint, 1894.

Excavation reports of J. Marshal, *Taxila* (Cambridge, 1951).

F.A. von Schiefer has translated a history of Buddhism in India written by a Tibetan monk Taranatha, *Geschichte des Buddhismum* in Indien (St Petersburg, 1869).

Fa Hsien's account of his travels in India, traslated by H.A. Giles, *The Travels of Fa-Hien* (Cambridge, 1923).

Fa Xian, *A Record of Buddhistic Kingdoms, Being an Account of the Chinese Monk Fa-Hien.* Trans by James Legge, Oxford: Clarendon Press, 1986.

Firdausi, *The Epic of the Kings: Shah-Nama.* Trans. by Reuben Levy, London: Routledge & Kegan Paul, 1967.

Grand View of Xinjiang's Cultural Relics and Historic Sites, Urumqi, 1999.

Greek accounts both of visitors and others have been collated and translated by J.W. MeCrindle in a series of books *Ancient India as described by Ktesias the Knidian* (Calcutta, 1882).

H.A. Giles, *The Travels of Fa-Hsien or Record of Buddhistic Kingdoms* (Tr.), Cambridge, 1923.

Herodotus, *The Histories,* Tr. Aubery de Selincourt, Penguin Books, 1954.

Herodotus's *History* (Oxford, 1913-14).

Ho Chang Chun, "Fa-hsien's Pilgrimage to Buddhist Countries", *Chinese Literature,* No. 3. 1956.

Hsuan Tsang's description of his visit to India, *On Yuan Chwang's Travels in India,* ed. Watters (London, 1904-5).

Ibn Battuta, *Travels in Asia and Africa* 1325-1354. Trans. by H.A.R. Gibb, London: The Broadway Travellers, George Routledge and Sons, 1929.

International Merv Project, The *Ancient Cities of Merv, Turkmenistan.* London: University College, 1996.

J.F. Fleet, *Inscriptions of the Early Gupta Kings,* CII, iii, London, 1888; Reprent, Indological Book House, Varanasi, 1963; Sten Konow, Kharosthi Inscriptions, CII, ii, Part I, Government of India, Central Publication Branch, Calcutta, 1929.

Jacobi, H., Trans., Gaina Sutras, Part I, Oxford, 1884.

Jaimini's Purvamimamsa-Sutra with the Bhasya of Sabara and the Tantravartika and Tup=tika of Kumarilabhatta, Anandasrama Series, Parts I-VI, Poona, 1930.

James Legge, Tr. *A Record of Buddhistic Kingdoms* (being an account of the Chinese monk Fa-hian's Travels), Oxford, 1886.

Jataka with commentary, Ed. V. Fausboll, 7 Vols. (Vol. 7, Index, by D. Anderson), London, 1877-97. Tr. Various hands, 6 vols., London, 1895-1907.

Jataka, ed. E.B. Cowell (Cambridge, 1893-1913).

Kautalya's Arthashastra edited by T. Ganapati Sastri and translated by R. Shamasastri (Mysore, 1958).

Konow. Sten, Tr., *Raja-Cekhara's Karpura Manjari*, Delhi, 1963.

M. Hussain has translated relevant sections of the *Rehla* of Ibn Batutah (GOS, cxxii, 1953).

Milindapanho, Ed. V. Trenckner, London, 1928, Tr. T.W. Rhys Davids, SBE, Oxford, 1890.

National Museum of Chinese History. *A Journey into China's Antiquity*. 4 vols., Beijing: Morning Glory Publishers, 1947.

Nizami of Ganja, *The Haft Paikar (The Seven Beauties)*. Trans. by C.E. Wilson, 2 vols., London: Probsthain & Co., 1924.

Pliny's *Natural History*, and Ptolemy's *Geography*, Translated by W.W. Tarn, *Hellenistic Civilization* (London, 1930).

Polo, Marco, *The Travels of Marco Polo The Venetian*. Trans. by William Marsden, New York: Doubleday and Co., 1948.

Reference to Ancient routes can be gathered from a variety of sources such as the *Jatakas*.

Research Center for Silk Roadology. Space Archeology. *Silk Roadology I*. Nara: 1995

Samuel Beal, *Travels of Fah-hian and Sung Yun* (Tr.), London, Trubner, 1869.

Sima. Qian, *Records of the Grand Historian: Shij*. 2 vols., trans. by Burton Watson, New York: Columbia University Press, 1993.

Si-yu-ki: Buddhist Records of the Western World, by Hiuen Tsiang. Trans. by Samuel Beal, 2 vols. in 1, London: Kegan Paul et al., 1884.

Stein, M. Aruel, Serindia-*Detailed Report of Explorations in Central Asia and Westernmost China*. Oxford: Clarendon Press, 1921.

Stein, M. Aurel, *Innermost Asia-Detailed report of explorations in Central Aisa*, Kan-su- and Eastern Iran. Oxford: Clarendon Press, 1928.

Studies in New China, *Xin Zhongguode kaogu Faxian he yanjiu/ Archaeological discoveries and studies in new China*, Institute of

Archaeological Studies of the Chinese Academy of Social Science, Beijing, 1984.

The inscriptions pertaining to the Gupta period edited and translated by J. Fleet in *Corpus Inscriptionum Indicarum*, Vol. III (Calcutta, 1888).

The major epigraphical evidence of Ashokan inscriptions, edited and translated by E. Hultzsch in *Corpus Inscriptionum Indicarum*, Vol. I (London, 1925).

The Silk Road and the World of Xuanzang, Asahi Shimbun 120th Anniversary Commemorative Exhibition, Osaka: Asahi Shimbun, 1999.

The Vishnu Purana, transl. H.H. Wilson (London, 1864-70).

Translations of Chinese material referring to India published in *Toung Pao*, XVI, 1915.

Treasures of Chang'an. Capital of the Silk Road: Exhibition catalogue, Hong Kong Museum of Art and the Overseas Exhibitions Department.

UNESCO, *Amir Temur in World History*, Paris, 1996.

UNESCO, *Mongolia's Tentative List: Cultural and Natural heritage*, 1996.

Vinaya Pitaka, Ed. H. Oldenberg, 5 vols., PTS, London, 1879-83. *The Book of Discipline*, Tr. I.B. Horner, 5 pts, SBB, London, 1938-52.

Zhou, Xuejun and Song, Weimin (ed.), *Archaeological Treasures of the Silk Road in Xinjaang Uygur Autonomous Region*. Exhibition catalogue, Shanghai Museum, Shanghai: Shanghai Translation Publishing House, 1998.

Primary Sources-II

A report on "Diplomacy of Silk Road" by Askar Akaev, President of the Kyrgyz Republic, *Foreign Policy Document of the Republic of Kyrgyzstan*, 1998.

A report on "EU/Ex-USSR: New TACIS Programme Approved", *European Report*, 7 January, 1999.

A report on "Road Safety in Asia and the Pacific:/ *ESCAP* / Asian Development Bank Seminar-cum-Workshop", 2-6 Sep., (Bangkok-New York: United. Nations, 1997).

An Interview with Andrew Kuchins, 'US-Russian Cooperation and the Future of Central Asia', in *World Focus*, March, 2004, vol. 25, Number 3, New Delhi.

GATT Yearbook Trade Policy Review, Geneva, GATT, Pub. Service, 1992 (Yearly Publication upto 2001).

GATT, Activities, *A Review of the work of the GATT,* Geneva, WTO, 1991 (Yearly publication upto 2000).

GATT, Annual Report of the Director General on International Trade and Trading System Geneva, GATT Pub. Service 1992-93.

GATT, Supplement No. 42, Basic Instruments and selected documents, Protocols, Decisions and Reports 1995 and Fifty-first Session, Geneva, GATT Pub., June 1998.

IMF, Annual Report on Exchange Arrangement and Exchange Restrictions, Washington DC, IMF Pub. Service, 1992 (Annual Report upto 2001).

IMF, *Azerbaijan: Economic Review,* Washington DC, April, 1993.

IMF, Direction of Trade Statistics, Year book, Washington, IMF Pub., 1992 (Yearly issues upto 2001).

IMF, *Economic Review: Kazakhstan,* Washington DC, June 1993.

IMF, *Economic Review: Kyrgyzstan,* Washington DC, May 1992.

IMF, *Economic Review: Tajikistan,* Washington DC, May 1992.

IMF, *Economic Review: Turkmenistan,* Washington DC, May 1994.

IMF, *Economic Review: Uzbekistan,* Washington DC, May 1992.

IMF, *Occasional Paper No. 183,* Economic Reforms in Kazakhstan, Kyrgyz Republic, Tajikistan, Turkmenistan and Uzbekistan, Aug., 31, 1999.

IMF, *Staff Country Report* No. 00/36 (series), Republic of Uzbekistan: Recent Economic Development, March 29, 2000.

IMF, summary proceedings, annual meeting, Washington DC, IMF, 1992 (Annual Publication upto 2001).

Material of the Baku Conference on 8th September 1998 by Rahman Dadman.

National Trade Data, *Commercial Overview of Uzbekistan,* United States Department of Commerce, Washington DC, 1994.

'Quarterly Country Reports and Annual Country Profiles: Kazakhstan, Turkmenistan, Uzbekistan, Kyrgyzstan and Tajikistan', *The Economist Intelligence Unit,* (London: 1998-2000).

Report of the UNESCO Programme and the WTO (World Tourism Organization) focusing on Central Asia, 1994.

Report of the World Bank of Silk Route Revival, New York, World Bank Pub., 1996.

The Economist Intelligence Unit, *Country Profile 1995-96: Uzbekistan,* London, 1995.

The Economist Intelligence Unit, *Country Report: Kazakhstan,* 3rd Oct., 1995, London, 1995.

The Economist Intelligence Unit, *Country Report: Kyrgyz Republic,* Ist Quarter 1996, London, 1996.

The Economist Intelligence Unit, *Country Report: Tajikistan,* 1st Quarter 1996, London, 1996.

The Economist Intelligence Unit, *Country Report: Turkmenistan,* 1st Quarter 1995, London, 1995.

The Economist Intelligence Unit, *Uzbekistan: Business Report,* 1st Quarter 1995. London, 1995.

UN, *Annual Bulletin* of Transport Statistics for Europe and North American, New York, UN Pub. 1992. (Annual Bulletin upto 2001).

UN, Annual Report on Trade and Development (New York and Geneva) Book Well, Delhi 1991 (Year Book upto 2001).

UN, Development Papers No. 19 Foreign Direct Investment in Selected Asian countries: Politics, related Institution-Building and Regional Cooperation, New York, 1998.

UN, Management and Financing of road maintenance: Report/ ESCAP/World Bank Seminar, 17-20 Sept., 1996.

UN, Road Safety in Asia and the Pacific: Report/ESCAP/ADB Seminar-cum-workshop, 2-6 Sept., Bangkok-New York: United Nations, 1997.

UN, Statistical Yearbook.

UN, World Economic and Social Survey: Trends and Policies in the World Economy, New York, Book well, Delhi, 2001.

UNIDO, Central Asian Republics: Azerbaijan, Turkmenistan, Uzbekistan: Industrial Reform and Restructuring, *Industrial Development Review,* vol. III, Vienna: EIU Pub., 1996.

UNIDO, Central Asian Republics: Kazakhstan, Kyrgyz Republic, Tajikistan: Industrial Report and Restructuring *Industrial Development Review* vol. I., Vienna: Published by the Economist Intelligence Unit, 1996.

World Bank *Kyrgyzstan: The transition to a market economy,* Washington DC, 1993.

World Bank, *Uzbekistan: An Agenda for Economic Reform,* Washington DC, Sep. 1993.

World Bank, Kazakhstan: *Economic Report,* Washington DC, 7 July 1994.

World Bank, *Kyrgyz, Republic:* Economic Report, Washington, DC, May 1994.

World Bank, *Tajikistan: Country Economic Memorandum,* Washington DC, 12 August, 1999.

World Bank, Trends in Developing Economies, Washington, DC, WB Pub., 1995.

World Bank, *Turkmenistan: Country Study, Economic Memorandum,* Washington DC, 7 Feb., 1994.

World Bank, *Turkmenistan: Country Study,* Washington DC, May 1994.

World Development Report, New York, World Bank Pub., Oxford Univ. Pres, 1992. (Yearly Pub., upto 2000).

World Markets Report: Tajikistan, DRI-WEFA, IMF, 5 Jan., 2000.

WTO, Annual Report, International Trade Statistic UN, Pub., New York, 1992 to 2000.

Secondary Sources

Books

Abazov, Rafiq, 'Independence Kyrgyzstan: 10 Difficult years on the Silk Road' *Eurasian Studies,* Special Issue, summer 2001, (Turkish Interview Cooperation Agency: Ankara).

Adshead, S.M. *Central Asia in World History* (New York: ST. Martin's Press, 1993).

Akiner, Shirin (ed.) *Cultural Change and Continuity in Central Asia* (London: Kegan Paul International, 1991).

Anne Wardell and James Watt, *When Silk was Gold* (New York: Abrams, 1997).

Arnolov, A. *On the Path of Cultural Progress,* (Moscow: Progress Pub., 1976).

Bagchi, P.C., *India and Central Asia* (Calcutta: National Council of Education, 1995).

Bakhtior A. Islamov, *The Central Asian States Ten years After: How to Overcome Traps of Development, Transformation and Globalization,* (Tokyo: Maruzen Co., Ltd., 2001).

Bakshi, Akhil, *Silk Road on Wheels* (New Delhi: Odyssey Pub., 2001).

Bamzai, P.N.K., *Kashmir and Central Asia* (New Delhi: Light and Life Pub., 1980).

Bangkok: National Culture Commission, *Ancient Trades and Cultural Contacts in Southeast Asia*, Bangkok. 1996

Basham, A.L., *A Cultural History of India*, (Delhi: Oxford University Press, 1984).

Basilow, Vladimir N. (ed.), *The Nomads of Eurasia*. University of Washington Press, 1989

Baumer, C., *Southern Silk Road: In the Footsteps of Sir Aurel Stein and Sven Hedin*. Bangkok: Orchid Press, 2000

Begley, V. and De Puma, R.D. (ed.), *Rome and India: The Ancient Sea Trade*. Madison Wisconsin: University of Wisconsin Press, 1991.

Bhattacharya, C., Art *of Central Asia: With Special Reference to wooden objects from the Nothern Silk Route*, (Delhi: Agam Prakashan, 1977).

Bhattacharya, Rakhee and Mishra, Binoda K (ed.), *A Journey through the Stilwell Road*, (New Delhi: Shipra Publications, 2011).

Boulger, D.C. *England and Russia in Central Asia* 2 vols. (London: W.H. Allen, 1879).

Boulnois L., *The Silk Road*, (London: George Allen & Unwin Ltd., 1963).

Boxer, C.R., *South China in the Sixteenth Century*, (London: Hakluyt Society, 1953).

Brown P., *Indian Architecture* (Buddhism and Hindu) (Bombay, 1949).

Bulliet, Richard, *The Camel and the Wheels* (New York: Columbia University Press, 1975).

Bury, J.B., *A History of the Later Roman Empire* (London: Macmillan and Co., 1989).

__________, *The Bolshevik Revolution*, 3 Vols. (Delhi: Macmillan India Ltd., 1961).

Cambridge Economic History of Europe, The Agrarian Life of the Middle Ages, Vol. I, (ed.) Postan, M.M., Cambridge University Press, 1966.

Cambridge Economic History of Europe, Trade and Industry in the Middle Ages, Vol. II, (eds.) Postan, M., and E.E. Rich, Cambridge University Press, 1952.

Carr, E.H., *What is History?*, (Delhi: Macmillan India Ltd., 1961).

Chakrabarti, D.K., *India An Archaeological History*, (London: Oxford University, 1999).

Chandra, Moti, *Trade and Trade Routes in Ancient India* (New Delhi: Abhinav Pub., 1977).

Chang, Hsing-Lang, (tr), *Historical Sources of Communications between the West and China* (Beijing: Chang-Hua-Shu-Chi, 1930).

Charles Worth, M.P., *Trade Routes and Commerce with Roman Empire* (Cambridge: Cambridge University Press, 1924).

Che, Muqi, *The Silk Road: Past and Present.* Beijing, Foreign Languages Press, 1989.

Chi, Hsi-ho., *Record of Hs - ho region,* (Shanghai: Commercial Press, 1936).

Chowdhury, S.N., *Muga Silk Industry,* (Guwahati: Peoples Pub., 1981).

Clark, G.N., *Early Modern Europe,* Oxford, 1976.

Colling Wood, R.G., *The Philosophy of History,* (London, 1985).

Colton, T.J., and Tucker, R.C., (ed.), *Patterns in Post-Soviet Leadership,* (Boulder: Westview Press, 1994).

Conze E. Conze, *Buddhism, Its Essence and Development,* (London, 1935).

Cummings, Sally N., *Power and Change in Central Asia,* (London: Rutledge Pub., 2002).

Cunningham, A., *Coins of Alexander's Successors in the East* (Oxford, 1914).

Cunningham, A., *The Ancient Geography of India* (Calcutta, 1924).

Cunningham, A., *The Ancient Geography of India: A Buddhist* Period Including the Campaigns of Alexander, and the Travels of Hwen-Thsang (Delhi: Low Price Pub., 1963).

Czuma, S.J., *Kushan Sculpture: Images from Early India,* Cleveland: Cleveland Museum of Art, 1985.

_______, *Human Records on Karakorum Highway,* (Lahore: Sang-E-Meel Pub., 1995).

_______, *Soviet Economic Development since 1917,* Rev. edition, London, 1963.

Dani, A.H. and Masson, V.M., *History of Civilizations of Central Asia, Vol. 1,* (Paris: UNESCO, 1992).

Dekmejian, R. Hrair, and Hovann H. Simonian, *Troubled. waters the Geopolitics of the Caspian Region,* (London, New York: I.B. Tauris Publishers, 2001).

Denis, Chambarlain (Tr.) *The Silk Road,* (New York: Dutton, 1972).

Dettke, Dieter, (ed.), *A Great Game No More: Oil, Gas, and Stability,* (Washington: Friedrich-Ebert-Stiftung, 1999).

Dobb, Maurice, *Studies in the Development of Capitalism,* Rev. edition, London, 1963.

Dorian, James P., *Oil and Gas in Russia and the Former Soviet Union,* (London: Financial Times Energy Publishing, 1997).

Dupree, A. et al, *A guide to the Kabul Museum. Kabul: Afghan Tourist Organization,* 1968.

Dupree, N. H, *An Historical Guide to Afghanistan. Kabul: Afghan Tourist Organization,* 1977.

Dupree, N.H., *The Road to Balkh. Kabul: Afghan Tourist Organization,* 1967.

Ebel, R., and Menon, R., (eds.), *Energy and Conflict in Central Asian and the Caucasus,* (New York: Rowman & Littlefield, 2000).

Eberhard, Wolfram, *A History of China,* (Berkeley and Los Angeles: University of California Press, 1969).

Edward, Allwarth, *Central Asia, A Century of Russian Rule* (New York, London, 1967).

Edward, Schafer, *The Golden Peaches of Samarkand,* (California, CUP, 1963).

Edwards Mathew, 'The New Great Game and the New Great Gamers: Disciples of Kipling', *Central Asian Survey,* (March, 2003) 22(1), 18-102, (London: Carfax Publication).

Engels, f., quoted by Elliott, J.H., *The Old World and the New 1492-1650, Cambridge Studies in Early Modern History,* Cambridge University Press, 1970a.

Florence, Day, *Silk of the Near East,* (Metro Political Museum of Art Bulletin, 1950).

Foltz, Richard C., *Religions of the Silk Road, Overland trade and Cultural Exchange from antiquity to the 15th century* (Houndmills: Macmillan Press, 1999).

______, *Mughal India and Central Asia* (Karachi: Oxford University Press, 1998).

Foucher, A., *Notes on the Ancient Geography of Gandhara (A Commentary on a chapter of Hiuan I Sung)* (Varanasi: Bhartiya Publishing House, 1974).

Gafurov and Others; *Kushan Studies in U.S.S.R.;* (Papers Presented by the Soviet Scholars at the UNESCO conference on History, Archaeology and culture of Central Asia in the Kushan period, Dushanbe 1968 with 18 plates); (Calcutta: Indian Studies Past and Present, 1968).

Gardner, P., The *Coins of the Greek and Scythic Kings of Bactria and India in the British Museum*, London: Trustees of the British Museum, 1886.

Gernet, Jacques, *A History of Chinese Civilisation*. Translated by J.R. Foster, Cambridge: CUP, 1982.

Goodrich, L. Carrington, *A Short History of the Chinese People*, (London: George Allen and Unwin Ltd., 1972).

Grabar, A., *Byzantium: Byzantine Art in the Middle Ages*. London: Methuen, 1996.

Grousset, R., *The Empire of the Steppes: A History of Central Asia*. Translated by Naomi Walford, (New Brunswick: Rutgers University Press, 1970).

Grousset, R., *The Empire of the Steppes: A History of Central Asia*. Translated by Naomi Walford, New Brunswick: Rutgers University Press, 1970.

Habib Irfan, Tapan Raychaudhuri, Dharma Kumar, *The Cambridge Economic History of India: c.1200-c.1750*, Cambridge University Press, 1982.

Hafeez, Malik, (ed.), *Central Asia – Its Strategic Importance and Future Prospects*, London: The Macmillan Press, Ltd., 1994).

Hallade, H., *The Gandhara Style and the Evolution of Buddhist Art*, London: Thames and Hudson, 1968.

Harmatta, Janos (ed.), *History of Civilizations of Central Asia. Vol. II. The development of Sedentary and nomadic civilization*. Paris: UNESCO Publishing, 1994.

He, Zhenguang (ed), *Xian: An Ancient Capital of China*. Beijing: Foreign Languages Press, 1990.

Hedin, Sven, *My Life as an Explorer*. New York: Garden City Publishing, 1925.

Hedin, Sven, *The Silk Road*. Translated by F.H. Lyon, New York: Dutton, 1938.

Hildinger, Erik, *Warriors of the Steppe: A Military History of Central Asia- 500 BC to 1700 AD*, (USA: Da Capo Press, 2001).

Hobsbawm, E.J., *Industry and Empire, From 1750 – Present Day, The Pelican Economic History of Britain*, Vol. I, 1969.

Hook, Brian, (ed.), *The Cambridge Encyclopedia of China*, (Cambridge: University Press, 1991), 2nd ed.

Hopkins, Clark, *The Discovery of Dura-Europos*. New Haven and London: Yale University Press, 1979.

Hopkirk, Peter, *Foreign Devils on the Silk Road: The Search for the Lost Cities and Treasurer of Chinese Central Asia,* (Oxford University Press, John Murry, 1980).

Hui Li, *The Life of Hiuen-Tsiang*. Trans. by Samuel Beal, London: Kegan Paul et al., 1914.

Ira, M., Lapidus, *A History of Islamic Societies,* (Cambridge: Cambridge University Press, 1988).

Jacques Garnet, *A History of Chinese Civilization,* [Translated. by J.R.Foster], (Cambridge: C.P.U., 1982).

Jain V.K., *Trade and Traders in Western India,* Munshiram Manoharlal, New Delhi, 1990.

Jalalzai, M.K., *Central Asia: Political Situation and Economic Opportunities* (Lahore: Frontier Post Pub., 1994).

James J. Reid, *Tribalism and Society in Islamic Iran,* (Malibu: Udena Publications, 1983).

Jha, D.N. & Shrimali, K.M., (ed.) *Pracheen Bharat Ka Itihas,* (New Delhi: Delhi University, 1997).

Jha, D.N., *Ancient India in Historical Outline,* (New Delhi: Manohar Publishers & Distributors, 1998).

Jidejian, Nina, *Sidon through the Ages*. Beirut: Dar El-Machreq Publishers, 1971.

Johannes, Kalter, *The Arts and Crafts of Turkistan* (London: Thames and Hudson, 1984).

Karagiannis, Emmanuel, 'The US-Iranian Relationship After 11 September 2001 and the Transportation of Caspian Energy', *Central Asian Survey*', June-Sep., 22(213), 151-162, (London: Carfax Publishing).

Kaul, B.K. Dembi (ed.) *Kashmir and Central Asia:* [Paper presented at the Seminar on Kashmir and Central Asia-Cultural contacts and Interactions, September 1-3, 1987] (Centre for Central Asian Studies, Kashmir University, 1989).

Kaushik, D., *Central Asia in Modern Times* (Moscow: Progress Pub, 1970).

______, *China and The Third World* (New Delhi: Sterling Publishers, Pvt. Ltd., 1975).

Kelly, Laurence, *Istanbul: A Traveller's Companion*. London: Constable, 1987.

Khan, S.A., *The East India Trade in the XVII Century – in its Political and Economic Aspects* (London: Humphrey Milford, Oxford University Press, 1923).

Kiani, M.Y. and Kleiss, W., *Iranian Caravanscrais.* Tehran: Cultural Heritage Organization of Iran, 1995.

Kinross, L., *The Ottoman Centuries,* (New York: Marrow Quill, 1977).

Knauer, E.R, *The Camel's Load in Life and Death: Iconography and ideology of Chinese pottery figurines from Han to Tang and their relevance to trace along the silk routes.* Zurich: Akanthus, 1998.

Knobloch, Edgar, *Beyond the Oxus: Archaeology, Art and Architecture of Central Asia,* (London: Ernest Benn Limited, 1972).

Kordosis, M., China and the Greek World: Hellenistic-Roman-Early Byzantine Period, (2nd c. BC- 6th c.AD), *Historicogeographica Melemata,* No. 2, Thessalonica. 1992.

Kosambi, D.D., *An Introduction to the Study of Indian History,* (Bombay, 1956).

_______, *The Culture and Civilization of Ancient India in Historical Outline,* (London, 1965).

_______, *Prachin Bharat ki Sanskrriti Aur Sabhyata,* (New Delhi: Raj Kamal Prakashan, 1992).

Krejci, J., *Civilizations of Asian and the Middle East before the European Challenge:* (London: 1990 Macmillan, 1990).

Lahiri, Nayanjot, *The Archaeology of Indian Trade Routes (up to c.200 BC),* Oxford University Press, New Delhi, 1992.

Laltimore, O., *Inner Asian Frontiers of China* (Oxford: Oxford University Press, 1998).

Law, B.C., *Geography of Early Buddhism* (London, 1932).

Lawton, J., *Samarkand and Bukhara.* London: Tauris Parke Books, 1991.

Le Strange, G., *Baghdad during the Abbasic Caliphate.* London: O.U.P., 1924 (first edition 1900). Levy, Reuben. A Baghdad Chronicle. Cambridge: Cambridge University Press, 1929.

LIu, G.K.C., The Silkworm and Chinese Culture, *Osiris.* 10, 129-193, 1952.

Lyndan Larauche, and others, *EIR's Special Report on the Eurasian Land Bridge: The New Silk Road-Locomotive for Worldwide Economic Development* (Washington D.C.: EIR News Service, Inc., Jan., 1997).

Maity, S.K., *Economic Life of Northern India,* (Calcutta: The World Press Private Ltd., 1957).

Majumdar,. R.C., Physical Features of Ancient Bengal, in B.C. Law, ed., *Acarya-Puspanjali Volume,* Calcutta, 1940.

Man-ch'un, Liu, *Silk Trade along the Silk Route from the Han to Tang,* (Lan Chou: People's Publisher, 1982).

Manz, Beatrice F., *Central Asian in Historical Perspective* (Boulder: Westview Press, 1994).

Marshal, Sir John, Taxila*: an illustrated account of archaeological excavations carried out at Taxila under the orders of the Government of India between the years 1913 and 1934,* Cambridge, 1951.

Marshall, Sir John, A *Guide to Taxila. Calcutta: Superintendent Government Printing,* 1918.

Meijer, F. and Nijf, O.V., *Trade, Transport and Society in the Ancient World* (London and New York: Routledge, 1992).

Melvin, N., *Uzbekistan: Transition to Authoritarianism on the Silk Road,* (Amsterdam and Reading: Harwood Academic Publishers, 2002).

Menon, Rajan, *New Russian Foreign Policy,* (New York, A Council of Foreign Relation Book, 1998).

Monnas. L., Granger-Taylor, H., *Ancient and Medieval Textiles.* Studies in Honour of Konald King, London, 1989.

Mote, F.W., *Imperial China: 900-1800 AD,* (London: Harvard University Press, 1999).

Mousavi, S.A., *The Hazaras of Afghanistan: An Historical, Cultural, Economic and Political Study,* Richmond, Surrey: Curzon Press, 1998.

Muthesium. A., *From Seek to Semite: aspects of Byzantine Silk Production,* 1989.

Myers, D.K., *Costume and Ceremonial Textiles of Bhutan, The Textile Museum Journal,* 1987.

Najafov, Dr Etibar, *The Restoration of the Silk Road as a Factor of Modernization,* (Baku: Baku Slavik University, 2000).

Nanavaty, M.M., 1965, *Silk, From Grub to Glamour,* Bombay, 1965.

Nishikawa Kyotaro (Director-General, Nara National Museum), *The Grand Exhibition of Silk Road Civilizations: The Route of Buddhist Art,* (Nara, 1988).

Nova, A., *An Economic History of the USSR,* 1992.

Osborn, R.D., *Islam Under the Khalifs of Baghdad.* London: Seeley, Jackson and Halliday, 1878.

Owen Lattimore, *Inner Asian Frontiers of China* (Oxford: Oxford University Press, 1988).

Paksoy, H.B., *Central Asia Reader: The rediscovery of History* (New York, London: M.E. Sharpe, 1994).

Pal, P., *The Ideal Image: The Gupta Sculptural Tradition and Its Influence,* New York: Asia Society and John Weatherhill, 1978.

Pandey, J.N., *Bhartiya Kala Avum Puratattva,* (Allahabad: Parmanaik Pub., 1996).

Pant, Girijesh, America's Caspian Oil Policy' in Shams-ud-Din (ed.), *Geopolitics and Energy Resources in Central Asia and Caspian Sea Region,* (New Delhi: Lancer pub., 2000).

Peimani, H., *Regional Security and The Future of Central Asia,* (Westport: Praeger, 1998).

Pierce, R., *Russian Central Asia, 1867-1917; A Study of Colonial Rule* (Breaking and Los Angeles, 1960).

Piotrovsky, M. (ed.), *Lost Empire of the Silk Road: Buddhist Art from Khara Khoto (X-XIII Century).* Lugano: Thyssen-Bornemisza Foundation, 1993.

Pliny, *Natural History,* [trans. H. Rackham], (Cambridge, Mass: Harvard University Press), 1956-62, XII.

Porada, Edith, *Ancient Iran: The Art of Pre-Islamic times.* London: Methuen, 1965.

Puri, B.N., *Buddhism in Central Asia,* (Delhi: Motilal Banarsi Das 1987).

Rahul, Ram, *China, Russia and Central Asia:* (New Delhi: Vikas Publishing House, 1995).

Rashid, A., *The Resurgence of Central Asia* (Karachi: Oxford University Press, 1994).

Ratchnevsky, P., *Genghis Khan: His Life and Legacy,* Trans. by T.N. Haining, (Oxford, U.K.: Blackwel Publishers, 1991).

Ray, Jayanta Kumar; Bhattacharya, Rakhee (ed.), *Sikkim's Tryst with Nathu La: What Awaits India's East and Northeast,* (New Delhi: Shipra Publications, 2009).

Raychaudhuri, H.C., *Political History of Ancient India* (Calcutta, 1953).

Reishauer, H.M., *Samuri and Silk – A Japanese and American Heritage* (Tokyo: Charles E. Tuttle Company, 1987).

Rice, D. Talbot, *Art of the Byzantine Era.* London: Thames and Hudson, 1963.

Rice, Tamara Talbot, *Everyday Life in Byzantium.* London: B.T. Batsford Ltd., 1967.

Riley, C.V., *The Silkworm, Being a brief Manual of instructions for the Production of Silk.* Washington, 1882.

Rossabi, Morris, *The Decline of the Central Asian Caravan and Trade* (Cambridge: Cambridge University Press, 1990).

Rostovtzeff, M., *History of the Ancient World* (London: Oxford University Press, 1945).

Rostovtzeff, M., *Social and Economic History of Roman Empire* (London: Oxford University Press, 1971).

Rowland, Benjamin, *Ancient Art from Afghanistan: Treasures from the Kabul Museum*, Exhibition Catalogue, New York: Asia Society, 1976.

Roy, Olivier, *The New Central Asia: The Creation of Nations*, (London: I.B. Tauris, 2000).

Rtveladze, E., *The Great Silk Road, Tashkent: Uzbek National Encyclopedias*, 1999.

Saha, Ksharika, *Buddhism in Central Asia* (Calcutta: Ferma Mukhopaothyay, 1970).

Sally, Wriggins, *Xuanzang: A Buddhist Pilgrims on the Silk Road* (Boulder: Westview Press, 1996).

Sankrityayana, Mahapandita Rahula, *History of Central-Asia: Bronze Age [200 BC] to Chengiz Khan [1227 AD]*, (New Delhi: New Age Pub. Ltd., Sep. 1964).

Sarkar, D.C., *Sericulture and Silk Industry in India*, (Indian Museum, Bulletin XII, 1977).

Sarkar, D.C., *Sericulture and Silk Industry in India, Indian Museum Bulletin*, XII, 7-75, 1977.

Sechin, J. and Van Jay Symons, *Peace, War and Trade Along the Great Wall* (Bloomington: Indiana University Press, 1989).

Shafi Iqbal M., *Silk Road to Sin Kiang*, (Lahore: Wajidalis Pub., 1988).

Shams-ud-Din, (ed.) *Geopolitics and Energy Resources in Central Asia and Caspian Sea Region* (New Delhi: Lancers Books, 2000).

Shaprio, L., *The History of the Communist Party of the Soviet Union*, (New Delhi: Macmillan, 1998).

Sharma, R.C., *Buddhist Art: Mathura School*, New Delhi: Wiley Eastern Press, 1995.

Sharma, R.S., *Ancient Pasts of India*, Oxford Pub., 2006.

Sharma, R.S., *Aspects of Political Ideas and Institutions in Ancient India*, (New Delhi: Motilal, Banarsi Das Publishers, 1959).

_______, *Indian Feudalism*, (New Delhi: Raj Kamal Publication Pvt. Ltd., 1993).

_______, *Material Culture and Social Formation in Ancient India*, (New Delhi: Macmillan India Ltd., 1983).

Shepherd, D.C. & W.B. Henning, *Zandaniji Identified.*, (Berlin: Fertschrift Ernst Kuhnel, 1959).

Siddiqui, Asiya (ed.) *Trade and Finance in Colonial India (1750-1860)* (Delhi: Oxford University Press, New York, 1995).

Singh, Mahavir, & Victor Krassilchtchikov (ed.), *Eurasian Vision*, (New Delhi, 2003).

Singh, Upinder, *A History of Ancient and Early Medieval India: From the Stone Age to the 12th Century*, Pearson, Delhi, 2009.

Skrine, C.P. *Chinese Central Asia* London: Methuen and Co., 1926.

Spink and Son, *Treasures from the Silk Road: Devotion, Conquest and Trade along Ancient Highways*, Exhibition Catalogue, London, 1999.

Starensier, Actele La Barre, *An Art Historical Study of the Byzantine Silk Industry*, (Columbia: Columbia University, 1982).

Stein, A., *Ancient Central Asian Tracks* (London: Oxford University Press, 1929).

Stein, Aurel, *Ancient Khotan* (Oxford, 1907).

Stiftung, Friedrich, Ebert, *A Great Game No More: Oil, Gas and Stability in the Caspian Sea Region*, (Washington: D.C., 1999).

Sultan, Muhesen, Dr. et al. (ed.), *Palmyra and the Silk Road. Activities of the International Colloquium*, 7-11 April 1992, Damascus, 1996.

Taran, W.W. *Greek's in Bactria and India*, (New Delhi: Munshiram Manoharlal, 1980).

_______, The *Greeks in Bactria and India* (Cambridge, 1951).

Taylor, H. Granger, *Two Silk Textiles from Rome and Some Thoughts on Roman Silk Weaving*, (Lyon, 1987).

Tennenbaum, Jonathan, et. al., 'The Eurasian Land-Bridge – The 'New Silk Road' locomotive for worldwide economic development', *Executive Intelligence Review*, Special Report, (Washington D.C.: January, 1997).

Thapar, R., *Asoka and the Decline of the Mauryas* (Oxford, 1907).

Thapar, Romila, *A History of India-I*, (London: Allen & Unwin Ltd., 1968).

_______, *Cultural Pasts: Essays in Early Indian History*, (New Delhi: Oxford University, 2000).

The Cambridge History of Iran, (Cambridge: Cambridge University Press, 1983).

Thomas, Burrow, *A Translation of Kharosti Documents from Chinese Turkistan*, (London: The Royal Asiatic Society, 1940).

Tikhvinsky, S.L., *China and Her neighbours: from Ancient Times to the Middle Ages* (Moscow: Progress Publishers, 1981).

Tordy Laszlo, *Mounted. Archers: The Beginning of Central Asian History*, (Durham: Durham Academic Press, 1997).

Tucker Jonathan, *The Silk Road: Art and History*, (New Delhi: Timeless Books, 2003).

Varadarajan, L., Indian *Textile Technology in the Pre-Industrial Period*, Indica, 1966.

Varron, A., The Origin and Rise of Silk, *Ciba Review*, II, 1938.

Wang Chung-Lo, *History of the Wei, Chin and Northern and Southern Dynasties*, (Shanghai: People's Publisher, 1979).

Warikoo, K., *Central Asia: Emerging New Order* (New Delhi: Har-Anand Pub., 1995).

_______, 'Central Asia and China: The Geopolitical Imperatives', in Shams-ud-Din (ed.) *Geopolitical and Energy Resources in Central Asia and Caspian Sea Region*, (New Delhi: Lancer Book, 2000).

_______, 'Russians in post Soviet Central Asia: Issues and concerns', in Touraj Atabahi and Sanjyat Mehendale (ed.) *Central Asia and the Caucasus: Transnationalism and Diaspora*, (New York and London: Routledge Pub. 2005).

Wheeler, G., *The Modern History of Soviet Central Asia*, (London, 1964).

Wheeler, Geaffrey, *Peoples of Soviet Central Asia* (London: Bodley Head, 1966).

Wheeler, Sir Mortimer, *Rome Beyond the Imperial Frontiers*. London: G. Bell and Sons, 1954.

White J. & Bunker, E., *Adornments for Eternity: Status and Rank in Chinese Ornament*. (Exhibition Catalogue, Denver, Denver Art Museum, 1994).

Williams, Paul, *Mahayana Buddhism: The Doctrinal Foundation*, (London: Rutledge Pub., 1989).

Winrow, Gareth M., *Turkey in Post-Soviet central Asia*, (London: Royal Institute of International Affairs, 1995).

Wood, E., Did *Marco Polo go to Chine?* London: Secker and Warburg, 1995.

Xinru, Liu, *Silk and Religion: An Exploration of Material Life and the thought of People, AD 600-1200* (Delhi, Bombay, Calcutta, Madras: Oxford University Press, 1996).

Xu, Yuan Zhong, *Golden Treasury of Chinese Poetry from Han to Sui (206BC-Ad 618)*. Beijing: Peking University Press, 1996.

Yang Hsuan-Chih, *Memories of Holy Places in Loyang,* (Shanghai: Ku-chi Ch'u-pan She, 1978).

Yang, Xiaoneng (ed.), *The Golden Age of Chinese Archaeology*. New Haven: Longon: Yale University Press, 1999.

Yu Ying-Shin, *Trade and Expansion in Han China* (Berkeley: University of California Press, 1997).

Zou, Zongxu, The *Land Within the Passes: A History of Xian*. Trans. by Susan Whitfield, London and New York: Viking, 1991.

Articles

Ahmar, Moonis, "Connecting two Asia's", *The News International,* Karachi, December 12, 1998.

_______, "Communication Linkage Between Central And South Asia: A case Study of Karakorum Highway (KKH)", *Eurasian Studies* 20, Special Issue, Summer 2001, p. 190.

Akcali, Pinar, "Islam as a 'Common Bond' in Central Asia", *Central Asian Survey,* vol. 17(2) June 1998, pp. 267-84.

Alam, Shah, "Iran's Hydrocarbon Profile: Production, Trade and Trend", *Strategic Analysis,* vol. 24(4) April 2001, pp. 119-34.

Ataov, Turkkaya, "Central Asia on the threshold of the 21st Century", *Himalayan and Central Asian Studies,* vol. 1(3) Oct.-Dec. 1997, pp. 66-75.

Bakshi, Jyotsna, "Russian Policy Towards Central Asia-I", *Strategic Analysis,* vol. 22(10) Jan. 1999, pp. 1577-80.

Baru, Sanjaya, "Economic Cooperation and Globalization", *China Report,* 39: 3 (2003), Sage Publications New Delhi, pp. 366-370.

Belokerenitsky, "Central Asia in the New Eurasian Geopolitics: Implications for Pakistan and Russia", *Pakistan Horizon,* vol. 48(3), July 1995, pp. 25-23.

Bransten, Jermy, "Central Asia/Caucasus: Silk Road Conference Agrees on Eurasian Corridor", *RFE/RL Weekday Magazine,* 9 September, 1993.

Central Asia Development in 1997, *World Focus,* vol. 19, No. 3, March 1998, pp. 21-23.

Central Asia Today, *World Focus,* vol. 21(8) Aug. 2000, pp. 3-24, (Series of Articles).

Central Asia: Developments in 1997, *World Focus,* vol. 19, No. 3, (New Delhi, March 1998), p. 14-21.

Chaitanya, R., "New Emerging Asian Alliance India, Iran and China", *Third Concept,* Oct.-Nov., 1996, pp. 15-19.

Chang, F.K., "China's Central Asian Power and Problems", China-Europe Relations, *World Focus,* April, vol. 17(4) 1996, pp. 22-23.

Coppieters, Bruno and Others, "Central Asian Region in a New International Environment", *NATO Review,* vol. 44(5) September 1996, pp. 26-31.

Cordier, Bruno De, "Economic Cooperation Organization: Towards a New Silk Road on the Ruins of the Cold War" *Central Asian Survey,* vol. 15(1) March, 1996, pp. 47-57.

Das, Rahul P., "Great Game Continued", *World Affairs,* vol. 4(3) July-September 2000, pp. 82-97.

Dash, P.L., "Pipelines Politics: Route options from Central Asian Oil Trade", *Economic and Political Weekly,* vol. 35(37) 9-15, September, 2000 pp. 3301-03.

Djalili, M.R., "In Search of New Friends: Iran and Central Asia's" *World Affairs,* vol. 1(1) January-March, 1997, pp. 102-15.

Dorian, James P. and Others, "Central Asia and Xinjiang, China: Emerging Energy, Economic and Ethnic Relations", *Central Aisan Survey,* vol. 16(4) December 1997, pp. 517-42.

Dunn, Michael, Collins, "Great Games and Small: Afghanistan, Tajikistan, and the New Geopolitics of South West Asia", *Middle East Policy* – 5, no. 2, May 1997, pp. 144-149.

Efegil, E. and Stone, L.A., "Iran's interests in Central Asia: A Contemporary Assessment", *Central Asian Survey,* vol. 41(9) September 2001, pp. 353-65.

Eggert, k., "Russia: Still Soul Searching", *World Today,* October 1999, pp. 6-7.

Evans, Michael C., "Europe's Strategic Role in the Caucasus and the Black Sea", *Strategic Review,* 27, no. 2, spring 1999, pp. 2-16.

Foltz, Richard, "Cultural Contacts Between Central Asia and Mughal India", *Central Asiatic Journal,* vol. 42(1), 1998, pp. 44-65.

Forsythe, R., "Politics of Oil in the Caucasus and Central Asia", *Adelphi Papers,* vol. 300, 1996, pp. 3-61.

Gentile, Michael, "Former Closed. Cities and Urbanisation in the FSU: An Exploration in Kazakhstan", *Europe-Asia Studies,* Vol.

56, No-2, (London: Carfax Publishing, March, 2004), pp. 265-271.

Gidadhubli, R.G., 'Russia: Oil Politics in Central Asia', *EPW,* (January 30-February 5, 1999), pp. 259-265.

Gleason, Gregory, "Inter-State Cooperation in Central Asia from the CIS to the Shanghi Forum", *Europe-Asia Studies,* vol. 53(7) November 2001, pp. 1077-95.

Hickok, M.R., "Other End of The Silk Road: Japan's Eurasian Initiative", *Central Asian Survey,* vol. 19(1) March, 2000, pp. 17-39.

Hiro, Dilip, "Turkmenistan and Iran: US Advice Ignored", *Middle East International,* no. 551, May 30, 1997, pp.18-25.

Hopkins, Keith, "Taxes and Trade in Roman Empire (200 BC-400 AD)" *Journal of Roman Studies,* vol. 19(1) March, 2000, pp. 17-39.

Hyman, Anthony, "Central Asian: Independence and After" *Round Table,* January 1997, pp. 67-79.

_______, "Central Asia's Relations with Afghanistan and South Asia", in Peter Ferdinand (ed.) *The New Central Asia and its Neighbors,* (London: Pinter Pub., 1994), pp. 86-93.

Islamov, B., and Parpiev, Z., "Challenges of Globalization and Exchange Rate-Policies in Central Asian Independent States", *Histotrubashi Journal of Economics,* vol. 41(1) June, 2000, pp. 27-52.

Jha, Manish, "Islam and Central Asia: A Case Study of Kazakhstan" *BIISS Journal,* vol. 20(2), April 1999, pp. 137-59.

Joshi, Nirmala, "Russia and Central Asia: The Strategic Dimension" *Strategic Analysis,* vol. 18(9): June 1998 pp. 1273-84.

Kapur, Vijay, "A Afghanistan And Central Asia: Differentiated. Challenges and Priorities in the Twenty First Century" in K. Warikoo (ed.), *Himalyan and Central Asian Studies,* vol. 8 Nos. 2-3, April-Sept. 2004, (New Delhi), pp. 10-14.

Kaser, Mechael, "Economic Transition in six Central Asian Economics", *Central Asian Survey,* vol. 20(3) March, 1997, pp. 5-26.

Kao-seng-chuan, "Biographies of Outstanding Monks", compiled. by Hui Chiao, *Tripitaka,* Vol. 50, pp. 321-336.

Kaul, T.N., "Towards a New Strategic partnership: India, China, and Russia", *Himalyayan and Central Asian Studies,* vol. 3(2-3) January-March, 1999, pp. 4-13.

Kaushik, D. "Islamic Fundamentalism in Central Asia: An Appraisal", *Himalayan and Central Asian Studies,* vol. 4(3-4) July-December, pp. 2000, 3-23.

_______, "Central Asia: The Balance Sheet of Ozodi" *World Focus,* vol. 19(3) March, 98, pp. 11-14.

_______, (ed.), *Contemporary Central Asia,* Vol. VI, Number 1-2 April-August, 2002. (New Delhi and Maulana Abul Kalam Institute of Asian Studies, Kolkata, India: Published jointly by the Central Asian Studies Foundation), pp. 20-25.

Kubick, Paul, "Regionalism, Nationalism and Real Politics in Central Asia", *Europe-Asian Studies,* vol. 49(4) June, 1997, pp. 637-55.

Kyrgyzstan, *Contemporary Central Asia,* vol. 11(2) September, 1998, pp. 1-70, (Series of Articles).

Leray, Rene, "European Union Policy and Action Toward Central Asia and Caspian Sea Countries", *A Great Game No More: Oil Gas and Stability in the Caspian Sea Region,* (ed.) Dieter Dettke (Washington, DC: Friedrich-Ebert-Stiftung, 1999), pp. 58-62.

Levi, Scott, "India, Russia and The Eighteenth Century Transformation of the Central Asian Caravans Trade", *Journal of the Economic and Social History of the Orient,* vol. 42(4) November 1999, pp. 519-48.

Lienig, Michael, "NATO, the Emerging 'Eurasian Triangle' and the Caucasus/Central Asia Region", *Contemporary Central Asia,* vol. 3(1) April, 1999, pp. 23-32.

Lukin, Alexander, "Image of China in Russian Boarder Regions", *Asean Survey* vol. 38(9), September, 1998, pp. 821-35.

Marylin M. Rhie, 'Aspects of the two Colossal Budhas at Bamiyan' Paper Presented in International Seminar on *Xuanzang and the Silk Route,* (Indira Gandhi National Centre for the Arts, New Delhi, January 17-19, 2003).

Melet, Yashin, "Economic relations with Kazakhstan and Kyrgyzstan", *Central Asian Survey,* vol. 17(2) June, 1998, pp. 229-52.

Meister Michael, "The Pearl Roundel in Chinese Textile Design", *Arts Orientalis,* Vol. VIII, 1970, pp. 255-67.

Miatra, Ramatanu, "Vajpayee's Historic Trip Strengthen India-China Ties", *EIR* (Washangton) July 4, 2003, vol. 30, no.26, pp. 40-44.

Mohan, C. Raja, "Central Asia's Pipeline Dreams', *The Hindu,* New Delhi, 12 October 1996; see also, 'India can join as pipeline", *The Times of India,* New Delhi, 20 April 1995.

Murarka, Dev, "Russia and China A Hollow Alliance", *Economic and Political Weekly,* vol. 32(31), August 1997, pp. 1955-58.

Mushtaq, A. Kaw, "Central Asian Contribution to Kashmir's Tradition of Religio-Cultural Pluralism", *Central Asiatic Journal,* 54(2010)2, Harrassowitz Verlag, Italy, 2010.

Najafov, Etibar, "Corelation between Culture and Civilization in the Social Development of Azerbaijan", *Proceedings of the International Education Society Conference,* (Urbana–Champaign, USA, Oct. 31-Nov. 2, 1997),

Orazov, M.B. and Khalova, G.O., "Foreign Economic Policy of Turkmenistan", *Contemporary Central Asia,* vol. 1(1), 1997, pp. 25-32.

ORBIS, vol. 41(3) Summer, 1997, pp. 401-25.

Palat, M.K., "Emergence of Central Asia", *Indian Historical Review,* July, vol. 18(1-2) 1991 & January 1992, pp. 76-92.

_______, "Shanghai Treaty: Readjusting of Chinese History" *China Report,* July-September 1996, pp. 233-50.

_______, "China's Central Asian Dilema" *Strategic Analysis,* June, vol. 22(3) 1998, pp. 399-408.

Palat, Madhavan, K., "Emergence of Central Asia" *Indian Historical Review* vol. 18(2) January 1992, pp. 76-92.

Pathak, S.K., 'Sanskritism had Moved. Forward the Silk Routes when Xuanzang Traversed', Paper presented in international seminar on, *Xuanzang and the Silk Route,* (IGNCA, New Delhi, January 17-19, 2003), pp. 5-9.

Patnaik, Ajaya, "Central Asia in Global Setting", in *World Focus,* Vol. 23, No. 6, (New Delhi, June, 2002), pp. 4-8.

Purcell, N., "Wine and Wealth in Ancient Italy" *Journal of Roman Studies,* vol. 75, 1985, pp. 10-23.

Rossabi, Morris, 'The Silk Road', *Education About Asia,* (Vol.4, November 1, Spring, 1999), pp. 1-18.

Rouche, Lyndon H. La, Jr., "World in Crisis Needs a new Monetary System", *Executive Intelligence Review,* December 21, 2001 issue.

Saidmuradov, K.M., "Reflection of Economy and Culture in Tajikistan" *Contemporary Central Asia,* vol. 1(1), 1997, pp. 19-24.

Schilling, W., "Return of Geopolitics in the Caucasus and Central Asia" *Aussen Politik,* vol. 49 4th Quarter 1998, pp. 50-55.

Scott, David, "Buddhist Response to Manichaeism: Mahayana Reaffirmation of Middle path" *History of Religion,* vol. 35(2) 1997, pp. 148-62.

Shams-ud-Din, "New Great Game in Central Asia", *International Studies,* vol. 34(3) September, 1997, pp. 329-41.

Sharifov, Abid, "New Life of the Ancient Silk Road", *Silk Road,* (Baku, 1998), No. 3.

Siddharth, Varadarajan, "India, China and the Asian Axis of Oil," *The Hindu,* January 24, 2006.

Stobdan, P., "China and Central Asia" *World Focus,* vol. 19(3) March, 1998, pp. 11-14.

_______, "Regional Security Issues in Central/South Asia and Potential for Cooperation" *Strategic Analysis,* vol. 22(10) January 1999, pp. 1561-76.

_______, "US Interest in Central Asia: New Agenda for Pakistan", *Strategic Analysis,* vol. 19(5) August, 1996, pp. 829-32.

Svante, E. Cornell & Maria Sultan, The Asian Connection: The new Geopolitics of Central Eurasia, *Marco Polo Magazine,* Venice, No. 6, 2000.

Swarn, Singh, "Shanghai Five Summit: Presenting a Parallel Paradigm for Cooperative Security", *Mainstream,* 29 vol. 38(32) July, 2000, pp. 8-16.

Talbott "Details of US Approach to Caucasus, Central Asia", *Strategic Digest,* vol. 27(9) September 1997, pp. 1378-83.

Tang, S., "Economic Integration in Central Asia" The Russian and Chinese Relationship", *Asian Survey,* vol. 40(2) March-April, 2000, pp. 360-76.

Tarock, Adm, "Iran's Policy in Central Asia", *Central Asian Survey,* vol. 16(2) June 1997, pp. 185-200.

Umamov, Alexander, "Central Asia in Russia's Post Soviet Policy", *Contemporary Central Asia,* vol. 12(3) December 1998, 39-43.

Varadarajan, Lotika, "Silk: The Extra Silk Route Story" [paper presented in International Seminar on 'Xuanzang and the Silk Route' on January 17-19, 2003, at Indira Gandhi National Centre for the Arts, New Delhi, Department of Culture, New Delhi, pp. 15-17.

Ved, Mahendra, "Silk Route Turns Destructive Drug Route", *World Focus,* vol. 21(8) August 2000, pp. 10-13.

Wardle, T., "The Indian Silk Culture Court" *Journal of International Affairs,* vol. 1, No. 18, pp. 1986.

Warikoo, K., "Central Asia and China: The Geopolitical Imperatives", in Shams-Ud-Din, (ed.) *Geopolitics and Energy*

Resources in Central Asia and Caspian Sea Region, (New Delhi: Lancer Books, 2000).

Zemin, Jiang, "Jiang calls for fair, equitable new int'l economic order", *China Daily,* September, 8, 2000, pp. 18-22.

Zhukov, S. and Reznikova, O., "Central Asia in World Politics and Economics", *Problems of Economics Transition,* vol. 38(8) December 1995, pp. 59-81.

Other Important Sources

BBC Summary of World Broadcasts Central Asia, 1991-2002.

Central Asia Report "A Weekly Survey of Developments in Kazakhstan, Kyrgyzstan, Tajikistan, Turkmenistan and Uzbekistan".

The New Encyclopedia Britannica (Chicago, Encyclopedia Britannica, Inc., 1995), S.9.

"The World Bank Group's Report" Washington, June 12, 2001.

Websites

www.cacianalyst.org
www.CPSS.org/cacianw/perca
www.muza.com.kg/slikroad
www.worlpaper.com/Archivewp
www.washington-report.org
www.washington.edu
www.aasianst.org
www.kyrgyzinvest.org
www.clemusarat.com
www.asiasource.org
www.mountaintravelsobeck.com
www.soros.org
www.silkroadproject.org
www.ess.uci.edu/~oliver/silk.html
www.alumni.calteck.edu/~pamlogan/silkroad
www.librarythinkquest.org
www.chinapage.com/silkroad
www.chnm.gmu.edu/SAS-silk-road-syllabus
www.thesouth-asian.com
www.azambassy.com

www.eurunion.org/news/speeches
www.g7report.com
www.idsa-india.org
www.schirmer.com/silkroad
www.amazon.com
www.milnet.com

Newspapers

Asian Times, London
Indian Express, New Delhi
Hindustan Times, New Delhi
New York Times, New York
Pravda, Moscow
Times of India, New Delhi
The Economic Times, New Delhi
The Hindu, New Delhi
The Dawan, Pakistan
The News International, Islamabad

Index